INTERNETWORKING LANs AND WANs
Concepts, Techniques and Methods

Internetworking is one of the fastest growing markets in the field of computer communications. However, the interconnection of LANs and WANs tends to cause significant technological and administrative difficulties. This book provides valuable guidance, enabling the reader to avoid the pitfalls and achieve successful connection.
1993 0 471 93568 9

THE MULTIPLEXER REFERENCE MANUAL

Designed to provide the reader with a detailed insight into the operation, utilization and networking of six distinct types of multiplexers, this book will appeal to practising electrical, electronic and communications engineers, students in electronics, network analysts and designers.
1993 0 471 93484 4

PRACTICAL NETWORK DESIGN TECHNIQUES

Many network design problems are addressed and solved in this informative volume. Gil Held confronts a range of issues including through-put problems, line facilities, economic trade-offs and multiplexers. Readers are also shown how to determine the numbers of ports, dial-in lines and channels to install on communications equipment in order to provide a defined level of service
1991 0 471 93007 5 (Book)
     0 471 92942 5 (Disk)
     0 471 92938 7 (Set)

NETWORK MANAGEMENT
Techniques, Tools and Systems

Techniques, tools and systems form the basis of network management. Exploring and evaluating these three key areas, this book shows the reader how to operate an effective network.
1992 0 471 92781 3

Please refer to the inside-back cover for further details

LAN PERFORMANCE

LAN PERFORMANCE
Issues and Answers
Second edition

Gilbert Held
4-Degree Consulting
Macon, Georgia,
USA

JOHN WILEY & SONS
Chichester ● New York ● Brisbane ● Toronto ● Singapore

CONTENTS

Preface   **xi**

Acknowledgements   **xiii**

1 LAN Performance Issues   1

1.1   Network Basics   1
1.2   Ethernet and Token-Ring Frame Operations   2
1.3   Estimating Network Traffic   3
1.4   The Impact of Remote Bridges and Routers   3
1.5   Determining Availability Levels   4
1.6   Ethernet Network Performance   5
1.7   Token-Ring Network Performance   6
1.8   Working with Images   7
1.9   Using Intelligent Switches   8
1.10 Transmission Optimization   8

2 Ethernet and Token-Ring Frame Operations   11

2.1 Ethernet Frame Operations   11
    2.1.1 Frame compostion   12
        Preamble field   13
        Start of frame delimiter field   13
        Destination address field   14
            I/G subfield   14
            U/L subfield   15
            Universal vs locally administered addressing   15
        Source address field   16
        Type field   17
        Length field   17
        Data field   17
        Frame check sequence field   18
        Fast Ethernet   18
    2.1.2 Fame overhead   19
2.2 Token-Ring Frame Formats   21

2.2.1 Frame compostion   22
    Starting/ending delimiters   23
      Differential Manchester encoding   23
      Non-data symbols   24
    Access control field   26
      The monitor bit   27
      Active monitor   29
    Frame control field   29
    Destination address field   30
      Universally administered address   30
      Locally administered address   31
      Functional address indicator   31
      Address values   32
    Source address field   33
    Routing information field   34
    Information field   34
    Frame check sequence field   35
    Frame status field   36
2.2.2 Frame overhead   36

3 Estimating Network Traffic   39

3.1 The Network Traffic Estimation Process   40
  3.1.1 The traffic estimation worksheet   40
    Workstation class   40
    Number of stations   40
    Column entries   41
  3.1.2 Developing a network traffic estimate   43
    Using the traffic estimate   43
      Required computations   43
      Networking printing considerations   45
      Graphic vs text transfer   47
  3.1.3 Network utilization considerations   48
  3.1.4 Planning for network growth   49
3.2 Network Modification   49
  3.2.1 Network subdivision considerations   50
  3.2.2 Inter- versus intra-network communications   52

4 Determining Remote Bridge and Router Delays and Buffer Memory Requirements   55

4.1 Waiting Line Analysis   56
  4.1.1 Basic components   56
  4.1.2 Assumptions   58
  4.1.3 Network applications   59
    Deciding on a queuing model   60
    Applying queuing theory   61
    Queuing theory designators   63
    Frame determination   64
    Time computations   65
4.2 Determining an Optimum Line Operating Rate   67
  4.2.1 Program QUEUE.BAS   67
  4.2.2 Utilization level versus line speed   68
  4.2.3 Selecting an operating rate   69
  4.2.4 Summary   70
4.3 Examining Single and Multiple Communications Circuits   71

4.3.1 Comparing the use of single- and dual-port equipment   71
>> Single circuit   72
>>> Notation   72
>> Computations   73
>> Dual circuits   75
>> Computations   75
>> General observations   76
>> Program QUEUE2.BAS   79

4.4 Buffer Memory Considerations   80
4.4.1 Average memory   81
4.4.2 Using probability   81
4.4.3 Six-step approach   83
4.4.4 Considering the maximum frame size   84
>> Program QVU.BAS   84
4.4.5 Summary   86

5 Using the Availability Level as a Decision Criterion   89

5.1 Availability   90
5.1.1 Component availability   90
>> MTBF and MTTR   90
5.1.2 System availability   92
>> Devices connected in series   92
>> Devices connected in parallel   94
>> Mixed topologies   96
5.1.3 Dual hardware versus dual transmission facilities   98
5.1.4 Evaluating disk mirroring   100
5.2 Automating Availability Computations   103
5.2.1 Program AVAIL.BAS   103
5.2.2 Program execution   105

6 Estimating Ethernet Network Performance   109

6.1 CSMA/CD Network Performance   110
6.1.1 Determining the network frame rate   110
>> Program EPERFORM.BAS   113
6.1.2 The actual Ethernet operating rate   116
>> Network utilization   117
>> Information transfer rate   118
6.2 Using Bridges to Adjust the Network   121
6.2.1 Predicting throughput   123
>> Linked LANs   123
>> Estimating data transfer time   124
>> Considering remote connections   125

7 Estimating Token-Ring Network Performance   129

7.1 Token-Ring Traffic Modeling   130
7.1.1 Model development   130
>> Propagation delay   131
>> 4 Mbps model   131
7.1.2 Exercising the model   133
>> Network modification   134
>> Varying the frame size   134
>> Adapter card considerations   136

7.1.3 General model development   136
           Program TPERFORM.BAS   138
           General observations   138
           Station effect upon network performance   142
    7.2 **Bridge and Router Performance Requirements**   144
       7.2.1 Local bridges   144
           Considering a performance range   145
           Considering the effect of network changes   145
       7.2.2 Remote bridges and routers   146
           Wide area network operating rate   146
           Program TRWAN.BAS   147
             Protocol overhead   148
             Data compression   148
           Internet traffic flow   150

8   **Working with Images   155**

    8.1 Image Basics   156
       8.1.1 Raster images   156
           Color depth   156
       8.1.2 Vector images   157
       8.1.3 Why images are a problem   158
           Storage considerations   158
           Transmission delays   159
    8.2 Examining Image Formats   160
       8.2.1 Common formats   160
             BMP   160
             GIF   162
             JPG   163
             PCX   164
             TIF   164
       8.2.2 Comparing storage requirements   166
           File format comparisons   168
           Examining visual image differences   170
           Considering JPG   171
       8.2.3 Additional image management operations   173
           Image cropping   173
           Color reduction   174
    8.3 Hardware Considerations   176
       8.3.1 LAN segmentation   176
       8.3.2 Upgrading adapter cards   177
       8.3.3 Upgrading the LAN infrastructure   178

9   **Using Intelligent Switches   179**

    9.1 Conventional Hub Bottlenecks   180
       9.1.1 Ethernet hub operation   180
       9.1.2 Token-Ring hub operation   182
       9.1.3 Bottleneck creation   183
    9.2 Switching Operations   183
       9.2.1 Bridge switching   184
       9.2.2 The switching hub   185
           Basic components   185
           Delay times   186
           Key advantages of use   187

9.2.3 Switching techniques   188
    Cross-point switching   188
    Store-and-forward   190
    Hybrid   193
    Port-based switching   194
    Segment-based switching   195

9.3 Switching Hub Features   197
9.3.1 Switching technique   197
9.3.2 Switching method   197
9.3.3 Backplane throughput   199
9.3.4 Port support   200
9.3.5 High speed port operation   200
    Fat pipe   202
    100BASE-T connection   203
    FDDI and ATM connections   203
9.3.6 Flow control support   205
    Backpressure   205
    Server software module   206
9.3.7 Statistics   206
9.3.8 Virtual LAN creation support   206

9.4 Networking Techniques   208
9.4.1 Network redistribution   208
9.4.2 Server segmentation   209
9.4.3 Network segmentation   211

10 Transmission Optimization Techniques   213

10.1 Filtering   214
10.1.1 Local versus remote filtering   214
10.1.2 Filtering methods   215
    Address field filtering   215
    Service access point filtering   216

10.2 Precedence and Express Queuing   217
10.2.1 First-in, first-out queuing   217
    Queuing problems   218
      Mixing file transfer and interactive sessions   219
      Workstation retransmissions   220
10.2.2 Precedence queuing   220
    Methods used   220
    Operation   221
10.2.3 Express queuing   222

10.3 Data Compression   222
10.3.1 Compression ratio   222
10.3.2 Compression methods   223
    Byte-oriented   223
    Statistical   224
    Dictionary-based   224
10.3.3 Performance considerations   225

10.4 Ethernet Frame Truncation   225
10.4.1 Overhead   225
10.4.2 Utilization example   226

10.5 Switched Network Use for Overcoming Congestion   226
10.5.1 Using bandwidth-on-demand inverse multiplexers   227
10.5.2 Dial-on congestion   228

10.6 Network Interface Card   228

10.6.1 Performance considerations   228
      DMA interface   229
      I/O mapping   229
      Shared memory   229
10.7 Change Network Routing and Advertising Protocol   230
10.7.1 Routing Protocol   231
10.7.2 Advertising Protocol   231
10.7.3 NLSP   233

Appendix A P(N) and P(N > K) Values for Single-Channel, Single-Server System   **235**

Appendix B 4 and 16 Mbps Token-Ring Network Performance Based upon the Network Operating Rate, Number of Network Stations, Frame Length and Total Cable Length   **247**

Index   267

PREFACE

In the prior edition of this book I noted that within many organizations LAN performance is discussed as frequently as the weather. However, unlike the weather, we have the ability to control and improve the performance of local area networks.

As I began to revise this book. I returned to my original outline several times to think about the issues I face as a network manager. I am responsible for establishing new LANs and expanding existing networks. I also need to provide the communications capability for users on different networks to communicate with one another or access a number of mainframe applications which reside on different computers. Naturally, I have a fixed budget. I therefore need to determine an optimum line rate to interconnect separate networks and I must decide whether to use multiport devices or dual devices for reliability. I need to estimate network traffic for networks that we plan to install but for which no prior traffic estimate exists, and evaluate the effect on the performance of Ethernet and Token-Ring networks as those network configurations change. In addition, I must plan to use effectively new technology, such as intelligent switches, 100 Mbps Ethernet LANs and full duplex Ethernet and Token-Ring network components. While performing those tasks I must also consider the impact of the transmission of images on other applications and develop solutions to maintain an acceptable level of network performance while supporting multimedia applications.

These other issues represent a core set of activities you will want to perform to ensure that your networks not only meet the requirements of your user community but in addition are not overconfigured. You will never hear an end-user complain that network performance is too good. Therefore it is likely that you will never be told that you have over-configured your network or transmission facilities. However, doing so can result in considerable over-expenditure.

In presenting various LAN performance issues, I have attempted to provide you with the tools to answer your specific networking requirements. To accomplish this goal, mathematical models of different LAN performance issues are developed. You can use these models to determine answers to your own networking requirements. Since the execution of some models is tedious and time-consuming, I have included several QBASIC programs that you can use to facilitate your computations.

Since a book must be finite in length, there may well be some issues which I have overlooked or, due to space constraints, have not been covered. If there is a particular issue you would like me to work on, please feel free to contact me and I will do my best to answer your questions. Perhaps your questions, as well as the answers to those questions, will result in their inclusion in a third edition of this book. As a professional author, I value your comments and encourage you to write to me directly or through my publisher.

Gilbert Held
Macon, GA

ACKNOWLEDGEMENTS

In several books I have alluded to the fact that the development of a book is a team effort, and this book is certainly no exception.

As the author, I am directly responsible for the contents of this book; however, the many processes involved from its acquisition through its production require the skills and efforts of many individuals. Thus, I would be remiss if I did not take the time to acknowledge those individuals who certainly contributed to the development and production of this book.

As an old-fashioned writer, I like to work with pen and paper and use my notebook computer for those really labor-intensive operations, such as developing programs whose execution saves hours or days of hand-held calculator effort. In addition, the use of pen and paper provides me with the ability to easily modify drawings, which is especially convenient when you encounter turbulence at 30 000 feet or when your notebook battery-low warning light illuminates. While it is easy for me to use pen and paper to develop a manuscript, it truly takes a special talent to turn that draft manuscript into a professional manuscript complete with camera-ready illustrations. Once again, I am indebted to Mrs Linda Hayes and Ms Junnie Heath for their fine efforts in preparing the manuscript for submission.

Once a manuscript has been submitted for production, a burden is removed from the author and placed on another individual, the production manager. Responsible for numerous items which somehow all get done, Mr Robert Hambrook and his team of professionals are again thanked by this author.

Last but certainly not least, the time spent writing a book places a considerable burden upon family life. Thus, my family's cooperation and understanding during the many evenings and weekends in which I worked on this book are truly appreciated.

LAN PERFORMANCE ISSUES

In this introductory chapter we will focus our attention on a core set of local area network performance issues. In doing so we will discuss why such issues are important for inter- and intra-network communications in the form of questions which we will want to answer when planning or expanding a network. Although we will leave it to future chapters in this book to answer questions raised in this chapter, our discussion of performance issues serves a dual purpose. First, it makes us aware of many factors which affect the performance of individual networking devices as well as the networks to which they are connected. Secondly, it makes us aware of the fact that performance can involve the tradeoff of many operating characteristics and that in some instances the modification of the operating characteristics of a networking device to enhance its performance may require adjustments to other features of that device and other networking devices and transmission facilities. Thus, we will note that local area network performance issues in many instances involve a detailed relationship between different network components as well as the transmission facilities used to provide a connection between separate networks.

1.1 NETWORK BASICS

Readers of this book are presumed to have a degree of familiarity with the basic operation and utilization of Ethernet and Token-Ring networks. Thus, this book was not written as an introductory text on local area networks nor on local area networking concepts. However, since Ethernet and Token-Ring network performance requires a degree of knowledge concerning the format of the frames and their composition, Chapter 2 in this book reviews both areas by borrowing relevant material from the author's previous books *Token-Ring Networks* and *Ethernet Networks* 2 edn, both published by John Wiley & Sons. In fact, you are encouraged to read the book most appropriate to the type of local area network you currently use or anticipate acquiring, or to read both books if you intend to establish or use mixed local area networks. Doing so will provide you with a greater appreciation for network performance issues.

Each of the previously mentioned books is focused on a specific type of local area network and provides a detailed examination of data flow on each network, the access protocol and network topology, the use of different network components, and the operation and utilization of bridges, routers, and gateways. By first reading those books you will obtain a better appreciation for the performance issues raised in the present book if your knowledge concerning the operation of either or both of those local area networks is not as detailed as you would like.

In the remainder of this chapter we will review the material in succeeding chapters with respect to the performance issues they raise. Thus, Sections 1.2 through 1.10 in this chapter can be considered previews to Chapters 2 through 10.

1.2 ETHERNET AND TOKEN-RING FRAME OPERATIONS

As mentioned above, material in Chapter 2 was first used in the author's books on Ethernet and Token-Ring networks. The key to understanding many performance-related issues is detailed knowledge of the frame format used on different local area networks – material which is presented in Chapter 2.

In Chapter 2 we will focus our attention on the fields of Ethernet and Token-Ring frames to include a discussion of Fast Ethernet. This will provide us with information necessary to understand the relationship between the overhead of a frame and the length of its information field. Doing so will assist us in understanding the effect of the frame length upon the efficiency of transmission on different types of local area networks. Thus, the primary focus of Chapter 2 is to provide readers with information that can be used in later chapters to answer such questions as what techniques can be used to adjust the length of local area network frames or their information transfer capability that can result in an improvement in the efficiency of transmission over the network. Other questions that we will tackle in later chapters which are related to the material presented in Chapter 2 include how to determine the effect of the frame length on bridge and router operations as well as on their buffer memory requirements.

1.3 ESTIMATING NETWORK TRAFFIC

If we already have a network in existence, there are a large number of tools that we can use to determine network traffic. Once this has been done we can use the results obtained from traffic monitoring to predict the effect of a network expansion, or use such information to estimate the traffic on a similar type network which is anticipated to be established. However, what can you do to estimate traffic if your organization plans to install its first local area network or a network in which the user community will significantly differ from the users of an existing corporate network? When those situations occur you have no baseline from which you can project network traffic – a situation which can result to a significant degree in a trial-and-error approach to networking unless you have a reasonable mechanism to follow to estimate network traffic.

In Chapter 3 we will turn our attention to methods you can use to estimate inter- and intra-network traffic. After discussing the need for developing a realistic traffic measurement technique, this chapter focuses its attention on the use of a traffic estimation worksheet which can facilitate the network traffic estimation process. This is followed by an example of the use of the worksheet to estimate the traffic load that will be placed on a network. In addition, this chapter examines how you can use the results obtained from the use of a traffic estimation worksheet to predict future network traffic growth, as well as how to analyze the potential effect of such growth upon your existing or planned local area network. Once the traffic estimation process has been reviewed it is used to illustrate how you can use these data to subdivide a network via the use of a local bridge to improve network performance. Thus, this chapter provides you with information concerning the traffic estimation process, as well as illustrating its use to improve the performance level of a network.

1.4 THE IMPACT OF REMOTE BRIDGES AND ROUTERS

What is the effect upon internet transmission when data flow must cross a pair of remote bridges or routers? The answer to this question can be quite complex and is based upon the use of waiting line analysis which is an alternative term to the more popular expression known as queuing theory.

In Chapter 4 we investigate the use of waiting line analysis to network traffic which must use remote bridges or routers to reach its destination. After reviewing some of the terms associated with queuing theory we will apply it to answering some key questions associated with the use of remote bridges and routers. Those questions include 'What is an optimum line operating rate for those devices, what is the effect of using single or multiple port devices, and what is the effect of altering the memory capacity of a bridge or router upon its servicing capacity?'.

Commencing in Chapter 4 we will begin to use a series of programs developed using Microsoft Corporation's QuickBASIC compiler to facilitate performing a series of repetitive and tedious computations. The selection of QuickBASIC was based upon the fact that it is very similar to QBasic which was included in MS-DOS version 5.0 and later versions of that operating system. In addition, readers with earlier versions of DOS can easily modify the QuickBASIC programs presented in this book to operate with the BASICA or GW-BASIC interpreters included on the DOS diskette. Thus, most readers should be able to use the programs presented in this book without additional cost.

To facilitate the use of the programs contained in this book the convenience diskette contains two versions of each program. One version, contained on a file with the extension .BAS, contains the source version of the program. If you have a QuickBASIC or QBasic compiler, you can easily modify these programs to reflect your specific networking environment and then compile and execute the modified program. With a little additional effort you can also use a BASICA or GW-BASIC interpreter to execute the programs presented in this book. For those readers who desire to execute programs without modification, a directly executable version of each program is also featured on the convenience diskette. These programs have the same filename as the source language versions of the programs presented in this book but have the extension .EXE. Although you cannot modify these directly executable programs, many of them operate based upon a variable input which allows you to adjust their use to your particular networking environment.

1.5 DETERMINING AVAILABILITY LEVELS

Depending on the activities performed by your organization, you may be required to incorporate a degree of redundancy into your internet structure. To do so you can simply acquire additional pairs of remote bridges or routers and connect them through the use of separate transmission facilities. As an alternative to duplicating certain network components you can also consider the use of multiport bridges and routers whose cost is considerably less than that of separate devices. However, what is the difference in the level of availability provided by the use of dual port devices compared with the use of separate devices? The answer to this question, as well as a detailed examination of the concept of availability, is the focus of Chapter 5.

In Chapter 5 the use of mean time before failure (MTBF) and mean time to repair (MTTR) information – usually available from vendor product specification sheets – is used to determine both component and system availability levels. Concerning the latter, a portion of this chapter illustrates how the availability level of a complex internet can be reduced to a series of simple computations.

Chapter 5 includes the use of a BASIC language program which can be used to facilitate tedious computations and provides you with the ability to compute the availability level of devices and transmission facilities connected in series or in parallel. This program also serves as a mechanism to compute the availability level of a mixed topology network. Using this program, or the calculation method described in Chapter 5, you can evaluate the costs and benefits in terms of network availability of alternative internet configurations.

1.6 ETHERNET NETWORK PERFORMANCE

Just how fast can frames flow on an Ethernet network? Although this question may appear to be taken from a technically oriented game show, in actuality the answer has a considerable bearing on the performance level of bridges and routers prior to those devices becoming possible network bottlenecks.

In Chapter 6 we turn our attention to the carrier sense multiple access with collision detection (CSMA/CD) network access protocol. By closely examining this protocol we can determine the maximum frame rate that can be supported on both 10 Mbps and 100 Mbps Ethernet networks based upon different frame lengths. This in turn provides us with the ability to determine if the performance level of a bridge or router listed by a manufacturer is an appropriate decision criterion for equipment acquisition. That is, if the performance level of a device is over a certain frame forwarding rate which represents the maximum frame rate that can be supported on an Ethernet network, the ability of a bridge or router to transfer frames beyond that rate is superfluous if the device supports only one communications circuit. Thus, the ability of one vendor's bridge or router to forward frames at a faster rate than another vendor's product might not be relevant when evaluating competitive products.

Once the Ethernet frame rate has been determined, Chapter 6 then presents you with an easy-to-use method to predict through-put between interconnected networks. This method permits you to estimate the best-case transfer time to upload or download files across connected networks, as well as to project the average time required to perform those activities.

1.7 TOKEN-RING NETWORK PERFORMANCE

The question asked above concerning how fast frames can flow on Ethernet networks is also applicable to Token-Ring networks. That is, if you can determine the flow of information on a Token-Ring network you can use this information to estimate the performance of the network as additional stations are added to the network. You can also use this information to determine the filtering and forwarding rates required by bridges and routers connected to a Token-Ring network prior to those devices potentially becoming a bottleneck and congesting the flow of data between networks. Last but not least, by determining the frame flow on a Token-Ring network you can use this information to develop a model to project internet transmission time. If the internet is to be created or was created through the use of a wide area network transmission facility, you can easily adjust the model to reflect different WAN operating rates. Then, you can determine an optimum wide area network operating rate that will satisfy your organization's internet communications require-ments without having to simply guess upon the selection of a WAN transmission facility or initiate an expensive trial-and-error process.

As might be expected from the first paragraph in this section, the initial focus of Chapter 7 is upon the development of a model to reflect the flow of frames on a Token-Ring network. Once this has been accomplished the model will be exercised to determine the frame-carrying capacity of a Token-Ring network under different operating conditions and network configurations.

The development of a Token-Ring traffic model will require the consideration of a large number of operating conditions and network configuration data. Some of the parameters that will have a bearing upon the flow of frames on a Token-Ring network include the number of stations on the network, the length of each lobe and the length of the ring, the average frame size, and the operating rate of the network. To facilitate our computations, we will again turn to the BASIC programming language and develop several programs as well as spreadsheet models to facilitate our computations. Both the Token-Ring program and Lotus spread-sheet model listings and results from executing each program are contained in this chapter. In addition, readers are referred to a set of tables contained in Appendix B which can be used to reduce the Token-Ring frame flow projection process to a simple table lookup operation.

Once the Token-Ring model has been developed and exercised this information is used as a foundation for determining bridge and router performance requirements. In doing so, frame flow information is used to project a range of performance that network devices should support as well as the effect of network changes upon the frame flow on a Token-Ring network.

1.8 WORKING WITH IMAGES

The old adage 'one picture is worth a thousand words' could be rewritten from the network manager's or administrator's per-spective as 'transporting images can ruin network performance and eliminate server storage'. Thus, advances in technology including methods for the transport and display of images can carry a significant price tag in terms of their data storage requirements and use of network bandwidth when transported on a network. How to minimize the effect of images on LAN performance, what techniques can be used to reduce their storage and transmission requirements, and how to convert images to more effective formats are a few of the questions that we must consider.

In Chapter 8 we turn our attention to the effect of images on network performance, including their storage and transport requirements. After first examining the characteristics of images which define their data storage and transmission time, we then turn our attention to a variety of methods that we can use to reduce their effect upon network performance. In doing so we will investigate both methods to restructure networks, as well as methods to restructure the manner by which images are stored and transported. This will provide us with knowledge of software and hardware based solutions that we can consider to minimize the effect of images upon LAN performance.

1.9 USING INTELLIGENT SWITCHES

Although local area networks are considered by many people to represent the most rapidly evolving area of communications technology, intelligent switches can be considered to represent the fastest growing segment of LAN technology. In the few years since the first edition of this book, intelligent switches have evolved from a curiosity into a multibillion-dollar market. Accompanying this growth is the incorporation of a large number of features and operational considerations that make their effective use a challenge. How to use switches effectively, what features can cause switches to become bottlenecks instead of improving network performance, and how are switches best used in a network, are important questions that must be answered for effective use of this networking device.

In Chapter 9 we focus our attention on the effective use of intelligent switches and answer those questions and more. To do so we will first review their basic operational characteristics, including different methods used to perform switching and the advantages and disadvantages associated with each method. Next, we will review the operational characteristics of different switch features to obtain an appreciation for their use in different network environments. In doing so we will examine the use of switches in several network configurations to obtain an appreciation of how this important network device can be effectively used.

1.10 TRANSMISSION OPTIMIZATION

Network administrators and managers are always looking for methods that can increase the performance of their network. In doing so, they must examine and compare the use of equipment manufactured by different vendors and determine if the features of such equipment provide the capability to optimize the use of the bandwidth on a network or a wide area network transmission facility. However, prior to examining the capability and functionality of local area networking equipment, it is important to understand the key techniques that can be used to optimize network and internet transmission. Thus, the purpose of Chapter 10 is to answer the question 'What are some of the key techniques available that can be used to optimize network and internet transmission?'.

In Chapter 10 we will examine features of bridges and routers developed by manufacturers to enhance transmission. Such features include the ability to filter frames, subdivide a queue into different areas to prioritize traffic, truncate frames, and use the switched network to overcome short periods of congestion. Concerning the latter, the use of the switched network as a supplement to the use of leased analog or digital transmission facilities to connect remote bridges or routers during peak periods of internet activity provides you with the ability to economize upon your internet design. That is, you can use the switched network to satisfy peak transmission periods and size the operating rate of the wide area network transmission facility for average internet traffic. Doing so may provide you with the ability to economize upon the cost of establishing or maintaining internet transmission facilities while maintaining or surpassing the transmission requirements of your organization.

ETHERNET AND TOKEN-RING FRAME OPERATIONS

The key to understanding local area network performance issues is a detailed level of knowledge concerning the flow of data on a network. To understand how data flows on a local area network we must examine the method by which information is carried within a frame and how different frame fields are used to provide such functions as routing, error detection and other network functions. Thus, the purpose of this chapter is to obtain a detailed understanding of the composition of Ethernet and Token-Ring frames, including their frame fields and the function of each field within a frame. This will provide us with the ability to understand the overhead associated with different network frames with respect to the field actually used to transport information, how network access occurs, network addressing considerations, and similar information that we must consider in attempting to determine problems that may occur when establishing or expanding a network or in attempting to connect two previously independent networks. In examining local area network frame operations, we will first focus our attention upon the frame format used on an Ethernet network and then examine the three types of transmission formats supported by a Token-Ring network.

2.1 ETHERNET FRAME OPERATIONS

In this section we will first look at the composition of different types of Ethernet frames. In actuality, there is only one Ethernet frame, whereas the CSMA/CD frame format standardized by the IEEE is technically referred to as an 802.3 frame. However, in this book we will collectively refer to CSMA/CD operations as Ethernet, and when appropriate indicate differences between Ethernet and the IEEE 802.3 Ethernet-based CSMA/CD standard by a comparison of the two. One such area worthy of a comparison is the frame format which differs between Ethernet and the IEEE 802.3 Ethernet-based CSMA/CD standard. Once we have obtained an understanding of the composition of Ethernet and IEEE 802.3 frames, we will examine the function of fields within each frame and then discuss the overhead of the frame with respect to its information transfer capability.

2.1.1 Frame composition

Figure 2.1 illustrates the general frame composition of Ethernet and IEEE 802.3 frames. A third type of frame that I would be remiss if I did not mention is the Fast Ethernet, 100BASE-TX frame. That frame differs from the IEEE 802.3 frame through the addition of a byte at each end to mark the beginning and end of the frame. Because those bytes do not alter the composition of the frame I will first focus my attention upon the fields within Ethernet and IEEE 802.3 frames, and then describe the bytes unique to Fast Ethernet. In comparing the format of Ethernet and IEEE 802.3 frames, you will note that they slightly differ. An Ethernet frame contains an eight-byte preamble, whereas the IEEE 802.3 frame contains a seven-byte preamble followed by a one-byte start of frame delimiter field. A second difference between the composition of Ethernet and IEEE 802.3 frames

Ethernet

Preamble	Destination Address	Source Address	Type	Data	Frame Check Sequence
8 bytes	6 bytes	6 bytes	2 bytes	46-1500 bytes	4 bytes

IEEE 802.3

Preamble	Start of Frame Delimiter	Destination Address	Source Address	Length	Data	Frame Check Sequence
7 bytes	1 byte	2/6 bytes	2/6 bytes	2 bytes	46-1500 bytes	4 bytes

Figure 2.1 Ethernet and IEEE 802.3 frame formats

concerns the two-byte Ethernet type field. That field is used by Ethernet to specify the protocol carried in the frame, enabling several protocols to be carried independently of one another. Under the IEEE 802.3 frame format, the type field was replaced by a two-byte length field which specifies the number of bytes that follow that field as data.

The differences between Ethernet and IEEE 802.3 frames, although minor, make the two incompatible with one another. This means that your network must contain either all Ethernet compatible network interface cards (NICs) or all IEEE 802.3 compatible NICs. Fortunately, the fact that the IEEE 802.3 frame format represents a standard resulted in most vendors now marketing 802.3 compliant hardware and software. Although a few vendors continue to manufacture Ethernet or dual functioning Ethernet/IEEE 802.3 hardware, such products are primarily used to provide organizations with the ability to expand previously developed networks without requiring the wholesale replacement of NICs. Although the IEEE 802.3 standard has essentially replaced Ethernet due to their similarities and the fact that 802.3 was based upon Ethernet, we will consider both to be Ethernet. Now that we have an overview of the structure of Ethernet and 802.3 frames, let us probe deeper and examine the composition of each frame field. In doing so we will take advantage of the similarity between Ethernet and IEEE 802.3 frames and examine the fields of each frame on a composite basis, noting the differences between the two when appropriate.

Preamble field

The preamble field consists of eight (Ethernet) or seven (IEEE 802.3) bytes of alternating 1 and 0 bits. The purpose of this field is to announce the frame as well as enable all receivers on the network to synchronize themselves to the incoming frame. In addition, this field by itself under Ethernet or in conjunction with the start of frame delimiter field under the IEEE 802.3 standard ensures that there is a minimum spacing period of 9.6 ms between frames for error detection and recovery operations.

Start of frame delimiter field

This field is only applicable to the IEEE 802.3 standard and can be viewed as a continuation of the preamble. In fact, the composition of this field continues in the same manner as the format of the preamble, with alternating 1 and 0 bits used for the first six bit positions of this one-byte field. The last two bit positions of this field are 11, which breaks the synchronization pattern and alerts the receiver that frame data follows.

Both the preamble field and the start of frame delimiter field are removed by the controller when it places a received frame in its buffer. Similarly, when a controller transmits a frame, it prefixes the frame with those two fields if it is transmitting an IEEE 802.3 frame or with a preamble field if it is transmitting a true Ethernet frame.

Destination address field

The destination address identifies the recipient of the frame. Although this may appear to be a simple field, in actuality this field can vary between IEEE 802.3 and Ethernet frames with respect to field length. In addition, each field can consist of two or more subfields whose settings govern such network operations as the type of addressing used on the LAN and whether or not the frame is addressed to a specific station or more than one station. To obtain an appreciation for the use of this field, let us examine how it is used under the IEEE 802.3 standard as one of the two field formats is applicable to Ethernet.

Figure 2.2 illustrates the composition of the source and destination address fields. As indicated, the two-byte source and destination address fields are only applicable to IEEE 802.3 networks, whereas the six-byte source and destination address fields are applicable to both Ethernet and IEEE 802.3 networks.

Although you can select either a two- or a six-byte destination address field, when working with IEEE 802.3 equipment, all stations on the LAN must use the same addressing structure. Today, almost all 802.3 networks use six-byte addressing because the inclusion of a two-byte field option was primarily designed to accommodate early LANs that use 16-bit address fields.

I/G subfield

The one-bit I/G subfield is set to a 0 to indicate the frame is destined to an individual station, and a setting of 1 indicates that the frame is addressed to more than one station. Here the latter situation indicates a group address.

One special example of a group address is the assignment of all 1s to the address field. Here the address, hex FFFFFFFFFFFF, is

(a) 2 byte field (IEEE 802.3)

(b) 6 byte field (Ethernet and IEEE 802.3)

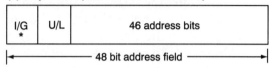

I/G bit subfield '0' = individual address '1' = group address
U/L bit subfield '0' = universally administrated addressing
'1' = locally administrated addressing

* set to '0' in source address field

Figure 2.2   Source and destination address field formats

recognized as a broadcast address and each station on the network will receive and accept frames with that destination address.

When a destination address specifies a single station, the address is referred to as a unicast address. A group address which defines multiple stations is known as a multicast address, whereas a group address which specifies all stations on the network is, as previously mentioned, referred to as a broadcast address.

U/L subfield

The U/L subfield is only applicable to the six-byte destination address field. The setting of this field's bit position indicates whether the destination address is an address that was assigned by the IEEE (universally administered) or assigned by the organization via software (locally administered).

Universal versus locally administered addressing

Each Ethernet Network Interface Card (NIC) contains a unique address burnt into its read-only memory (ROM) at the time of manufacture. To ensure that this universally administered address is not duplicated, the IEEE assigns blocks of addresses to each manufacturer. Those addresses normally include a three-byte prefix which identifies the manufacturer and is assigned by the IEEE, as well as a three-byte suffix which is assigned by the adapter manufacturer to its NIC. For example, the prefix hex 02608C identifies an NIC manufactured by 3Com, and a prefix of hex 008002 identifies an NIC manufactured by Digital Equipment Corporation.

Although the use of universally administered addressing eliminates the potential for duplicate network addresses, it does not provide the flexibility obtainable from locally administered addressing. For example, under locally administered addressing, you can configure mainframe software to work with a predefined group of addresses via a gateway PC. Then, as you add new stations to your LAN you simply use your installation program to assign a locally administered address to the NIC instead of using its universally administered address. As long as your mainframe computer has a pool of locally administered addresses which includes your recent assignment, you do not have to modify your mainframe communications software configuration. Because the modification of mainframe communications software typically requires a recompile and reload activity to be performed, doing so requires the attached network to become inoperative for a short period of time. As a large mainframe may service hundreds to thousands of users, such changes are normally performed late in the evening or during a weekend, making the changes for the use of locally administered addressing more responsive to users than the changes required when universally administered addressing is used.

Source address field

The source address field identifies the station that transmitted the frame. Similar to the destination address field, the source address can be either two or six bytes in length.

The two-byte source address is supported only under the IEEE 802.3 standard and requires the use of a two-byte destination address, with all stations on the network required to be set to two-byte addressing field use. The six-byte source address field is supported by both Ethernet and the IEEE 802.3 standard. When a six-byte address is used, the first three bytes represent the address assigned by the IEEE to the manufacturer for incorporation into each NIC's ROM. The vendor then normally assigns the last three bytes to each of its NICs.

Type field

The two-byte type field applies only to the Ethernet frame. This field identifies the higher-level protocol contained in the data field. Thus, this field tells the receiving device how to interpret the data field.

Under Ethernet, multiple protocols can exist on the LAN at the same time, and Xerox served as the custodian of Ethernet address ranges licensed to NIC manufacturers as well as defining the protocols supported by the assignment of type field values. Under the IEEE 802.3 standard, the type field was replaced by a length field which precludes compatibility between pure Ethernet and 802.3 frames.

Length field

The two-byte length field applies only to the IEEE 802.3 standard and defines the number of bytes contained in the data field. Under both Ethernet and IEEE 802.3 standards, the minimum size frame must be 64 bytes in length from preamble through FCS fields. This minimum size frame was required to ensure that there was sufficient transmission time to enable Ethernet NICs to accurately detect collisions based upon the maximum Ethernet cable length specified for a network and the time required for a frame to propagate the length of the cable. The minimum frame length of 64 bytes and the possibility of using two-byte addressing fields mean that each data field must be a minimum of 46 bytes in length.

Data field

As previously discussed, the data field must be a minimum of 46 bytes in length to ensure that the frame is at least 64 bytes in length. This means that the transmission of one byte of information must be carried within a 46-byte data field and results in the padding of the remainder of the field if the information to be placed in the field is less than 46 bytes in length. Although some publications subdivide the data field to include a PAD subfield, the latter actually represents optional fill characters that are added to the information in the data field to ensure a length of 46 bytes. The maximum length of the data field is 1500 bytes, which results in the use of multiple frames to transport full screen images and almost all file transfers.

Frame check sequence field

The frame check sequence (FCS) field is applicable to both Ethernet and the IEEE 802.3 standard and provides a mechanism for error detection. Each transmitter computes a cyclic redundancy check (CRC) which covers both address fields, the type/length field and the data field. The transmitter then places the computed CRC in the four-byte FCS field.

The CRC is developed by treating the composition of the previously mentioned fields as one long binary number. The n bits to be covered by the CRC are considered to represent the coefficients of a polynomial $M(X)$ of degree $n-1$. Here, the first bit in the destination address field corresponds to the X^{n-1} term, whereas the last bit in the data field corresponds to the X^0 term. Next, $M(X)$ is multiplied by X^{32} and the result of that multiplication process is divided by the following polynomial:

$$G(X) = X^{32} + X^{26} + X^{23} + X^{22} + X^{16} + X^{12} + X^{11} + X^{10}$$
$$+ X^8 + X^7 + X^5 + X^4 + X^3 + X + 1$$

Readers should note that the term X^n represents the setting of a bit to a 1 in position n. Thus, part of the generating polynomial $X^5 + X^4 + X^3 + X^1$ represents the binary value 110111.

The result of the division produces a quotient and remainder. The quotient is discarded and the remainder becomes the CRC value placed in the four-byte FCS field. This 32-bit CRC reduces the probability of an undetected error to 1 bit in every 4.3 billion, or approximately 1 bit in $2^{32} - 1$ bits.

Once a frame has reached its destination, the receiver uses the same polynomial to perform the same operation upon the received data. If the CRC computed by the receiver matches the CRC in the FCS field, the frame is accepted. Otherwise, the receiver discards the received frame, as it is considered to have one or more bits in error. The receiver will also consider a received frame to be invalid and discard it under two additional conditions. Those conditions occur when the frame does not contain an integral number of bytes and when the length of the data field does not match the value contained in the length field. Obviously the latter condition applies only to the 802.3 standard because an Ethernet frame uses a type field instead of a length field.

Fast Ethernet

As discussed earlier in this section the frame format of Fast Ethernet duplicates the IEEE 802.3 frame with the exception of

SSD 1 byte	Preamble 7 bytes	SFD 1 byte	Destination Address 6 bytes	Source Address 6 bytes	L/T 2 bytes	Data 45 to 1500 bytes	FCS 1 byte	ESD

Legend: SSD Start of Stream Delimiter
SFD Start of Frame Delimiter
L/T Length (IEEE 802.3) /Type (Ethernet)
ESD End of Stream Delimiter

Figure 2.3   Fast Ethernet frame. The 100BASE-TX frame differs from the IEEE 802.3 frame through the addition of a byte at each end to mark the beginning and ending of the stream delimiter

the use of prefix and suffix bytes that surround the frame. The prefix bit is known as the Start of Stream Delimiter (SSD), while the suffix byte is known as the End of Stream Delimiter (ESD).

The SSD is used to align a received frame for subsequent decoding, whereas the ESD is used as an indicator that data transmission has terminated normally and a properly formed stream has been transmitted. Figure 2.3 illustrates how the SSD and ESD bytes are used to 'frame' the IEEE 802.3 frame. At the 100 Mbps operating rate of 100BASE-TX the frames are known as streams, which accounts for the names of the two delimiters.

In comparing the Fast Ethernet to Ethernet and IEEE 802.3 frame formats illustrated in Figure 2.1, you will note that apart from the starting and ending stream delimiters, the Fast Ethernet frame duplicates the older frames. Another difference between the two is not shown, as it is not actually observable from a comparison of frames, since this difference is associated with the time between frames. Ethernet and IEEE 802.3 frames are Manchester encoded and have an interframe gap of $9.6\,\mu s$ between frames. In comparison, the Fast Ethernet 100BASE-TX frame is transmitted using 4B5B encoding, and idle codes are used to mark a $0.96\,\mu s$ interframe gap. Both the SSD and ESD fields can be considered to fall within the interframe gap of Fast Ethernet frames. Thus, computation between Ethernet/IEEE 802.3 and Fast Ethernet becomes simplified, as the latter has an operating rate 10 times the former and an interframe gap one-tenth of the former.

2.1.2 Frame overhead

As previously indicated in this section, each Ethernet and Fast Ethernet frame consists of six fields (if we consider the preamble and start of frame delimiter as one field and do not consider the SSD and ESD fields, as they are considered to fall within the interframe gap), of which only one field actually transports information. That data field must contain a minimum of 46 bytes even if the frame is transporting a single character response to a client–server query. Thus, the overhead associated with an Ethernet frame depends upon both the fixed length of the frame fields that do not carry information as well as the number of characters carried in the data field, which can vary from one to 1500 bytes.

If we assume six-byte addressing which is applicable to almost all modern Ethernet networks, the number of fixed overhead bytes per frame is 26, consisting of eight preamble bytes, six destination and six source address bytes, two bytes for the type or length field, and four bytes for the FCS field.

A one-byte response carried in the data field must be padded by the addition of 37 fill characters when six-byte addressing is used. In this situation the overhead required to carry a one-byte character is 26 plus 37, or 63 bytes.

Now consider the situation in which you have 38 bytes of data to transmit. Here the 38 bytes would not require the addition of pad characters, because the frame length when using six-byte addressing would be 64 bytes which is the minimum frame length. Thus, 38 bytes of data would result in a frame overhead of 26 bytes.

Table 2.1 summarizes the overhead associated with transporting information in Ethernet frames as the number of bytes of information varies from one to the maximum 1500 bytes the frame can carry. As indicated in Table 2.1, this overhead can vary considerably, ranging from a high of 6300% to a low of 1.7% when the maximum length data field is used to transport information.

Table 2.1 Ethernet frame overhead

Information carried in data field (bytes)	Frame overhead (bytes)	Percent overhead
1	63	6300.0
38	26	68.4
39	26	66.7
64	26	40.6
128	26	20.3
256	26	10.2
512	26	5.1
1024	26	2.5
1500	26	1.7

One question you might have by now is how you can use the overhead information presented in Table 2.1 to your advantage to increase network performance. The data contained in Table 2.1 can be extremely important for network performance if your organization is developing client–server applications. For example, assume that your programming staff is developing screens to be displayed on a user's workstation in which the client enters information which is then transmitted to the server to initiate different activities. If there is a choice between generating a screen display which results in the transmission of a small number of characters to the server or generating a lesser number of screen displays and transmitting the fields of several screens at one time, the latter is preferable as it results in a lower overhead. This in turn will reduce the number of frames carried on the network. Since each version of Ethernet requires a fixed time gap between frames, reducing the number of frames increases the efficiency of the data flow. Although altering the transmission of data carried by frames will probably not result in any noticeable increase in network performance if your network only has a handful of workstations, more notable results can be expected to be observed if your network has a large number of stations that perform client–server operations on a regular basis.

2.2 TOKEN-RING FRAME FORMATS

Three types of frame format are supported on a Token-Ring network: token, abort, and frame. The token format as illustrated at the top of Figure 2.4 is the mechanism by which access to the ring is passed from one computer attached to the network to another device connected to the network. Here the token format consists of three bytes, of which the starting and ending delimiters are used to indicate the beginning and end of a token frame. The middle byte of a token frame is an access control byte. Three bits are used as a priority indicator, three bits are used as a reservation indicator, and one bit is used for the token bit, and another bit position functions as the monitor bit. When the token bit is set to a binary 0 it indicates that the transmission is a token. When it is set to a binary 1 it indicates that data in the form of a frame are being transmitted.

The second Token-Ring frame format signifies an abort token. In actuality there is no token, since this format is indicated by a starting delimiter followed by an ending delimiter. The transmission of an abort token is used to abort a previous transmission. The format of an abort token is illustrated in Figure 2.4b.

(a) Token format

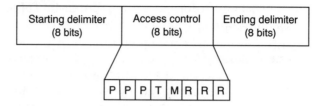

(b) Abort token format

Starting delimiter	Ending delimiter

(c) Frame format

Starting delimiter (8 bits)	Access control (8 bits)	Frame control (8 bits)	Destination address (48 bits)	Source address (48 bits)	Routing information (optional)

Information variable	Frame check sequence (32 bits)	Ending delimiter (8 bits)	Frame status (8 bits)

Figure 2.4 a: Token, b: abort, and c: frame formats. P = priority bits, T = token bit, M = monitor bit, R = reservation bits

The third type of Token-Ring frame format occurs when a station seizes a free token. At that time the token format is converted into a frame which includes the addition of frame control, addressing data, an error detection field and a frame status field. The format of a Token-Ring frame is illustrated in Figure 2.4c.

2.2.1 Frame composition

By examining each of the fields in the Token-Ring frame we can examine the token and token abort frames due to the commonality of fields between each frame. Note that, excluding the optional routing field, there is a total of 21 bytes of overhead associated with a Token-Ring frame.

Starting/ending delimiters

The starting and ending delimiters mark the beginning and ending of a token or frame. Each delimiter consists of a unique code pattern which identifies it to the network. To understand the composition of the starting and ending delimiter fields requires us to review the method by which data are represented on a Token-Ring network using Differential Manchester encoding.

Differential Manchester encoding

Figure 2.5 illustrates the use of Differential Manchester encoding, comparing its operation to non-return to zero (NRZ) and conventional Manchester encoding.

At the top of Figure 2.5, NRZ coding illustrates the representation of data by holding a voltage low ($-V$) to represent a binary 0 and high ($+V$) to represent a binary 1. This method of signaling is called non-return to zero, because there is no return to a 0 V position after each data bit is coded.

One problem associated with NRZ encoding is the fact that a long string of 0 or 1 bits does not result in a voltage change. Thus, to determine that bit m in a string of n bits of 0s or 1s is set to a 0 or 1 requires sampling at predefined bit times. This in turn requires each device on a network using NRZ encoding to have its own clocking circuitry.

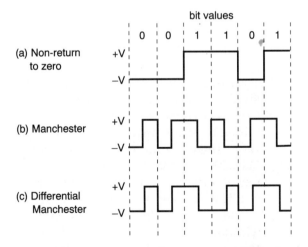

Figure 2.5 a: Non-return to zero (NRZ), b: Manchester, and c: Differential Manchester encoding. In Differential Manchester encoding, the direction of the signal's voltage transition changes whenever a binary 1 is transmitted but remains the same for a binary 0

To avoid the necessity of building clocking circuitry into devices requires a mechanism for encoded data to carry clocking information. One method by which encoded data carries clocking information is obtained from the use of Manchester encoding which is illustrated in Figure 2.5b. In Manchester encoding, each data bit consists of a half-bit time signal at a low (negative) voltage (−V) and another half-bit time signal at the opposite (positive) voltage (+V). Every binary 0 is represented by a half-bit time at a low voltage and the remaining half-bit time at a high voltage. Every binary 1 is represented by a half-bit time at a high voltage followed by a half-bit time at a low voltage. By changing the voltage for every binary digit, Manchester encoding ensures that the signal carries self-clocking information.

In Figure 2.5c, Differential Manchester encoding is illustrated. The difference between Manchester encoding and Differential Manchester encoding occurs in the method by which binary 1s are encoded. In Differential Manchester encoding, the direction of the signal's voltage transition changes whenever a binary 1 is transmitted, but remains the same for a binary 0. The IEEE 802.5 standard specifies the use of Differential Manchester encoding and this encoding technique is used on Token-Ring networks at the physical layer to transmit and detect four distinct symbols: a binary 0, a binary 1 and two non-data symbols.

Non-data symbols

Under Manchester and Differential Manchester encoding two possible code violations that can occur. Each code violation produces what is known as a non-data symbol and is used in the Token-Ring frame to denote starting and ending delimiters similar to the use of the flag in an HDLC frame. However, unlike the flag whose bit composition, 01111110, is uniquely maintained by inserting a 0 bit after every sequence of five set bits and removing a 0 following every sequence of five set bits, Differential Manchester encoding maintains the uniqueness of frames by the use of non-data J and non-data K symbols. This eliminates the bit stuffing operations required by HDLC.

The two non-data symbols each consist of two half-bit times without a voltage change. The J symbol occurs when the voltage is the same as that of the last signal, and the K symbol occurs when the voltage becomes the opposite of that of the last signal. Figure 2.6 illustrates the occurrence of the J and K non-data symbols based upon different last-bit voltages. Readers will note in

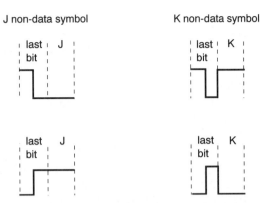

Figure 2.6 J and K non-data symbol composition. J and K non-data symbols are distant code violations that cannot be mistaken for data

comparing Figure 2.6 to Figure 2.5c that the J and K non-data symbols are distinct code violations that cannot be mistaken for either a binary 0 or a binary 1.

Now that we have an understanding of the operation of Differential Manchester encoding and the composition of the J and K non-data symbols, we can focus our attention upon the actual format of each frame delimiter.

The start delimiter field marks the beginning of a frame. The composition of this field is the bits and non-data symbols JK0JK000. The end delimiter field marks the end of a frame as well as denoting whether or not the frame is the last frame of a multiple frame sequence using a single token or if there are additional frames following this frame. The format of the end delimiter field is JK1JK1IE, where I is the intermediate frame bit. If I is set to 0, this indicates that it is the last frame transmitted by a station. If I is set to 1, this indicates that additional frames follow this frame. E is an Error-Detected bit. The E bit is initially set to 0 by the station transmitting a frame, token or abort sequence. As the frame circulates the ring, each station checks the transmission for errors. Upon detection of a Frame Check Sequence (FCS) error, inappropriate non-data symbol, illegal framing, or another type of error, the first station that detects the error will set the E bit to a value of 1. Since stations keep track of the number of times they set the E bit to a value of 1, it becomes possible to use this information as a guide to locating possible cable errors. For example, if one workstation accounted for a very large percentage of E bit settings in a 72-station network, there is a high degree of probability that there is a problem with the lobe cable to that workstation. The problem could be a crimped cable or a loose connector, and it represents a logical place to commence an investigation in an attempt to reduce E bit errors.

Access control field

The second field in both token and frame formats is the access control byte. As illustrated in Figure 2.4a, this byte consists of four subfields and it serves as the controlling mechanism for gaining access to the network. When a free token circulates around the network the access control field represents one-third of the length of the frame since it is prefixed by the start delimiter and suffixed by the end delimiter.

The lowest priority that can be specified by the priority bits in the access control byte is zero (000), and the highest is seven (111), providing eight levels of priority. Table 2.2 lists the normal use of the priority bits in the access control field. Workstations have a default priority of three, and bridges have a default priority of four.

To reserve a token, a workstation inserts its priority level in the priority reservation subfield. Unless another station with a higher priority bumps the requesting station, the reservation will be honored and the requesting station will obtain the token. If the token bit is set to 1, this serves as an indication that a frame follows instead of the ending delimiter.

A station that needs to transmit a frame at a given priority can use any available token that has a priority level equal to or less than the priority level of the frame to be transmitted. When a token of equal or lower priority is not available, the ring station

Table 2.2 Priority bit settings

Priority bits	Priority	
000	0	Normal user priority, MAC frames that do not require a token and response type MAC frames
001	1	Normal user priority
010	2	Normal user priority
011	3	Normal user priority and MAC frames that require tokens
100	4	Bridge
101	5	Reserved
110	6	Reserved
111	7	Specialized Station Management

can reserve a token of the required priority through the use of the reservation bits. In doing so the station must follow two rules. First, if a passing token has a higher priority reservation than the reservation level desired by the workstation, the station will not alter the reservation field contents. Secondly, if the reservation bits have not been set or indicate a lower priority than that desired by the station, the station can now set the reservation bits to the required priority level.

Once a frame has been removed by its originating station, the reservation bits in the header will be checked. If those bits have a non-zero value, the station must release a non-zero priority token, with the actual priority assigned based upon the priority used by the station for the recently transmitted frame, the reservation bit settings received upon the return of the frame, and any stored priority.

Upon occasion, the Token-Ring protocol will result in the transmission of a new token by a station prior to that station having the ability to verify the settings of the access control field in a returned frame. When this situation arises, the token will be issued according to the priority and reservation bit settings in the access control field of the transmitted frame.

Figure 2.7 illustrates the operation of the priority (P) and reservation (R) bit fields in the access control field. In this example, the prevention of a high-priority station from monopolizing the network is illustrated by station A entering a Priority-Hold state. This occurs when a station originates a token at a higher priority than the last token it generated. Once in a Priority-Hold state, the station will issue tokens that will bring the priority level eventually down to zero as a mechanism to prevent a high-priority station from monopolizing the network.

The monitor bit

The monitor bit is used to prevent a token with a priority exceeding zero or a frame from continuously circulating on the Token-Ring. This bit is transmitted as a 0 in all tokens and frames, except for a device on the network which functions as an active monitor and thus obtains the capability to inspect and modify that bit. When a token or frame is examined by the active monitor it will set the monitor bit to 1 if it was previously found to be set to 0. If a token or frame is found to have the monitor bit already set to 1 this indicates that the token or frame has already made at least one revolution around the ring and an error condition has occurred, usually caused by the failure of a station

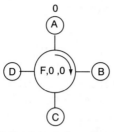

(a) Station A generates a frame
using a non-priority token P,R = 0,0

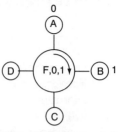

(b) Station B reserves a priority 1 in the
reservation bits in the frame P,R = 0,1;
Station A enters a priorty-hold state.

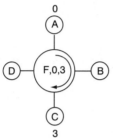

(c) Station C reserves a priority of 3,
overriding B's reservation of 1; P,R = 0,3.

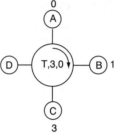

(d) Station A removes its frame and
generates a token at reserved
priority level 3; P,R = 3,0.

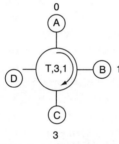

(e) Station B repeats priority token and makes a
new reservation of priority level 1; P,R = 3,1.

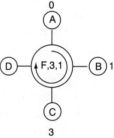

(f) Station C grabs token and transmits a frame
with a priority of 3; P,R = 3,1.

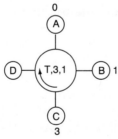

(g) Upon return of frame to Station C
it's removed. Station C generates a
token at the priority just used; P,R = 3,1.

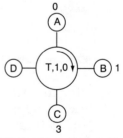

(h) Station A in a priority-hold state grabs token
and changes its priority to 1; P,R = 1,0.
Station A stays in priority-hold state until
priority reduced to 0.

Legend:

(A),(B),(C),(D) = stations

Numeric outside station identifier
indicates priority level.

Figure 2.7 Priority and reservation field utilization

to remove its transmission from the ring or the failure of a high-priority station to seize a token. When the active monitor finds a monitor bit set to 1 it assumes that an error condition has occurred. The active monitor then purges the token or frame and releases a new token onto the ring. Now that we have an understanding of the role of the monitor bit in the access control field and the operation of the active monitor on that bit, let us focus our attention upon the active monitor.

Active monitor

The active monitor is the device that has the highest address on the network. All other stations on the network are considered as standby monitors and watch the active monitor.

As previously explained, the function of the active monitor is to determine if a token or frame is continuously circulating the ring in error. To accomplish this the active monitor sets the monitor count bit as a token or frame goes by. If a destination workstation fails or has its power turned off the frame will circulate back to the active monitor, where it is then removed from the network. In the event that the active monitor should fail or be turned off, the standby monitors watch the active monitor by looking for an active monitor frame. If one does not appear within seven seconds, the standby monitor that has the highest network address then takes over as the active monitor.

Frame control field

The frame control field informs a receiving device on the network of the type of frame that was transmitted and how it should be interpreted. Frames can be either logical link control (LLC) or reference physical link functions according to the IEEE 802.5 media access control (MAC) standard. A media access control frame carries network control information and responses, and a logical link control frame carries data.

The eight-bit frame control field has the format FFZZZZZZ, where FF are frame definition bits. The upper part of Table 2.3 indicates the possible settings of the frame bits and the assignment of those settings. The ZZZZZZ bits convey MAC buffering information when the FF bits are set to 00. When the FF bits are set to 01 to indicate an LLC frame, the ZZZZZZ bits are split into two fields, designated rrrYYY. Currently, the rrr bits are reserved for future use and are set to 000. The YYY bits indicate the

Table 2.3 Frame control field subfields

F bit settings	Assignment
00	MAC frame
01	LLC frame
10	Undefined (reserved for future use)
11	Undefined (reserved for future use)

Z bit settings	Assignment[a]
000	Normal buffering
001	Remove ring station
010	Beacon
011	Claim token
100	Ring purge
101	Active monitor present
110	Standby monitor present

[a]When F bits set to 00, Z bits are used to notify an adapter that the frame is to be expressed buffered.

priority of the LLC data. The lower portion of Table 2.3 indicates the value of the Z bits when used in MAC frames to notify a Token-Ring adapter that the frame is to be expressed buffered.

Destination address field

Although the IEEE 802.5 standard is similar to Ethernet in that it supports both 16-bit and 48-bit address fields, IBM's implementation requires the use of 48-bit address fields and almost all Token-Ring networks use six-byte address fields today. The destination address field is made up of five subfields as illustrated in Figure 2.8. The first bit in the destination address identifies the destination as an individual station (bit set to 0) or as a group of one or more stations (bit set to 1). The latter provides the capability for a message to be broadcast to a group of stations.

Universally administered address

Similarly to Ethernet, the Token-Ring universally administered address is a unique address permanently encoded into an adapter's ROM. Because it is placed into ROM, it is also known as a burnt-in address. The IEEE assigns blocks of addresses to

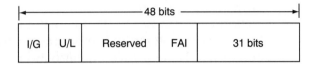

Figure 2.8 Destination address subfields. The reserved field contains the manufacturer's identification in 22 bits represented by 6 hex digits.
I/G = individual or group bit address identifier, U/L = universally or locally administered bit identifier, FAI = functional address indicator

each vendor manufacturing Token-Ring equipment, which ensures that Token-Ring adapter cards manufactured by different vendors are uniquely defined. Some Token-Ring adapter manufacturers are assigned universal addresses that contain an organizationally unique identifier. This identifier consists of the first six hex digits of the adapter card address and is also referred to as the manufacturer identification. For example, cards manufactured by IBM will begin with the address hex 08005A or hex 10005A, whereas adapter cards manufactured by Texas Instruments will begin with the address hex 400014.

Locally administered address

A key problem with the use of universally administered addresses is the requirement to change software coding in a mainframe computer whenever a workstation connected to the mainframe via a gateway is added or removed from the network. To avoid constant software changes, locally administrated addressing can be used. This type of addressing temporarily overrides universally administrated addressing; however, the user is now responsible for ensuring the uniqueness of each address.

Functional address indicator

The functional address indicator (FAI) subfield in the destination address identifies the function associated with the destination address, such as a bridge, active monitor or configuration report server.

The functional address indicator indicates a functional address when it is set to 0 and the I/G (Individual/Group) bit position is set to 1, the latter indicating a group address. This condition can only occur when the U/L (Universally/Locally administered) bit position is also set to 1 and results in the ability to generate locally administered group addresses that are called functional addresses. Table 2.4 lists the functional addresses defined by the IEEE. Currently, 14 functional addresses have been defined out of a total of 31 that are available for use, with the remaining addresses available for user definitions or reserved for future use.

Address values

The range of addresses that can be used on a Token-Ring primarily depends upon the settings of the I/G, U/L and FAI bit positions. When the I/G and U/L bit positions are set to 00 the manufacturer's universal address is used. When the I/G and U/L bits are set to 01, individual locally administered addresses are used in the defined range listed in Table 2.4. When all three bit positions are set, this situation indicates a group address within the range contained in Table 2.5. If the I/G and U/L bits are set to 11 but the FAI bit is set to 0, this indicates that the address is a functional address. In this situation the range of addresses is bit-sensitive, permitting only those functional addresses previously listed in Table 2.4.

In addition to the previously mentioned addresses, there are two special destination address values that are defined. An address of all 1s (hex FFFFFFFFFFFF) identifies all stations as

Table 2.4 IEEE Token-Ring functional addresses

Active monitor	hexC000 0000 0001
Ring Parameter Server	hexC000 0000 0002
Network Server Heartbeat	hexC000 0000 0004
Ring Error Monitor	hexC000 0000 0008
Configuration Report Server	hexC000 0000 0010
Synchronous Bandwidth Manager	hexC000 0000 0020
Locate–Directory Server	hexC000 0000 0040
NETBIOS	hexC000 0000 0080
Bridge	hexC000 0000 0100
IMPL Server	hexC000 0000 0200
Ring Authorization Server	hexC000 0000 0400
LAN Gateway	hexC000 0000 0800
Ring Wiring Concentrator	hexC000 0000 1000
LAN Manager	hexC000 0000 2000
User-defined	hexC000 0000 8000
	through hexC000 4000 0000

Table 2.5 Token-Ring addresses

| | Bit settings | | | |
	I/G	U/L	FAI	Address/address range
Individual, universally administered	0	0	0/1	Manufacturer's serial no.
Individual, locally administered	0	1	0	hex4000 0000 0000 to hex4000 7FFF FFFF
Group address	1	1	1	hexC000 8000 0000 to hexC000 FFFF FFFF
Functional address	1	1	0	hexC000 0000 0001 to hexC000 0000 2000
All stations broadcast	1	1	1	hexFFFF FFFF FFFF
Null address	0	0	0	hex0000 0000 0000

destination stations. If a null address is used in which all bits are set to 0 (hex 000000000000), the frame is not addressed to any workstation. In this situation it can only be transmitted but not received, enabling you to test the ability of the active monitor to purge this type of frame from the network.

Source address field

The source address field always represents an individual address which specifies the adapter card responsible for the transmission. The source address field consists of three major subfields as illustrated in Figure 2.9. When locally administered addressing occurs, only 24 bits in the address field are used since the 22 manufacturer identification bit positions are not used.

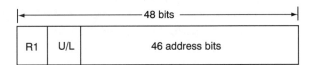

Figure 2.9 Source address field. The 46 address bits consist of 22 manufacturer identification bits and 24 universally administered bits when the U/L bit is set to 0. If set to 1, a 31-bit locally administered address is used with the manufacturer's identification bits set to 0. RI = routing information bit identifier, U/L = universally or locally administered bit identifier

The routing information (RI) bit identifier identifies the fact that routing information is contained in an optional routing information field. This bit is set when a frame will be routed across a bridge using IBM's source routing technique.

Routing information field

The routing information field (RIF) is optional and is included in a frame when the RI bit of the source address field is set. Figure 2.10 illustrates the format of the optional routing information field. If this field is omitted, the frame cannot leave the ring on which it originated under IBM's source routing bridging method. Under transparent bridging, the frame can be transmitted onto another ring. The routing information field is of variable length and it contains a control subfield and one or more two-byte route designator fields when included in a frame, as the latter are required to control the flow of frames across one or more bridges.

The maximum length of the routing information field supported by IBM is 18 bytes. Since each routing information field must contain a two-byte routing control field, this leaves a maximum of 16 bytes available for use by up to eight route designators. As illustrated in Figure 2.10, each two-byte route designator consists of a 12-bit ring number and a four-bit bridge number. Thus, a maximum total of 16 bridges can be used to join any two rings in an Enterprise Token-Ring network.

Information field

The information field is used to contain Token-Ring commands and responses, as well as to carry user data. The type of data carried by the information field depends upon the F bit settings in the frame type field. If the F bits are set to 00 the information field carries media access control (MAC) commands and responses that are used for network management operations. If the F bits are set to 01 the information field carries logical link control (LLC) or user data. Such data can be in the form of portions of a file being transferred on the network or an electronic mail message being routed to another workstation on the network. The information field is of variable length and can be considered to represent the higher level protocol enveloped in a Token-Ring frame.

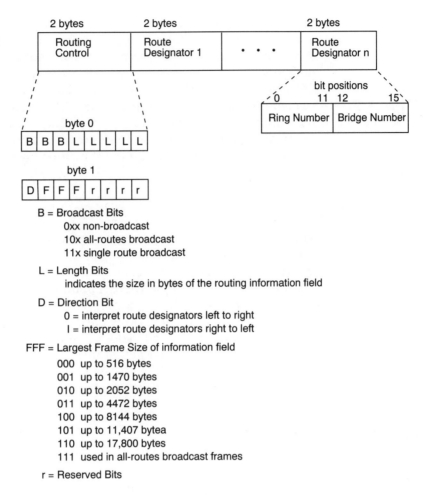

Figure 2.10 Routing information field

In the IBM implementation of the IEEE 802.5 Token-Ring standard the maximum length of the information field depends upon the Token-Ring adapter used and the operating rate of the network. Token-Ring adapters with 64 Kbytes of memory can handle up to 4.5 Kbytes on a 4 Mbps network and up to 18 Kbytes on a 16 Mbps network.

Frame check sequence field

The frame check sequence field contains four bytes which provide the mechanism for checking the accuracy of frames flowing on the network. The cyclic redundancy check data included in the frame check sequence field covers the frame control, destination address, source address, routing information and information fields. If an adapter computes a cyclic redundancy check that does not match the data contained in the frame check sequence field of a frame, the destination adapter discards the frame information and sets an error bit (E-bit) indicator. This error bit indicator, as previously discussed, actually represents a ninth bit position of the ending delimiter and serves to inform the transmitting station that the data were received in error.

Frame status field

The frame status field serves as a mechanism to indicate the results of a frame's circulation around a ring to the station that initiated the frame. Figure 2.11 indicates the format of the frame status field. The frame status field contains three subfields that are duplicated for accuracy purposes because they reside outside of CRC checking. One field (A) is used to denote if an address was recognized, and a second field (C) indicates if the frame was copied at its destination. Each of these fields is one bit in length. The third field (rr), which is two bit positions in length, is currently reserved for future use.

2.2.2 Frame overhead

Unlike Ethernet, which requires the use of fill characters to produce a minimum length frame of 64 bytes, there are no such restrictions on a Token-Ring frame. Although this makes the computation of the Token-Ring frame overhead more direct, this is only true when a frame does not contain a routing information field. If it does, then the length of that field, which can be up to 18 bytes, will affect the overhead of frames that traverse more than one Token-Ring network.

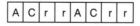

A = Address-Recognized Bits
C = Frame-Copied Bits
r = Reserved Bits

Figure 2.11 Frame status field. The frame status field denotes if the destination address was recognized and if the frame was copied. Since this field is outside CRC checking its subfields are duplicated for accuracy

Table 2.6 Token-Ring frame overhead

Information field (bytes)	Frame overhead (bytes)	Percent overhead
1	21	2100.0
32	21	65.6
64	21	32.8
128	21	16.4
256	21	8.2
512	21	4.1
1 024	21	2.1
2 048	21	1.0
4 096	21	0.5
4 500	21	0.5
8 192	21	0.3
16 384	21	0.1

If we focus our attention upon frames limited to being carried on a single network, as indicated in Figure 2.4c, the overhead of a Token-Ring frame is 21 bytes. This overhead is applicable to both 4 and 16 Mbps Token-Ring networks.

Table 2.6 illustrates the overhead of Token-Ring frames as the information field varies in length from 1 to 16 384 bytes. As previously noted, the maximum information field length is 4500 bytes for a 4 Mbps Token-Ring network and 18 000 bytes for a 16 Mbps Token-Ring network.

In examining the overhead associated with information fields whose lengths are under 512 bytes, we can express concerns with respect to network performance which are similar to those found with short Ethernet data fields. That is, if your organization is in the process of developing client–server applications, network performance can be improved by developing client–server displays and transmitting a grouping of information to the server rather than a series of short groups of data. Although there is no predefined time gap between Token-Ring frames as there is with Ethernet frames, the lower operating rate of a 4 Mbps Token-Ring frame increases the probability of poor performance with a lesser number of clients accessing a server and repeatedly transmitting short responses to server application program queries. Thus, you may be able to improve the performance of your Token-Ring network, as well as extend its ability to service additional users without degrading network performance, by designing application programs to take advantage of the structure of network frames.

3

ESTIMATING
NETWORK TRAFFIC

Although there are a large number of hardware and software products that can be used to obtain network utilization information, the use of those products obviously requires an existing network. If you're planning the installation of a new network, you cannot use a performance monitor to measure network utilization until the network has been established. At that time you might notice a high level of utilization, requiring the network to be subdivided through the use of a local bridge or switching hub to provide a better level of performance to local area network users. Thus, it is important to understand how you can estimate network traffic and use the results of that traffic estimation process to determine whether or not you should consider the subdivision of the network via the use of a local bridge, switching hub or similar communications device to enhance the performance level of each network segment.

In this chapter we will first focus our attention upon developing a methodology to estimate network traffic on a local area network. In doing so we will develop a traffic estimation worksheet and use that worksheet to project the average and peak traffic that could be carried on a network. Next, we will turn our attention to the typical average and peak utilization levels of Ethernet and Token-Ring networks, discussing utilization levels which, when exceeded, may indicate a decision criterion for network subdivision. This will be followed by an example that illustrates how the use of a local bridge can make performance on each part better than if a network was not subdivided Because Chapter 9 is directly focused upon the use of switching hubs, we will defer a discussion of the use of this communications device until that chapter.

3.1 THE NETWORK TRAFFIC ESTIMATION PROCESS

Assuming that you do not have access to monitoring equipment to analyze an existing local area network or that your network is in a planning stage, you can develop a reasonable estimate of traffic by considering the functions each network user performs. To facilitate the traffic estimation process you can group a number of network users together into a 'workstation class' category and perform your computations for a single workstation. Then, you can multiply the results of that computation by the number of workstations grouped into the specific workstation class to obtain an estimate of network traffic for a similar group of network users. You can then repeat this process for each workstation class you define and add the traffic estimate for all workstation classes to obtain an estimate of the average traffic that will be carried on the entire network.

3.1.1 The traffic estimation worksheet

As mentioned at the beginning of this chapter, you can expedite the traffic estimation process through the use of a worksheet. Figure 3.1 illustrates the general format of a traffic estimation worksheet you can consider to facilitate your network traffic estimation process. Prior to illustrating how you can use the worksheet, let us first review the meaning of each entry in the worksheet.

Workstation class

The workstation class identifies a specific category of local area network user. Normally you will use the occupational category of a group of persons for that entry. Typically, but not always, that entry reflects their average usage of the LAN. Examples of some common workstation classes include secretary, engineer, accountant, payroll clerk, application programmer, and so on.

Number of stations

The number of stations entry on the worksheet permits you to indicate the number of workstations that fall into a specific workstation class. Thus, you would normally have one worksheet for each defined workstation class.

Workstation Class _____   Number of Stations _____

Activity Performed	Message Size in Bytes	Number of Frames/ Msg	Frame Size in Bytes	Frequency /Hr	Resulting Bit Rate (bps)*
					Subtotal bps=

Total for all workstation class:

_____ = # stations _____ * subtotal bps _____ = _____

•Note:
$$\text{bit rate (bps)} = \frac{\text{frames/message * frame size * 8 bits/byte * frequency/hour}}{3600 \text{ seconds/hour}}$$

Figure 3.1   Traffic estimation worksheet

Column entries

Turning our attention to the column entries, you will note six specific column headings. The first column provides you with the ability to define the major activities performed by a workstation in the given class. Examples of major workstation activities include loading programs and data files residing on the network server, saving data files to the server, transmitting and receiving electronic mail, and directing print jobs to a network printer. Although the worksheet contains nine rows, you can add additional rows if you wish to define more than nine specific activities for a particular workstation class.

The Message Size column references the average number of bytes in a particular event performed by the defined activity. For example, suppose that the transmission of electronic messages is expected to average 1800 characters. Thus, the message size in bytes would be entered as 1800.

Although several articles and technical manuals read by the author indicate the direct use of the message size, doing so results in a degree of inaccuracy. Even though the use of a traffic estimation worksheet, as its name implies, results in an estimate of network traffic, we can reduce the degree of inaccuracy by considering the fact that Ethernet, Fast Ethernet, Token-Ring and other types of LAN frames have a degree of overhead. That degree of overhead can range in scope from a few percent for large message sizes to 30–50% or more for small size messages, due to the failure of the authors of those articles and technical manuals to consider the fact that a message must be encapsulated into one or more local area network frames and that each frame contains a number of fields that wrap around the encapsulated information. Thus, you must consider the number of frames used to carry a message as well as the frame size. Here the latter includes the overhead fields that contain the preamble (Ethernet) or starting delimiter (Token-Ring), source and destination addresses, and other frame information. As previously noted in Chapter 2, the overhead associated with Ethernet and Fast Ethernet frames can vary from a low of 26 bytes when 38 or more bytes of information are carried in the data field to as many as 63 bytes when that field carries only one character of information. In comparison, a Token-Ring frame which is not routed between rings has a fixed overhead of 21 bytes.

The fifth column contained in the traffic estimation worksheet is used to place your estimate of the frequency per hour in which the row activity is performed. Even if this activity is performed only once per day, such as the remote load of a diskless workstation, you can express the frequency on an hourly basis. For example, if you expect an activity to occur once a day and expect the workstation user to work an eight-hour day, then the frequency per hour becomes 1/8, or 0.125.

The last column in the traffic estimation worksheet contains the resulting bit rate computed for the specific activity entered on the row. As indicated by the footnote at the bottom of the worksheet, the bit rate in bps is determined by the following equation:

bit rate (bps)
$$= \frac{\text{frames/message} \times \text{frame size} \times 8 \times \text{frequency/hour}}{3600 \text{ seconds/hour}}$$

Once you have computed the resulting bit rate for each activity, you can sum the results of those computations to obtain the bit rate for all activities for one workstation in the class of workstations you are working with. To complete your computation for the workstation class, you would then multiply the number of workstations in the class by the summed bit rate, as indicated in the lower portion of Figure 3.1. Next, you would complete the traffic estimation process by computing a total bit rate for each remaining workstation class and then sum the total for each workstation class to obtain a network traffic estimate.

3.1.2 Developing a network traffic estimate

Since the best way to illustrate the network traffic estimation process is by example, let us do so. Assume that you want to install a Token-Ring local area network that will operate at 4 Mbps. Suppose that this network is intended to support 50 design engineers; 30 technicians; 40 general support personnel in accounting, personnel, finance, sales, and marketing; 10 managers; and 10 secretaries. Thus, you would probably consider completing a series of six traffic estimation worksheets to cover each of the six general categories of users planned for the Token-Ring network. As an alternative, you might decide to complete separate traffic estimation worksheets for accounting, personnel, finance, sales and marketing personnel, instead of grouping them into a general support personnel class of network users. If you do this, you would then be required to complete a total of nine traffic estimation worksheets instead of five.

Using the traffic estimation worksheet

Figure 3.2 illustrates the completion of a traffic estimation worksheet for the design engineer class of workstation users. In completing this worksheet it was assumed that the average design engineer will perform a core set of seven local area network functions. Those functions are listed under the Activity Performed column in Figure 3.2, and range in scope from loading a program which resides on a network server to loading and saving graphic images, sending and receiving messages, and printing both graphic images and text data on a printer to be connected to the Token-Ring network.

Required computations

To illustrate the computations used for the completion of the traffic estimation worksheet, let us consider the load program

Workstation Class   Design Engineer   Number of Stations   50

Activity Performed	Message Size in Bytes	Number of Frames/ Msg	Frame Size in Bytes	Frequency /Hr	Resulting Bit Rate (bps)*
load program	512 K	117	4521	5	5878
load graphic image	1024 K	233	4521	3	7023
save graphic image	1024 K	233	4521	3	7023
send message	0.5 K	1	533	2	3
receive message	0.5 K	1	533	2	3
print graphic image	1024 K	233	4521	3	7023
print text data	0.5 K	1	533	4	6
				Subtotal bps=	26959

Total for all workstation class:

  Design Engineer = # stations   50 * subtotal bps   26959   = 1,347,950

•Note:

bit rate (bps) = $\dfrac{\text{frames/message * frame size * 8 bits/byte * frequency/hour}}{\text{3600 seconds/hour}}$

Figure 3.2   Completed traffic estimation worksheet

activity entry row. Here it was assumed that programs which occupy an average of 512 kbytes of storage on the network server will be loaded five times each hour. Although this program loading frequency may appear high, many engineering programs actually consist of a series of overlays, and the loading of one program could easily result in the loading of five modules each hour, as the design engineer accesses different program features in performing the design effort.

If the size of the program or program module loaded into the workstation is 512 kbytes, then the actual size of the program is 512×1024 bytes per K, or 524 288 bytes.

On a 4 Mbps Token-Ring network the maximum length of the information field in a frame which contains the program data transported from the server to the workstation is 4500 bytes. Thus, 524 288 bytes in the program divided by 4500 bytes that can be carried in a frame result in 117 frames that will be required to transport the program. Although the information field is 4500 bytes, the actual frame size will be 4521 bytes since there are 21 overhead bytes in a Token-Ring frame. Based upon the preceding calculations, the resulting bit rate attributed to the load program activity becomes

bit rate (bps)

$$= \frac{117 \text{ frames} \times 4521 \text{ bytes/frame} \times 8 \text{ bits/byte} \times 5/\text{hour}}{3600 \text{ seconds/hour}} = 5878$$

If we anticipate installing an Ethernet or Fast Ethernet network, we would consider data field sizes ranging from a minimum of 46 to a maximum of 1500 bytes, with interactive responses of less than 46 characters resulting in a data field of 46 bytes due to the padding of that field. Then, the overhead of the Ethernet frame would result in a total frame size of 72 bytes (46 for the data field plus 26 bytes of overhead) when the message size is less than or equal to 46 bytes, and would increase to 1526 bytes when the data field is filled to its maximum of 1500 bytes.

In performing the above computation, readers will note that it was not precise, because the number of frames was rounded to 117 and it did not consider the fact that the last frame does not actually carry 4500 bytes. For file transfers, program loads and print jobs, you can safely disregard the fact that the last frame used to carry an activity may have an information field whose length is less than 4500 bytes. This is because doing so results in a maximum divergence of 10 bps over an hour for the activity being computed for each occurrence of the activity. For example, 4500 bytes × 8 bits/byte results in a 4 Mbps Token-Ring information field carrying a maximum of 36 000 bits which when divided by 3600 seconds per hour is 10 bps. Thus, your activity projection would be off by a maximum of 50 bps, which is less than 1%. Since you are estimating network traffic, a good rule of thumb to follow is to ignore the fact that the last frame's information field used to carry an activity may be partially filled unless the activity is performed more than 50 times per hour. The latter may represent the use of an application performed by clerical personnel entering batches of data concerning personnel file updates, corporate receipts and disbursements, and similar type work.

Network printing considerations

One item worthy of mention concerning the activity entries in Figure 3.2 involves network printing. If your network infrastructure is designed so that file servers function as print servers, as shown in the top portion of Figure 3.3, the computations shown

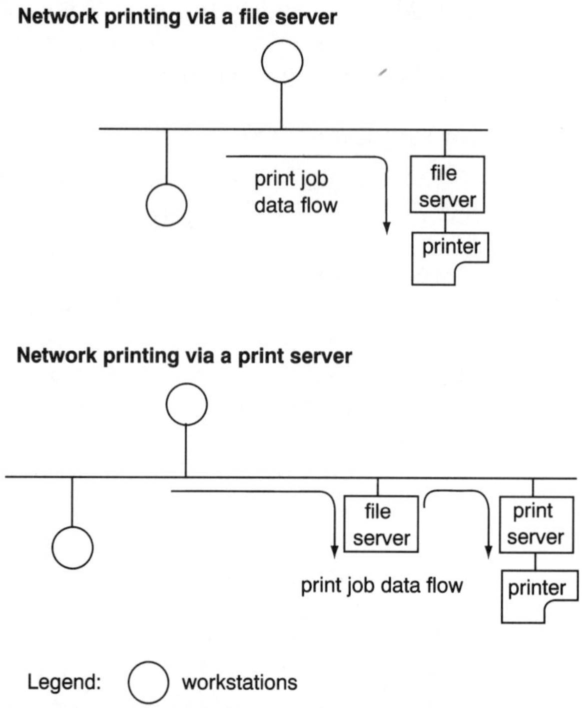

Network printing via a file server

Network printing via a print server

Legend: ◯ workstations

Figure 3.3 The method of printing can double network traffic, resulting from the execution of a print job

for network printing are correct. However, many networks are constructed using separate print servers. When this occurs a print job transmitted by a network user first flows from his or her workstation to the file server where it is placed in a print queue. Then the file server transmits the print job from the queue to the print server, as illustrated in the lower portion of Figure 3.3. Under this network printing configuration the print job is transmitted twice, first from the workstation to the file server and then from the file server to the print server. If your network infrastructure is to use separate print servers, you would then double the resulting bit rate for each print job computed in a traffic estimation worksheet.

To further illustrate the completion of the traffic estimation worksheet illustrated in Figure 3.2, let us examine the load and save graphic image entries and the send and receive message activities. In addition, to further illustrate the computations involved in completing the worksheet, the resulting bit rate computations for each activity will also indicate the significant difference in the effect of graphic versus text information transfer on a local area network.

Graphic versus text transfer

Since the entries for loading and saving a graphic image are the same, you can compute one entry and use the resulting bit rate computation for each activity. Similarly, you can do the same for sending and receiving messages.

For each graphic image activity let us assume that the image consists of a file of 1024 K bytes. Thus, the file size is 1024×1024 bytes per K, or 1 048 576 bytes. When carried by a 4500 byte information field, this results in the use of 1 048 576 bytes/4500 bytes/frame, or 233 frames, to transport the graphic image. Since there are 21 overhead bytes in each frame, the actual frame length is 4521 bytes. Based upon a frequency of three images loaded or saved per hour, each graphic image activity bit rate computation is as follows:

bit rate (bps)

$$= \frac{233 \text{ frames} \times 4521 \text{ bytes/frame} \times 8 \text{ bits/byte} \times 3/\text{hour}}{3600 \text{ seconds/hour}} = 7023$$

Now let us turn our attention to the send and receive message activities. For each activity we assumed the message size is 0.5 K, or 512 bytes. Thus, the entire message can be transported by one Token-Ring frame that has a 512 byte information field. Since there are 21 overhead bytes per Token-Ring frame, the frame size is 533 bytes. Based upon a frequency of two messages sent or received per hour, each message activity's bit rate computation becomes

bit rate (bps)

$$= \frac{1 \text{ frame} \times 533 \text{ bytes/frame} \times 8 \text{ bits/byte} \times 2/\text{hour}}{3600 \text{ seconds/hour}} = 3$$

In comparing the resulting bit rate of a graphic image activity to that of an electronic message activity, note the significant difference: here each graphic image activity has in excess of 2000 times the resulting bit rate associated with a message. Even if the message was doubled in size to 1024 bytes, the graphic image would have a bit rate 1000 times that of the message. If you consider the fact that a super-VGA monitor color graphic image can easily exceed 1 Mbytes and that most electronic mail messages are relatively short, consisting of one or two paragraphs and typically less than 100 words, this explains why text-based electronic mail has a negligible effect upon LAN performance in comparison to the transmission of graphic images.

Table 3.1 Projected network traffic by workstation class

Workstation class	Bit rate (bps)
Design engineers	1 347 950
Technicians	422 500
General support personnel	238 750
Managers	83 920
Secretaries	146 750
Total estimated bit rate	2 239 870

Returning to Figure 3.2, note that the subtotal bps of 26 959 represents the average network traffic for one workstation used by a design engineer. Since there are 50 workstations used by design engineers, the total bit rate is 26 959 × 50, or 1 347 950 bps. Now that we have completed the traffic estimation worksheet for one workstation class, we would perform similar computations for each of the remaining five workstation classes. To facilitate our analysis, let us assume that the results of the computations for the six workstation classes are as summarized in Table 3.1.

3.1.3 Network utilization considerations

In examining the projected network traffic summarized in Table 3.1, note that the total bit rate of 2.23 Mbps represents a projected utilization level of 2.23/4.0, or 55%, of the available network bandwidth. Although this may not appear to be a sufficiently high level of network utilization that would result in excessive transmission delays, in actuality the transmission capability of a Token-Ring network depends upon several variables, including the number of stations on the network, the average length of frames transmitted on the network, and the total length of cable used to form the network.

Under certain variable relationships the capability of a Token-Ring network to transport data can be as low as one-half of the network's operating rate. Although Chapter 7 contains specific information concerning the development and execution of a mathematical model to determine the information-carrying capacity of a Token-Ring network, we can generalize the findings of that chapter by noting that when possible you should attempt to keep the utilization level of a Token-Ring network to a maximum of 70% of its operating rate. Doing so will preclude the occurrence of excessive response times. For an Ethernet local area network the utilization level should be kept to 40 to 50% of the network's operating rate. The rationale for an Ethernet local area network having a lower utilization level threshold than a Token-Ring network is due to the difference in the access method used by each network. Ethernet access is not predictable and can result in collisions which require a random time delay in which no station on the network can transmit data. In comparison, network access on a Token-Ring network is predictable since a station can only transmit when it is able to acquire a free token.

A second difference between the transmission capability of each network concerns the method of frame transmission used on each network. On an Ethernet network there is a minimum fixed delay period of time between frame transmissions. In comparison, transmission can occur on a Token-Ring network as soon as a station acquires a free token. Readers are referred to Chapter 6 for specific information concerning the flow of data on Ethernet and Fast Ethernet local area networks.

3.1.4 Planning for network growth

In addition to estimating traffic that will be carried by a network, it is equally important to consider network growth. Doing so permits you to determine if a network structure will be able to accommodate a buildup in workstation usage of the network and/or an increase in network users over a period of time.

To illustrate how you can consider network growth, let us assume that your organization anticipates additional hiring that will increase the design engineering staff by 5%, management personnel by 10%, and the secretarial staff by 20%. To consider the potential effect of adding workstations to the network to accommodate the additional hiring you could use a network growth worksheet similar to the one contained in Table 3.2. This worksheet was completed based upon the projected network traffic contained in Table 3.1 and the previously discussed projections for additional employees.

3.2 NETWORK MODIFICATION

It has been noted that the bit rate on the Token-Ring network was projected to be approximately 55% of the available network bandwidth. Based upon the projected network growth, the bit rate is expected to increase to 2.34 Mbps, which would be 2.34/4.0, or approximately 59% of the available network bandwidth. Thus, the

Table 3.2   Network growth worksheet

Workstation class	Estimated bit rate (bps)	Projected growth rate (%)	Projected bit rate (bps)
Design engineers	1 347 950	5	1 415 348
Technicians	422 500	0	422 500
General support personnel	238 750	0	238 750
Managers	83 920	10	92 312
Secretaries	14 750	20	176 100
Total projected bit rate			2 345 010

relatively high level of network utilization is projected to worsen over time if one network is used to provide a communications capability for both existing and anticipated employees. To alleviate potential problems associated with a high level of network utilization one of the first modifications to a network infrastructure that you should consider is the installation of dual networks interconnected by a local bridge.

The use of a bridge to subdivide a network into two or more interconnected segments essentially doubles your effective bandwidth prior to considering inter-segment communications, a topic which is discussed in the next section of this chapter. Since the cost of a two-port bridge is usually considerably less expensive than an intelligent switch or router, from a cost perspective most network modification efforts begin by examining a network with respect to its subdivision into segments via a bridge.

3.2.1 Network subdivision considerations

In examining the entries in the completed traffic estimation worksheet contained in Figure 3.2, you will note that the vast majority of network usage associated with workstations used by design engineers involves the loading of programs and graphic images as well as the saving and printing of graphic images. Thus, it appears that the requirement of design engineers to interact with other network users through the transmission and reception of electronic mail messages is relatively limited with respect to their total projected transmission on the local area network. Therefore it appears that you could safely place all design engineers on one Token-Ring network, and all other network users could be placed on a second Token-Ring network.

If the network is subdivided as previously indicated, the network supporting the design engineers would have a utilization level of 1.415/4.0, or approximately 35%, including the projected growth in the design engineering staff. The second network which would support all other network users would have a utilization level of 0.93/4.0, or approximately 23%, including projected growth in management and secretarial employees. Although this network subdivision does not provide an equal distribution of network usage, it does minimize inter-LAN communications due to the limited communications between design engineers and other organizational employees.

Figure 3.4 illustrates the resulting subdivided Token-Ring network in which it is assumed that all design engineers are placed on network A. This method of subdivision minimizes inter-LAN communications and reduces the forwarding rate the local bridge has to support.

As an alternative to placing all design engineers on network A, let us assume that you wish to consider network subdivision by placing half of the employees on each network. Although this would more evenly balance the utilization level of each network, what would be the effect upon inter-LAN communications? Unless you could distribute the programs and graphic images used by design engineers onto servers on each network, the design engineers on network B would require a significant amount of communications with the server located on network A. Although we did not analyze the activities of other classes of network users, we can safely assume that any subdivision in which a class of workstation users is subdivided onto two or more interconnected networks will result in a high level of inter-LAN communications, unless the programs that users access are located on servers on each network. Because the cost of a program license to operate on separate servers typically exceeds the cost of a program

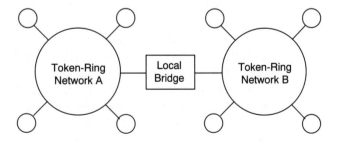

Figure 3.4 Resulting subdivided network. By placing all design engineers on Token-Ring network A, communications between network A and network B are minimized

license to operate on one server, the additional cost associated with the separation or subdivision of users within a workstation class is normally not recommended. Thus, most organizations should consider the subdivision of network users based upon the class of user.

3.2.2 Inter- versus intra-network communications

One area which remains to be discussed concerning local area network traffic is the relationship between inter- and intra-network communications. This is especially important if your organization previously established separate local area networks and now has a requirement to interconnect those networks.

If you previously estimated traffic carried by separate networks or have access to monitoring equipment you can estimate or determine the actual data flow on separate networks. However, what can you expect to occur when you internet two or more networks together?

Unless you use a poor design philosophy and require workstations on one network to access many applications on a server on a different network, the majority of transmission will be local with respect to each LAN. In fact, the interconnection of separate networks usually results in traffic following what is commonly referred to as the 80/20 rule. That rule states that when separate networks are interconnected, intra-LAN communications will account for 80% or more of communications traffic, whereas 20% or less of the traffic on a network will require the services of a bridge or router to flow between networks.

The effect of the 80/20 rule should be taken into consideration when estimating the potential effect on bandwidth resulting from the segmentation of a network. To illustrate the effect of the 80/20 rule, or a variation of the percentages of that rule to better fit your organization's operational requirements, consider Figure 3.5. This example illustrates the effect on the bandwidth of a segmented network from inter-LAN communications. In this example it was assumed that the initial utilization level of network A was projected to be 50%, and that of network B was projected to be 55%. It was also assumed that 80% of all traffic on each network segment would be local and remain on the segment from which it was placed on the network, whereas 20% of the traffic on each segment would be destined to a device on the other segment. This means that at an expected 50% utilization level, 0.50×0.20 or 10% of the utilization of network A will flow onto network B. Similarly, if network B has an expected utilization

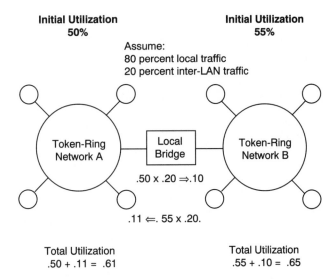

Initial Utilization
50%

Initial Utilization
55%

Assume:
80 percent local traffic
20 percent inter-LAN traffic

Token-Ring
Network A

Local
Bridge

Token-Ring
Network B

.50 x .20 ⇒.10

.11 ⇐. 55 x .20.

Total Utilization
.50 + .11 = .61

Total Utilization
.55 + .10 = .65

Figure 3.5 The effect upon the bandwidth of a segmented network resulting from inter-LAN communications

level of 55% then 0.55×0.20 or 11% of the utilization of network B can be expected to flow onto network A. Since both networks are considered to represent the same type of Token-Ring network, the inter-LAN communications results in an increase in the utilization of network A to 61% and an increase in the utilization of network B to 65%. Thus, it is extremely important to consider the effect of inter-LAN communications, as such communication not only represents a consumption of bandwidth on the initial network that a frame is placed in, but, in addition, a consumption of bandwidth for each network that it is placed in.

4

DETERMINING REMOTE BRIDGE AND ROUTER DELAYS AND BUFFER MEMORY REQUIREMENTS

One of the major problems associated with the use of remote bridges and routers is the delay that those devices introduce into linked networks. This delay results from the fact that a local area network operating rate is normally an order of magnitude or higher than the wide area network operating rate used to connect LANs via the use of remote bridges or routers. A second major problem associated with the use of remote bridges and routers concerns the selection of an appropriate amount of buffer memory for installation in each device. If too little memory is installed in such devices, the probability that memory will be filled when a frame arrives for forwarding increases. This in turn results in the inability of a bridge or router to service the frame, causing the originating network station to periodically regenerate the frame or a timeout to occur which results in the termination of an existing communications session. Thus, an insufficient amount of buffer memory can result in both extended network delays as well as an increase in network traffic.

In this chapter we will first focus our attention upon the use of queuing theory to determine the delays associated with the use of remote bridges and routers. Next, we will investigate modifying the operating rate of communications circuits used to connect remote bridges and routers. Doing so will enable us to examine the effect of different communications circuit operating rates upon equipment delays, as well as to understand that beyond some operating rates further increases in the operating rate of a communications circuit have an insignificant effect upon equipment and network performance. Once we have obtained an appreciation for the use of queuing theory to determine an acceptable operating rate for wide area network transmission facilities linking LANs, we will examine a related problem. That problem involves the use of queuing theory to determine whether to use single or multiple communications circuits when connecting remote LANs with respect to their ability to service frames arriving at a remote bridge or router connected to single or multiple circuits. In examining this problem we will expand our knowledge of queuing theory to cover multiple channel, single-phase queuing systems, as such systems represent the flow of data through a remote bridge or router connected to multiple communications circuits. In concluding this chapter we will turn our attention to the use of queuing theory to determine the minimum amount of buffer storage remote bridges and routers should contain to provide a predefined level of performance. In doing so we will develop a six-step approach that readers can follow to select equipment with a sufficient amount of buffer storage to satisfy their specific organizational networking requirements.

4.1 WAITING LINE ANALYSIS

Queuing theory, the formal term for waiting line analysis, can be traced to the work of A. K. Erlang, a Danish mathematician. His pioneering work spanned several areas of mathematics, including the dimensioning or sizing of trunk lines to accommodate long-distance calls between telephone company exchanges. Readers are referred to the present author's book *Practical Network Design Techniques*, published by John Wiley & Sons, for specific information concerning the application of Erlang's work conducted during the 1920s to the sizing of ports on modern multiplexers and concentrators. In this chapter we will bypass Erlang's sizing work to concentrate upon the analysis of waiting lines.

4.1.1 Basic components

Figure 4.1 illustrates the basic components of a simple waiting line system. The input process can be considered as the arrival of

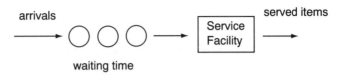

Figure 4.1 Basic components of a simple waiting line system. When the arrival rate exceeds the service rate a waiting line or queue forms

people, objects or frames of data. The service facility performs some predefined operation upon arrivals, such as collecting tolls from passengers in cars arriving at a toll booth, or converting a local area network frame into an SDLC or HDLC frame by a remote bridge or router for transmission over a wide area network transmission facility. If the arrival rate temporarily exceeds the service rate of the service facility, a waiting line known as a queue will form. If a waiting line never exists, this fact implies that the server is idle or an excessive service capacity exists.

The waiting line system illustrated in Figure 4.1 is more formally known as a single-channel, single-phase waiting line system. The term *single channel* refers to the fact that there is one waiting line, and the term *single phase* refers to the fact that the process performed by the service facility occurs once at one location. One toll booth on a highway or a single port remote bridge connected to a local area network and a wide area network are two examples of single-channel, single-phase waiting line systems.

Figure 4.2 illustrates three additional types of waiting line systems. Here the term *multiple channel* refers to the fact that arrivals are serviced by more than one service facility and results in multiple paths or channels to those service facilities. The term *multiple phase* refer the fact that arriving entities are processed by multiple service facilities.

One example of a multiple-phase service facility would be a toll road in which drivers of automobiles are serviced by several series of toll booths. Any reader who drove on the Petersburg–Richmond, VA, turnpike during the 1980s is probably well aware of the large number of 25¢ toll booths that you seem to encounter every few miles. Another example of a multiple-phase service would be the routing of data through a series of bridges and routers. Since the computations associated with multiple phase systems can become quite complex and, as we will shortly note, we can analyze most networks on a point-to-point basis as a single-phase system, we will primarily restrict our examination of queuing models to single-phase systems in this chapter.

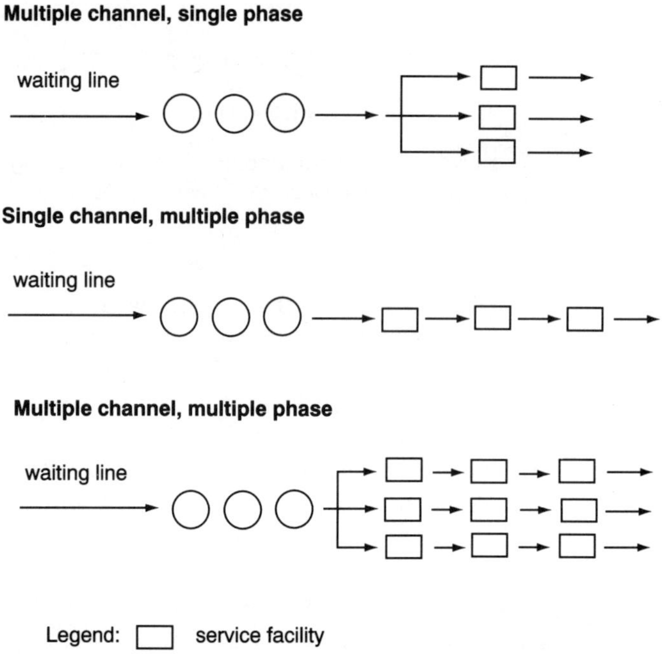

Multiple channel, single phase

waiting line

Single channel, multiple phase

waiting line

Multiple channel, multiple phase

waiting line

Legend: ☐ service facility

Figure 4.2 Other types of waiting line systems. In addition to single-channel, single-phase waiting line systems, other systems include multiple channel, single phase; single channel, multiple phase; and multiple channel, multiple phase

4.1.2 Assumptions

Queuing theory is similar to many other types of mathematical theory in that it is based upon a series of assumptions. Those assumptions are primarily focused upon the distribution of arrivals and the time required to service each arrival.

Both the distribution of arrivals and the time to service them are normally represented as random variables. The most common distribution used to represent arrivals is the Poisson distribution:

$$P(n) = \frac{\lambda^n e^{-\lambda}}{n!}$$

where:

$P(n) =$ probability of n arrivals
$\lambda =$ mean arrival rate
$e = 2.718\,28$
$n! = n$ factorial $= n \times (n - 1) \times \ldots \times 3 \times 2 \times 1$

One of the more interesting features of the Poisson process concerns the relationship between the arrival rate and the time between arrivals. If the number of arrivals per unit time is Poisson-distributed with a mean of λ, then the time between arrivals is distributed as a negative exponential probability distribution with a mean of $1/\lambda$. For example, if the mean arrival rate per 10 minute period is 3, then the mean time between arrivals is 10/3, or 3.3 minutes.

4.1.3 Network applications

Through the use of queuing theory or waiting time analysis, we can examine the effect of different wide area network circuit operating rates upon the ability of remote bridges and routers to transfer data between local area networks, and the effect of different levels of buffer memory on their ability to transfer data. In doing so we can obtain answers to such critical questions as 'What is the average delay associated with the use of a remote bridge or router?', 'What is the effect upon those delays by increasing the operating rate of the wide area network circuit?', 'When does an increase in the wide area network circuit's operating rate result in an insignificant improvement in bridge or router performance?', 'How much buffer memory should a remote bridge or router contain to avoid losing frames?', and similar questions. To illustrate the application and value of queuing theory to network problems, let us look at an example of its use.

Assume that you are planning to interconnect two geographically dispersed local area networks through the use of a pair of remote bridges, as illustrated in Figure 4.3. In this example a Token-Ring network at one location will be connected to an Ethernet LAN at another location. Today most remote bridges support both RS-232 and V.35 interfaces, permitting the bridge to be connected to modems or higher speed data service units (DSUs) which are used with digital transmission facilities. This opens a Pandora's box concerning the type of circuit to use to connect a pair of remote bridges, analog or digital, and the operating rate of the circuit.

Fortunately, we can use queuing theory to determine an optimum line operating rate to interconnect the two LANs illustrated in Figure 4.3.

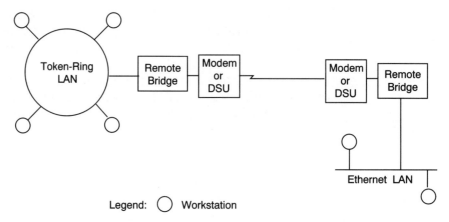

Legend: ◯ Workstation

Figure 4.3 Internet consisting of two LANs connected via a pair of remote bridges. One of the most common problems facing network designers is to select an appropriate line operating rate to interconnect geographically dispersed networks

Deciding on a queuing model

In applying queuing theory to the network configuration illustrated in Figure 4.3 you would be correct in stating that it resembles a single-channel multiple-phase waiting line system similar to the second example shown in Figure 4.2. However, prior to deciding on a queuing model to use, let us consider the delays associated with each phase of the network shown in Figure 4.3.

If data are routed from the Token-Ring network to the Ethernet network the primary delay occurs when a frame attempts to gain access to the bridge connected to the Token-Ring LAN and use its encapsulation services to be placed onto the wide area network. If the memory of the bridge is not full, the frame is placed into memory at the LANs operating rate and after a delay based on the number of frames preceding that frame in memory, it is transmitted bit-by-bit at the wide area network operating rate which is typically an order of magnitude lower than the LAN operating rate. If the memory of the bridge is full the frame is discarded and the workstation that originated the frame must then retransmit it, further adding to the delay in the frame reaching its destination. At the Ethernet site the frame is received on a bit-by-bit basis and the primary delay encountered is the time required to buffer the frame for placement on the Ethernet LAN.

Because multiple frames result in one following another, there is a degree of overlap between receiving frame $n + 1$ and placing the received frame n onto the network. In addition, because the WAN operating rate is but a fraction of the LAN operating rate, the delay associated with the destination bridge becomes primarily one of latency and is negligible with respect to the bridge at the transmit side of the interconnected network. Owing to this we can simplify our computations by assuming the second phase of the single-channel multiple-phase model does not exist, reducing the network to a single-channel single-phase model. Similarly, data flowing from the Ethernet to the Token-Ring network have a primary delay attributable to the bridge connected to the Ethernet network. Thus, data flow in either direction can be analyzed using a single-channel single-phase queuing model.

Applying queuing theory

Let us assume that, based upon prior knowledge obtained from monitoring the transmission between locally interconnected LANs, you determined that approximately 10 000 frames per day can be expected to flow from one network to the other network. Let us also assume that the average length of each frame was determined to be 1250 bytes.

Based upon our assumption that 10 000 frames will flow between each LAN we must convert that frame rate into an arrival rate. In doing so let us further assume that each network is active for only eight hours per day and both networks are in the same time zone. Thus, a transaction rate of 10 000 frames per eight-hour day is equivalent to an average arrival rate of 10 000/ (8 × 3600), or 0.347 222 frames per second. In queuing theory this average arrival rate (AR) is the average rate at which frames arrive at the service facility for forwarding across the wide area network communications circuit.

Previously we said that through monitoring it had been determined that the average frame length was 1250 bytes. Since a LAN frame must be converted into a WAN frame or packet for transmission over a wide area network transmission facility, the resulting frame or packet will usually result in the addition of header and trailer information required by the protocol used to carry the LAN frame. Thus, the actual length of the wide area network frame or packet will exceed the length of the LAN frame. For our computational purposes, let us assume that 25 bytes are added to each LAN frame, resulting in the average transmission of 1275 bytes per frame.

Since the computation of an expected service time requires an operating rate, let us first assume that the wide area network communications circuit illustrated in Figure 4.3 operates at 9600 bps. Then the time required to transmit one 1275 byte frame or packet becomes 1275 bytes/frame × 8 bits/byte ÷ 9600 bps, or 1.0625 seconds. This time is more formally known as the expected service time and it represents the time required to transmit a frame whose average length is 1250 bytes on the LAN and 1275 bytes when converted for transmission over the wide area network transmission facility. Given that the expected service time is 1.0625 seconds, we can easily compute the mean service rate (MSR). That rate is the rate at which frames entering the remote bridge destined for the other local area network are serviced, and it is 1/1.0625, or 0.9411765 frames per second.

So far we have computed two key queuing theory variables, the arrival rate and the mean service rate. Note that the service rate computation was dependent upon the initial selection of a wide area network circuit operating rate which was initially selected as 9600 bps.

Figure 4.4 illustrates the results of our initial set of computations for one portion of our internet. Since we assumed that 10 000 frames per eight-hour day flow in each direction we can simply analyze one-half of the internet. This simplification is facilitated by the fact that we are also assuming that the average frame size flowing in each direction is the same or nearly equivalent. If this is not true, such as for inter-network communications restricted to network users on one LAN accessing a server on another network resulting in relatively short queries in one direction followed by long frames carrying responses to those queries, then our assumption would fall by the wayside. In this type of situation you would analyze the traffic flow in each

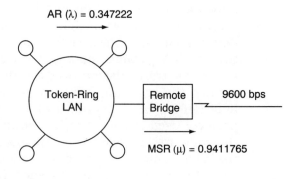

AR (λ) = 0.347222

Token-Ring LAN

Remote Bridge

9600 bps

MSR (μ) = 0.9411765

Legend:
AR or   λ   arrival rate
MSR or   μ   mean service rate

Figure 4.4 Initial computational results. The mean service rate, MSR, or μ in queuing theory terms, depends upon the operating rate of the line

direction and select a line operating rate that meets your requirements for serving the worst case transmission direction in terms of frame rate and frame size. However, if the traffic flow is even or nearly even in terms of frame rate and frame size you can restrict your analysis to one direction. This is because full duplex communications circuits operate at the same data rate in each direction, once you determine the required operating rate in one direction you have also determined the operating rate of the circuit.

Queuing theory designators

In examining Figure 4.4, note that queuing theory designators are indicated in parentheses. Thus, in a queuing theory book the average arrival rate of 0.347 222 transactions or frames per second would be indicated by the expression $\lambda = 0.347\,222$. Similarly, the mean service rate in queuing theory books is designated by the symbol μ.

Although the mean service rate exceeds the average arrival rate, upon occasion the arrival rate will result in a burst of data which exceeds the capacity of the bridge to service frames. When this situation occurs, queues are created as the bridge accepts frames and places those frames it cannot immediately transmit into memory buffers or temporary storage areas. Through the use of queuing theory, we can examine the expected time for frames to flow through the bridge and adjust the circuit operating rate accordingly. In addition, we can also use queuing theory to determine the amount of buffer memory a remote bridge or router should have to minimize the potential for the loss of frames to a specific probability.

As previously discussed, the use of remote bridges or routers can be considered to represent a single-channel, single-phase queuing model. The utilization of the service facility (p) is obtained by dividing the average arrival rate by the mean service rate. That is,

$$p = \frac{\text{AR}}{\text{MSR}} = \frac{0.347222}{0.9411765} = 0.3689$$

Thus, the use of a circuit operating at 9600 bps results in an average utilization level of approximately 37%. Readers should note that in queuing theory texts the preceding equation will be replaced by $p = \lambda/\mu$, where λ is the symbol used for the average arrival rate, while μ is the symbol used for the mean service rate.

Since the utilization level of the service facility (remote bridge) is AR/MSR, the probability that there are no frames in the bridge, P_0, becomes

$$P_0 = 1 - \text{AR/MSR, or } 1 - \lambda/\mu$$

For the remote bridge connected to a 9600 bps circuit we then obtain

$$P_0 = 1 - 0.37 = 0.63$$

Thus, for 63% of the time there will be no frames in the bridge's buffers awaiting transmission to the distant network.

Frame determination

For a single-channel, single-phase system the mean number of units expected to be in the system is equivalent to the average arrival rate divided by the difference between the mean service rate and the arrival rate. In queuing theory the mean or expected number of units in a system is normally designated by the letter L. Thus,

$$L = \frac{\text{AR}}{\text{MSR} - \text{AR}} = \frac{\lambda}{\mu - \lambda}$$

Returning to our networking example, we can determine the mean or expected number of frames that will be in the system, including frames residing in the bridge's buffer area or flowing down the wide area network transmission facility, as follows:

$$L = \frac{0.347}{0.941 - 0.347} = 0.585$$

Thus, on average we can expect approximately six-tenths of a frame to reside in the bridge's buffer and on the transmission line.

If we multiply the utilization of the service facility by the expected number of units in a system we obtain the mean number of units in the queue or, in common English, the queue length. The queue length is denoted by Lq and thus becomes

$$Lq = p \times L = \frac{\text{AR}^2}{\text{MSR(MSR} - \text{AR)}} = \frac{\lambda^2}{\mu(\mu - \lambda)}$$

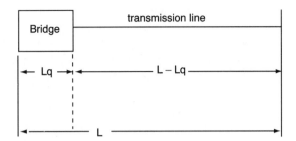

Figure 4.5 Temporary frame storage relationship. The mean number of frames in the system (L) is the sum of the frames stored in the bridge (Lq) and flowing on the transmission line (L − Lq)

Again returning to our network example, we obtain

$$Lq = \frac{(0.347)^2}{0.941 \times (0.941 - 0.347)} = 0.216$$

Based upon the above, we can expect on average 0.216 frames to be queued in the bridge for transmission when the operating rate of the wide area network is 9600 bps and 10 000 frames per eight-hour day require remote bridging. Since we previously determined that there were 0.585 frames in the system, this means that the difference, (0.585 − 0.216) or 0.369 frames, is flowing on the transmission line at any particular point in time. We can visualize the locations where frames are temporarily stored by examining Figure 4.5 which illustrates the relationship between L, Lq and $L - Lq$. Here Lq corresponds to the buffer memory of the bridge and L corresponds to the system consisting of the bridge and transmission line. Thus, $L - Lq$ then corresponds to the frames or portion of a frame flowing on the transmission line.

The preceding information also provides us with data concerning the average expected utilization of the wide area network transmission facility. Since the frame length is 1275 bytes and 0.369 frames can be expected to be flowing on the circuit at any point in time, this means the line can be expected to hold 1275 bytes/frame × 0.369 frames, or 470.5 bytes. This is equivalent to 3764 bits on a line planned to operate at 9600 bps, or a circuit utilization level of approximately 39%.

Time computations

In addition to computing information concerning the expected number of frames in queues and in the system, queuing theory provides us with the tools to determine the mean time in the system and the mean waiting time. In queuing theory, the mean waiting time is designated as the variable W, and the mean waiting time in the queue is designated as the variable Wq.

The mean time in the system W is

$$W = \frac{1}{\text{MSR} - \text{AR}} = \frac{1}{\mu - \lambda}$$

For our bridged network example, the mean time for which a frame can be expected to reside in the system can be computed as follows:

$$W = \frac{1}{0.941 - 0.347} = 1.68 \text{ seconds}$$

By itself this tells us that we can expect an average response time of approximately 1.7 seconds for frames that must be bridged from one local area network to the other if our wide area network transmission facility operates at 9600 bps. Whether this is good or bad depends upon how you view a 1.7 second delay.

The last queuing item we will focus our attention upon is the waiting time associated with a frame being queued. That time, Wq, is equivalent to the waiting time in the system multiplied by the utilization of the service facility. That is,

$$Wq = p \times W = \frac{\text{AR}}{\text{MSR}} \times \frac{1}{(\text{MSR} - \text{AR})} = \frac{\text{AR}}{\text{MSR}(\text{MSR} - \text{AR})}$$

In terms of queuing theory, Wq then becomes

$$Wq = \frac{\lambda}{\mu(\mu - \lambda)}$$

Similarly to the manner in which frame storage relationships were shown with respect to the bridge and transmission line, we can illustrate the relationship of waiting times. Figure 4.6 illustrates the relationship between W, Wq and $W - Wq$ with respect to the bridge and transmission line. Here Wq corresponds to the waiting time for a frame to pass through the bridge, whereas W is the total frame waiting time including the transit time through the bridge and across the transmission line. Thus, $W - Wq$ corresponds to the time required for a frame to transit the transmission line.

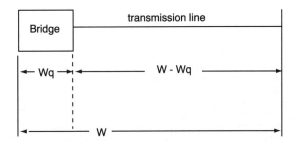

Figure 4.6 Waiting time relationships. The mean time in the system (W) is the sum of the time in the bridge (Wq) and the time for the frame to flow down the transmission line (W − Wq)

One more time let us return to our bridged network example. In doing so, we obtain

$$Wq = \frac{0.347}{0.941 \times (0.941 - 0.347)} = 0.621 \text{ seconds}$$

Note that we previously determined that a frame can be expected to reside for 1.68 seconds in our bridged system, including queue waiting time and transmission time. Since we computed the queue waiting time to be 0.621 seconds, the difference between the two, 1.68 − 0.621, or approximately 1.06 seconds, is the time required to transmit a frame over the 9600 bps wide area network transmission facility.

4.2 DETERMINING AN OPTIMUM LINE OPERATING RATE

Although we could recompute each of the previously computed variables based upon different line operating rates, we can just as easily write a program to perform such tedious operations.

4.2.1 Program QUEUE.BAS

Figure 4.7 lists the statements of a BASIC language program appropriately named QUEUE.BAS. The execution of this program is shown in Figure 4.8 which displays the values for eight queuing theory parameters based upon line speeds ranging from 4800 bps to 1.536 Mbps. The latter line speed represents the effective operating rate of a T1 circuit, because 8000 bps of the 1.544 Mbps operating rate of that circuit is used for framing and is not available for the actual transmission of data.

```
REM PROGRAM QUEUE.BAS
CLS
REM AR=arrival rate
REM MSR=mean service rate
REM L=mean (expected) number of frames in system
REM Lq=mean number of frames in queue
REM W=mean time (s) in system
REM Wq=mean waiting time (s)
REM EST= expected service time
transactions = 10000           'transactions per day
avgframe = 1275                'average frame size
hrsperday = 8
AR = transactions / (8 * 60 * 60)
DATA 4800,9600,19200,56000,64000,128000,256000,384000,768000,1536000
FOR i = 1 TO 10
READ linespeed(i)
est(i) = avgframe * 8 / linespeed(i)
msr(i) = 1 / est(i)
utilization(i) = AR / msr(i)
prob0(i) = 1 - (AR / msr(i))
L(i) = AR / (msr(i) - AR)
Lq(i) = AR ^ 2 / (msr(i) * (msr(i) - AR))
W(i) = 1 / (msr(i) - AR)
Wq(i) = AR / (msr(i) * (msr(i) - AR))
NEXT i
PRINT "Line Speed  EST    MSR      Po         p        L       Lq       W        Wq"
FOR i = 1 TO 10
PRINT USING " #######  #.#### ###.## "; linespeed(i); est(i); msr(i);
PRINT USING " #.#####   .#####"; prob0(i); utilization(i);
PRINT USING "  #.#####  #.#####  #.#####   #.#####"; L(i); Lq(i); W(i); Wq(i)
NEXT i
PRINT
PRINT "where:"
PRINT
PRINT " EST= expected service time  MSR = mean service rate"
PRINT " Po=probability of zero frames in the system  p = utilization"
PRINT " L= mean number of frames in system Lq = mean number in queue"
PRINT " W= mean waiting time in system  Wq = mean waiting time in queue"
```

Figure 4.7   Program listing of QUEUE.BAS

4.2.2 Utilization level versus line speed

In examining the values of the queuing parameters listed in Figure 4.8, let us focus our attention upon the utilization level, P, and the mean waiting time in the queue, Wq. At 4800 bps note that the utilization level is approximately 74%, and the waiting time in the queue is almost six seconds! Clearly, linking the two local area networks via remote bridges operating at 4800 bps provides an unacceptable waiting time due to the high utilization level of the remote bridge.

Line Speed	EST	MSR	Po	p	L	Lq	W	Wq
4800	2.1250	0.47	0.26215	.73785	2.81457	2.07672	8.10596	5.98096
9600	1.0625	0.94	0.63108	.36892	0.58459	0.21567	1.68363	0.62113
19200	0.5313	1.88	0.81554	.18446	0.22618	0.04172	0.65141	0.12016
56000	0.1821	5.49	0.93676	.06324	0.06751	0.00427	0.19444	0.01230
64000	0.1594	6.27	0.94466	.05534	0.05858	0.00324	0.16871	0.00934
128000	0.0797	12.55	0.97233	.02767	0.02846	0.00079	0.08196	0.00227
256000	0.0398	25.10	0.98617	.01383	0.01403	0.00019	0.04040	0.00056
384000	0.0266	37.65	0.99078	.00922	0.00931	0.00009	0.02681	0.00025
768000	0.0133	75.29	0.99539	.00461	0.00463	0.00002	0.01334	0.00006
1536000	0.0066	150.59	0.99769	.00231	0.00231	0.00001	0.00666	0.00002

where:

EST= expected service time MSR = mean service rate
Po=probability of zero frames in the system p = utilization
L= mean number of frames in system Lq = mean number in queue
W= mean waiting time in system Wq = mean waiting time in queue

Figure 4.8 Execution results of program QUEUE.BAS

As the line speed connecting the remote bridges is increased, each bridge is able to service frames at a higher processing rate. Since the average arrival rate is fixed, increasing the line operating rate should lower the utilization level of the bridge as well as the time for which a frame resides in the queue. Our expectation is verified by the results of the execution of QUEUE.BAS shown in Figure 4.8. Note that, as expected, both the utilization level and mean waiting time in the queue decrease as the line speed increases.

4.2.3 Selecting an operating rate

At the beginning of this chapter it was mentioned that queuing theory could be used to determine the operating rate of transmission lines for linking remote bridges and routers. In actuality, such usage will not produce a 'magic number'. Instead, the use of queuing theory can provide you with a range of values from which you can make a logical decision. For example, returning to Figure 4.8, a line operating rate of 4800 bps is clearly unacceptable. However, what can we say concerning an operating rate of 9600 bps, 19 200 bps, 56 000 bps and so on?

To provide some 'food for thought', Figure 4.9 shows the probability of a bridge containing zero frames (e.g. having empty buffers) and the utilization level of the bridge based upon the 10 line operating rates that were considered. Note that at a line

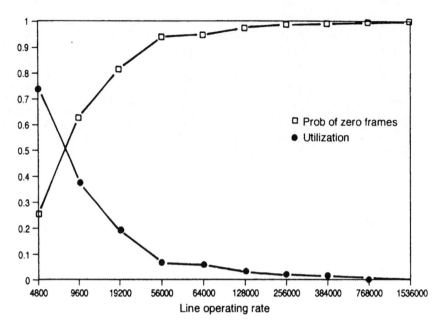

Figure 4.9 Probability of zero frames versus utilization

operating rate above the 56–64 kbps range, further reductions in
the utilization level of the bridge and an increase in the probability
of zero frames in the system is essentially insignificant. Thus, you
would more than likely restrict your line operating rate to a
maximum of 56–64 kbps in this example. From Figure 4.8, note
that doing so only marginally decreases the waiting time in the
queue from 0.12 seconds at 19 200 bps to 0.012 seconds at
56 kbps. Thus, if you were fairly certain that your application
would not grow, you would probably install an analog leased line
operating at 19 200 bps, as the cost of that line is normally less
than the cost of a digital line operating at 56 or 64 kbps. If you
expect further growth in the use of remote bridges, you would
probably install a more expensive 56 or 64 kbps digital line.

4.2.4 Summary

To correctly apply queuing theory to interconnecting local area
networks you must first obtain knowledge about the number of
transactions and the average frame size of each transaction that
will flow to the other network. Once this has been accomplished
you must estimate the growth in the average frame size to reflect
the addition of header and trailer information required by the

wide area protocol to carry your LAN frame. This then provides you with the ability to compute the average arrival rate of frames as well as the mean service rate of a remote bridge or router. Then, you can easily compute the additional queuing parameters previously discussed in this section and recalculate those parameters for different transmission line operating rates whose examination will enable you to select an appropriate operating rate to interconnect your LANs.

4.3 EXAMINING SINGLE AND MULTIPLE COMMUNICATION CIRCUITS

One of the more common decisions facing a network designer is whether to use single or multiple communications circuits when connecting remote local area networks via the use of bridges or routers. Obviously, from a reliability point of view multiple circuits are preferable to the use of a single circuit. However, from a performance point of view, are two circuits, each with one-half of the transmission capacity of a single circuit, better than the use of a single transmission path? This is the question that will be examined in this section, while leaving an investigation of the gain in availability and reliability of multiple circuits over single circuits and other network configurations for Chapter 5.

4.3.1 Comparing the use of single- and dual-port equipment

Figure 4.10 illustrates the use of single and dual port remote bridges to connect an Ethernet local area network to a distant Token-Ring local area network. Suppose that the single port remote bridges are connected to data service units (DSUs) that operate at 19 200 bps, whereas the multiport remote bridges are connected to two DSUs, each operating at 9600 bps. Although each pair of bridges has access to an aggregate transmission capacity of 19 200 bps, does the use of single and dual transmission paths in which the single path operates at twice the rate of each dual transmission path provide an equivalent level of service? To answer this question let us return to the use of queuing theory. In doing so, let us assume that the number of transactions estimated to flow between local area networks is 21 600 per eight-hour day. Let us also assume that the average frame size, including communications framing for transmission, is 1200 bytes.

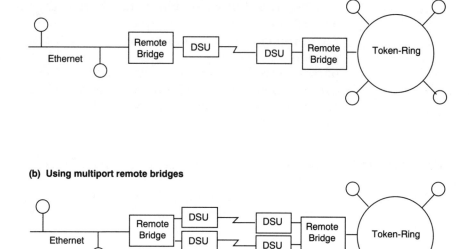

(a) Using single port remote bridges

(b) Using multiport remote bridges

Legend: DSU = data service unit

⬭ = network stations

Figure 4.10   Comparing the use of a: single- and b: dual-port (or multiport) remote bridges. If the single communications circuit in a operates at twice the data rate of each of the multiple circuits shown in b, does each network config-uration provide an equal level of service?

Single circuit

The single circuit communications link illustrated in Figure 4.10a more formally represents what is known as an M/M/1 queuing system.

Notation

The notation M/M/1 is actually a shorthand abbreviation of the form A/B/C which is used by queuing theorists to describe queuing problems. The letter used in the A position represents the statistical characteristics of the arrival rate of items to be serviced, such as customers approaching a teller or frames flowing to a bridge. A probability density function (pdf), such as the Poisson pdf, is typically used to describe a customer arrival rate. One of the most commonly used is the exponential pdf, which is denoted as M in queuing theory shorthand notation. The exponential pdf is defined as

$$p(t) = \lambda e^{-\lambda t}$$

This pdf is equivalent to saying that arriving customers behave as if they were not aware of each other's existence, i.e. occur randomly. Thus, the arrival process is a process without memory and the shorthand abbreviation M used to denote an exponential arrival rate actually refers the fact that the arrivals are 'memoryless'.

Readers should note that systems with an exponential inter-arrival distribution result in a Poisson arrival rate distribution. In fact, the probability that exactly n customers will arrive in a period of time is given by the equation

$$P(n, t) = \frac{\lambda t^n e^{-\lambda t}}{n!}$$

The above equation is the Poisson probability function. Thus, an exponential interarrival time distribution which is memoryless and denoted in queuing shorthand notation by M is generated by a Poisson process in which the arrival of any customer is independent of the arrival of previous customers.

Returning to the A/B/C notation format used to describe a queuing problem, B represents the statistical characteristics of the server. A server which operates without regard to the length of a queue, e.g. does not get tired, has its behavior described by an exponential service time distribution. Thus, such servers are also 'memoryless' and the letter M is used in position B to describe the characteristics of our server. Finally, the letter C in the queuing problem shorthand description format represents the number of servers. Thus, the numeric 1 was used in our shorthand queuing abbreviation for position C to complete our description of the queuing model in Figure 4.10a.

Computations

Based upon 21 600 transactions occurring in an eight-hour day, the arrival rate becomes

$$\lambda = \frac{21\,600}{8 \times 3600} = 0.75 \,\text{per second}$$

Since it was assumed that the average frame size is 1200 bytes, the expected service time when the line operates at 19 200 bps becomes $1200 \times 8/19\,200$, or 0.5 seconds. Thus, the service rate becomes

$$\mu = \frac{1}{\text{expected service time}} = \frac{1}{0.5} = 2 \text{ per second}$$

The utilization of the server (p) is the arrival rate divided by the service rate. Thus,

$$p = \frac{\lambda}{\mu} = \frac{0.75}{2} = 0.375$$

The probability that there are no frames in the system (P_0) is one minus the utilization. Thus,

$$P_0 = 1 - \frac{\lambda}{\mu} = 1 - 0.375 = 0.625$$

Let us continue and compute the mean number of frames expected in the system (L) and the mean length of the queue (Lq). Doing so, we obtain

$$L = \frac{\lambda}{\mu - \lambda} = \frac{0.75}{2 - 0.75} = 0.6$$

$$Lq = \frac{\lambda^2}{\mu(\mu - \lambda)} = \frac{p^2}{1 - p} = \frac{(0.375)^2}{1 - 0.375} = 0.225$$

Thus, we can expect 0.6 frames to be in the system, and 0.225 frames on average will be in the queue. Now let us focus our attention upon waiting times: the mean time waiting (Wq) and the mean time waiting in the system (W). Those two parameters are computed as follows:

$$Wq = \frac{\lambda}{\mu(\mu - \lambda)} = \frac{0.75}{2(2 - 0.75)} = 0.3 \text{ seconds}$$

$$W = \frac{1}{\mu - \lambda} = \frac{1}{2 - 0.75} = 0.8 \text{ seconds}$$

Note that the difference between the average waiting time in the system of 0.8 seconds and the average waiting time in the queue of 0.3 seconds is 0.5 seconds. That time is exactly the expected service time for a 1200 byte frame to be carried on a 19 200 bps

transmission circuit. Now that the basic queuing-related performance elements for the single path circuit have been computed, let
us focus our attention upon the use of dual transmission circuits.

Dual circuits

The dual transmission path illustrated in Figure 4.10 represents
an M/M/2 queuing system in which the numeric indicates that
there are two servers or, in our example, two channels or circuits.
   Although you would normally think of a server as a device with
memory which enables queues to form, you can also treat each
circuit as a server. In doing so, each remote bridge then provides
the buffer memory for the formation of queues for service or
placement onto each communications circuit. Here the use of two
channels or communication circuits can be considered to
represent a queuing system which is more formally referred to
as a multiple-channel, single-phase queuing system.

Computations

In computing the queuing parameters note that the arrival rate of
0.75 frames per second remains the same. However, since each
circuit now operates at 9600 bps the expected service time is
1200 bytes $\times$ 8 bits/byte $\div$ 9600 bytes, or 1 second. Thus, the
service rate, μ, is 1/1, or 1 frame per second per transmission
line.
   For a multiple-channel, single-phase system, utilization is
computed as follows, where s is the number of servers

$$p = \frac{\lambda}{s\mu} = \frac{0.75}{2 \times 1} = 0.375$$

So far everything appears to be equivalent between a single
transmission line and two lines in which each of the latter
operate at one-half the rate of the former.
   In a multiple-channel, single-phase queuing system, the probability that there are no frames in the system (P_0) is determined
using the following formula:

$$P_0 = \frac{1}{\displaystyle\sum_{n=0}^{s-1} \left[\frac{(\lambda/\mu)^n}{n!}\right] + \frac{(\lambda/\mu)^s}{s!(1 - \lambda/s\mu)}}$$

where s represents the number of servers and $n!$ and $s!$ represent n and s factorial where factorial n represents the value $m \times (m-1) \times (m-2)\dots 1$. The results of the computations for our two-server model to obtain the probability that there are no frames in the system are as follows:

$$P_0 = \cfrac{1}{1 + 0.75 + \cfrac{(0.75)^2}{2(1 - 0.75/2)}}$$

$$= \frac{1}{1 + 0.75 + 0.45} = \frac{1}{2.2} = 0.45$$

This means that there is a 45% probability that both servers do not contain any frames at any point in time.

Now that P_0 has been computed, we can use our prior computations in equations developed for multiple-channel, single-phase systems for other queuing parameters of interest. Those four parameters, Lq, L, W and Wq, are computed as follows:

$$Lq = \frac{P_0(\lambda/\mu)^2 p}{S!(1-p)^2} = \frac{0.45(0.75)^2 \times 0.365}{2(1 - 0.375)^2} = 0.1215$$

$$L = Lq + \frac{\lambda}{\mu} = 0.1215 + \frac{0.75}{1} = 0.8715$$

$$Wq = \frac{Lq}{\lambda} = \frac{0.1215}{0.75} = 0.162$$

$$W = Wq + \frac{1}{\lambda} = 0.162 + 1 = 1.162$$

General observations

So far we have made a number of computations. Now let us compare our previous computations and use the comparison between single and dual server models to make some general observations. Table 4.1 compares the queuing computations for the single and dual communications paths illustrated in Figure 4.10.

In comparing the entries in Table 4.1 between the single and dual path scenarios, let us first focus our attention upon P_0, the probability that there is no frame in the system. Note that the single path has a higher probability that there is no frame in the system than the dual path. The reason for this can be explained by examining Figure 4.11 which indicates how

Table 4.1 Comparing single and dual path queuing values

Parameter	Single path	Dual path
Arrival rate (λ)	0.75	0.75
Service rate (μ)	2	1
Utilization (p)	0.375	0.375
Probability no frame in system (P_0)	0.625	0.45
Mean number of frames in system (L)	0.6	0.87
Mean length of queue (Lq)	0.225	0.12
Mean time in system (W)	0.3	1.162
Mean waiting time (Wq)	0.8	0.162

transmission gaps can occur on two paths each operating at a fraction of a single path.

Suppose that a 2400 byte frame arrives at a server connected to a single 19 200 bps data circuit. As indicated in the upper portion of Figure 4.11, one 19 200 bps circuit could transmit the first 2400 byte frame in precisely one second. If a second frame shows up precisely one second later, the first frame would have been transmitted and the transmission of the second frame can then commence. If a second frame shows up just a fraction of a second after the first frame, the second frame will be queued for

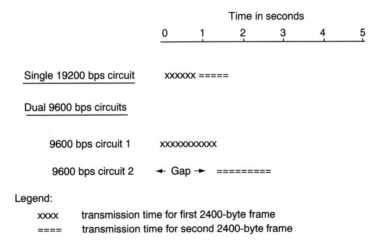

Legend:
xxxx   transmission time for first 2400-byte frame
====   transmission time for second 2400-byte frame

Figure 4.11 Transmission gaps commonly occur on multiple circuits. The use of multiple circuits operating at a fraction of the operating rate of a single circuit can be expected to result in more transmission gaps for the same frame arrival rate to a service facility

transmission. Then, once the first frame has been transmitted the second frame will immediately follow the first frame. In fact, the second frame can arrive at any time up to one second after the first frame without a transmission gap occurring. Now consider a similar situation in which two 2400 byte frames arrive one second apart at a bridge connected to two communications circuits. The first frame requires two seconds for transmission, and the second 9600 bps circuit is unoccupied for one second until the second frame arrives and is then transmitted on the second circuit since the first circuit is occupied. Because there is no way to split a frame between circuits, there is no way to fill the gap that occurred. The one second gap illustrated in the lower portion of Figure 4.11 represents half the longest duration gap based upon the previous assumptions. If a second frame arrived two seconds after the first, a two second period of time would occur in which one circuit was not occupied. Similarly, if the second frame followed the first by 0.5 seconds, the gap would be reduced to a 0.5 second duration. As illustrated in this example, the use of two queuing systems each with half the capacity of a single system will almost always have a lower level of performance due to the higher probability of occurrence of transmission gaps.

By comparing the single and dual path queuing values listed in Table 4.1, readers will note that there are other significant differences between a single circuit operating at X bps and two circuits each operating at $X/2$ bps. For example, the mean number of frames in the system less the mean length of the queue tells us the mean number of frames on the circuit or circuits. Here the use of a single path would result in $0.6 - 225$, or 0.375 frames, and the dual path would have $0.87 - 0.12$, or 0.75 frames. This means that the mean number of frames in a two-circuit system is twice the number of frames found in a single circuit system, a situation that we would intuitively expect.

Another area of difference between the single and dual circuit configurations concerns waiting times. Although the mean waiting time in the queue is less for a two-circuit configuration as it provides two paths for transmitting frames, its mean system time considerably exceeds that of a single path system. What this tells us is that the use of multiple circuits provides a larger 'moving storage' facility for frames than a single circuit system; however, the end result is that although queuing time (Wq) is reduced, the total time in the system (W) is increased. Thus, discounting availability considerations, a choice between a single circuit operating at X bps and two circuits each operating at $X/2$ bps should be made in favor of the single circuit.

Program QUEUE2.BAS

> To facilitate computations associated with two-channel, single-phase queuing systems, the program QUEUE.BAS was modified. The results of that modification provide queuing statistics for a two-channel, single phase queuing system for line rates ranging from 4800 bps to 1.536 Mbps. This program modification was renamed QUEUE2.BAS and its statements are listed in Figure 4.12. In addition to revising the program to compute two-channel, single-phase queuing system statistics, the program was also modified to accept daily transactions, operational hours per day, and an average frame size as user input.

```
REM PROGRAM QUEUE2.BAS
CLS
PRINT "PROGRAM QUEUE2.BAS - STATISTICS FOR TWO CHANNEL SINGLE PHASE QUEUE"
PRINT
REM AR=arrival rate
REM MSR=mean service rate
REM L=mean (expected) number of frames in system
REM Lq=mean number of frames in queue
REM W=mean time (s) in system
REM Wq=mean waiting time (s)
REM EST= expected service time
INPUT "Enter transactions per day      : "; transactions
INPUT "Enter operational hours per day : "; hrs
INPUT "Enter average frame size        : "; frame
AR = transactions / (hrs * 60 * 60)
DATA 4800,9600,19200,56000,64000,128000,256000,384000,768000,1536000
FOR I = 1 TO 10
READ linespeed(I)
est(I) = frame * 8 / linespeed(I)
MSR(I) = 1 / est(I)
UTILIZATION(I) = AR / (2 * MSR(I))
PROBO(I) = 1 / (1 + (AR / MSR(I)) + (AR / MSR(I)) ^ 2 / (2 * (1 - (AR / (2 * MSR(I))))))
Lq(I) = PROBO(I) * (AR / MSR(I)) ^ 2 * UTILIZATION(I)
Lq(I) = Lq(I) / (2 * (1 - UTILIZATION(I)) ^ 2)
L(I) = Lq(I) + AR / MSR(I)
Wq(I) = Lq(I) / AR
W(I) = Wq(I) + 1 / MSR(I)
NEXT I
PRINT "Line Speed   EST    MSR      Po        p        L        Lq        W        Wq"
FOR I = 1 TO 10
PRINT USING " ######   #.#### ###.## "; linespeed(I); est(I); MSR(I);
PRINT USING " #.##### #.#####"; PROBO(I); UTILIZATION(I);
PRINT USING "  #.##### #.##### #.#####    #.#####"; L(I); Lq(I); W(I); Wq(I)
NEXT I
PRINT
PRINT "where:"
PRINT
PRINT " EST= expected service time  MSR = mean service rate"
PRINT " Po=probability of zero frames in the system  p = utilization"
PRINT " L= mean number of frames in system Lq = mean number in queue"
PRINT " W= mean waiting time in system  Wq = mean waiting time in queue"
```

Figure 4.12   Program listing QUEUE2.BAS

```
PROGRAM QUEUE2.BAS - STATISTICS FOR TWO CHANNEL SINGLE PHASE QUEUE

Enter transactions per day      : ? 21600
Enter operational hours per day : ? 8
Enter average frame size        : ? 1200
Line Speed  EST     MSR     Po       p        L        Lq       W        Wq
      4800  2.0000    0.50  0.14286  0.75000  3.42857  1.92857  4.57143  2.57143
      9600  1.0000    1.00  0.45455  0.37500  0.87273  0.12273  1.16364  0.16364
     19200  0.5000    2.00  0.68421  0.18750  0.38866  0.01366  0.51822  0.01822
     56000  0.1714    5.83  0.87919  0.06429  0.12910  0.00053  0.17214  0.00071
     64000  0.1500    6.67  0.89349  0.05625  0.11286  0.00036  0.15048  0.00048
    128000  0.0750   13.33  0.94529  0.02813  0.05629  0.00004  0.07506  0.00006
    256000  0.0375   26.67  0.97227  0.01406  0.02813  0.00001  0.03751  0.00001
    384000  0.0250   40.00  0.98142  0.00938  0.01875  0.00000  0.02500  0.00000
    768000  0.0125   80.00  0.99067  0.00469  0.00938  0.00000  0.01250  0.00000
   1536000  0.0063  160.00  0.99532  0.00234  0.00469  0.00000  0.00625  0.00000

where:

    EST= expected service time  MSR = mean service rate
    Po=probability of zero frames in the system  p = utilization
    L= mean number of frames in system Lq = mean number in queue
    W= mean waiting time in system  Wq = mean waiting time in queue

Press any key to continue
```

Figure 4.13 Execution results of program QUEUE2.BAS

Figure 4.13 illustrates an example of the results of executing QUEUE2.BAS. In this example the program was executed using 21 600 transactions per eight-hour day with an average frame size of 1200 bytes.

4.4 BUFFER MEMORY CONSIDERATIONS

Most bridges and routers are modular devices whose feature selection list may contain more entries than a restaurant menu. Among the features from which you can normally select is a series of different memory modules which govern the buffer area in which frames can be queued when the frame arrival rate temporarily exceeds the service rate of the bridge or router.

Although the cost of memory has significantly declined over the past few years, a wild guess can still be costly from an operational perspective. Thus, we will conclude this chapter by examining how you can use queuing theory to make an educated estimate of the amount of buffer memory that should be installed in remote bridges and routers.

4.1.1 Average memory

Previously, we have determined the mean length of the queue, denoted as *Lq*. By multiplying the value of *Lq* by the average frame size you can determine the average amount of buffer memory that will be occupied. Unfortunately, this results in the average amount of buffer memory required and means that half the time more memory will be required. Thus, to obtain a more meaningful mechanism to estimate buffer memory requirements you must consider another method to determine the use of buffer memory. That method is obtained by computing the probability of different numbers of frames in a queuing system.

4.4.2 Using probability

The probability of *n* units (P_n) in a single-channel, single-server system is obtained from the following formula:

$$P_n = \left(\frac{\lambda}{\mu}\right)^n \left(1 - \frac{L}{\mu}\right) = p^n(1 - p)$$

The probability of *k* or more units ($P_{n>k}$) in a single-channel, single-server system is given by the formula

$$P_{n>k} = \left(\frac{\lambda}{\mu}\right)^k = p^k$$

To illustrate the use of the preceding formulas, let us return to our prior computations in which the utilization level was determined to be 0.375. Figure 4.14 lists the statements of a BASIC program labeled UNITS.BAS which you will use to compute the value of *P(N)* and *P(N > K)* as *N* and *K* vary from 0 to 20 for a single-channel, single-server system. This program was written to accept any server utilization level, which provides you with the ability to use it to satisfy the computational requirements associated with a specific situation.
Figure 4.15 illustrates the results obtained from the execution of the program UNITS.BAS with a server utilization level of 0.375, which is equivalent to 37.5%. In examining the data listed in Figure 4.15, note the relationship between *P(N)* and *P(N > K)*. That is, *P(N)* provides the probability for a specific number of units or (for our example) frames in a system, while *P(N > K)*

```
REM PROGRAM UNITS.BAS TO COMPUTE PROBABILITY OF N UNITS IN SYSTEM
REM AND PROBABILITY OF K OR MORE UNITS IN SYSTEM
CLS
PRINT "PROGRAM TO COMPUTE PROBABILITY OF N UNITS AND K OR MORE UNITS IN SYSTEM"
DIM P(20), K(20)
INPUT "Enter utilization level of server"; P
PRINT "PROBABILITY OF N UNITS     PROBABILITY K OR MORE UNITS"
PRINT " N      P(N)                K       P(N>K)"
FOR N = 0 TO 20
P(N) = P ^ N * (1 - P)
K(N) = P ^ N
PRINT USING "### #.########            ###    #.########"; N; P(N); N; K(N)
NEXT N
END
```

Figure 4.14   Program listing of UNITS.BAS

provides the probability that there are K or more units in the system. Thus, there is a 62.5% probability that there are no frames in the system ($P(N = 0)$), while as expected there is a probability of unity that there are zero or more frames in the system. Although you could use either column of probabilities as a decision criterion for determining the amount of buffer space you need in your bridge or router, you will shortly note that the second column provides a more direct value.

In attempting to determine the size of the buffer space you require, the question you must answer is 'How big should the buffer be to satisfy a predefined probability level of X%?'. Then, once you have defined the probability level you can answer the question. For example, assume that you want a buffer size big enough to store 99.9% of the occurrences when the arrival rate exceeds the service rate. To accomplish this you can directly use the right-hand columns listed in Figure 4.15 in which the probability of K or more units is tabulated for K varying from 0 to 20. To obtain a level of 99.9% of the occurrences is equivalent to not being able to handle 0.1% of the occurrences, which would be displayed as 0.001 in the second P column of Figure 4.15. Note that when K is 7, $P(N > K)$ is 0.00104284, or slightly more than 0.1%. Thus, you must select K equal to 8 to satisfy your requirement for handling 99.9% of the occurrences in which the frame arrival rate exceeds the service rate of the bridge or router. Thus, through the use of Figure 4.15 you would want the bridge or router to be capable of storing or queuing up to eight frames. Since the frame length was defined as 1200 bytes, your memory storage requirement becomes 1200 bytes/frame $\times$ 8 frames, or 9600 bytes for this particular situation.

```
PROGRAM TO COMPUTE PROBABILITY OF N UNITS AND K OR MORE UNITS IN SYSTEM
Enter utilization level of server? .375
PROBABILITY OF N UNITS     PROBABILITY K OR MORE UNITS
   N      P(N)              K          P(N>K)
   0  0.62500000           0    1.00000000
   1  0.23437500           1    0.37500000
   2  0.08789063           2    0.14062500
   3  0.03295898           3    0.05273438
   4  0.01235962           4    0.01977539
   5  0.00463486           5    0.00741577
   6  0.00173807           6    0.00278091
   7  0.00065178           7    0.00104284
   8  0.00024442           8    0.00039107
   9  0.00009166           9    0.00014665
  10  0.00003437          10    0.00005499
  11  0.00001289          11    0.00002062
  12  0.00000483          12    0.00000773
  13  0.00000181          13    0.00000290
  14  0.00000068          14    0.00000109
  15  0.00000025          15    0.00000041
  16  0.00000010          16    0.00000015
  17  0.00000004          17    0.00000006
  18  0.00000001          18    0.00000002
  19  0.00000001          19    0.00000001
  20  0.00000000          20    0.00000000
```

Figure 4.15 Execution results of program UNITS.BAS with a server utilization level of 0.375

4.4.3 Six-step approach

The steps required to determine queuing storage requirements can be summarized as follows.

(1) Determine the average frame arrival and average server service rates.
(2) Determine the utilization level of the server.
(3) Determine the level of service you want the server to provide with respect to storing or queuing frames for transmission when the frame arrival rate exceeds the server's service rate.
(4) Determine the probability of K or more units in the system for a range of values.
(5) Determine the probability that $N > K$, where K represents the level of service you want the server to provide, and locate that value in the computed range of probabilities. Then, extract the value of K which represents the number of frames that must be queued.

(6) Multiply the average or maximum frame length by the number of frames that must be queued. Note that multiplying by the average frame length results in obtaining the average buffer storage required for a given level of probability, and multiplying by the maximum frame length supported by your LAN results in obtaining a buffer storage value which will satisfy all situations for the predefined probability level.

4.4.4 Considering the maximum frame size

Although the first five steps are relatively self-explanatory, the sixth step may be confusing to some readers. So let us take a moment prior to proceeding and focus our attention upon the last step.

Previously you determined that your bridge or router should have 9600 bytes of buffer storage to queue 99.9% of the occurrences in which the frame arrival rate exceeds the server's service rate. In actuality, the prior computation was based upon an average frame length of 1200 bytes. Thus, the amount of buffer storage that you computed satisfies an average of 99.9% of the occurrences in which the frame arrival rate exceeds the server's service rate. If you wish to obtain a buffer storage value which fully satisfies your probability requirement, you must then use the maximum frame size supported by the local area network you are using or anticipate installing. For example, if you are using an Ethernet or IEEE 802.3 LAN, its maximum frame size is 1500 bytes (excluding overhead preamble and addressing and CRC bytes), whereas the use of a 4 Mbps or 16 Mbps Token-Ring LAN would result in a maximum frame size of 4500 or 18 000 bytes, respectively.

Program QVU.BAS

To facilitate performing another set of calculations, the program QVU.BAS was developed. Figure 4.16 lists the statements contained in this program which computes the buffer requirements for Ethernet and 4 and 16 Mbps Token-Ring networks based upon different server utilization levels ranging up to 99.0%. Readers can easily modify this program to obtain buffer requirements for other server utilization levels or to slightly expand frame sizes to better reflect the overhead associated with transmitting a frame using a specific wide area network protocol.

```
REM PROGRAM QVU.BAS TO COMPARE QUEUE LENGTH VERSUS SERVER UTILIZATION LEVEL
CLS
FRAME = 1500
LPRINT "ANALYSIS OF BUFFER STORAGE REQUIREMENTS"
LPRINT "MAXIMUM ETHERNET FRAME SIZE = 1500 BYTES"
LPRINT "MAXIMUM 4MBPS TOKEN-RING FRAME SIZE  = 4500 BYTES"
LPRINT "MAXIMUM 16MBPS TOKEN-RING FRAME SIZE =18000 BYTES"
LPRINT
LPRINT "UTILIZATION   LENGTH OF QUEUE    BUFFER REQUIREMENTS IN BYTES"
LPRINT " PERCENT         IN FRAMES         ETHERNET   4MBPS T-R  16MBPS T-R"
FOR P = 0! TO .9 STEP .1
LQ = P ^ 2 / (1 - P)
B = INT(LQ * FRAME + .99)
T4 = INT(LQ * 4500 + .99)
T16 = INT(LQ * 18000 + .99)
LPRINT USING "###.##        ####.###          ########"; P * 100; LQ; B;
LPRINT USING "  ######## ########"; T4; T16
NEXT P
FOR P = .91 TO .99 STEP .01
LQ = P ^ 2 / (1 - P)
B = INT(LQ * FRAME + .99)
T4 = INT(LQ * 4500 + .99)
T16 = INT(LQ * 18000 + .99)
LPRINT USING "###.##        ####.###          ########"; P * 100; LQ; B;
LPRINT USING "  ######## ########"; T4; T16
NEXT P
END
```

Figure 4.16 Program listing of QVU.BAS

```
ANALYSIS OF BUFFER STORAGE REQUIREMENTS
MAXIMUM ETHERNET FRAME SIZE = 1500 BYTES
MAXIMUM 4MBPS TOKEN-RING FRAME SIZE  = 4500 BYTES
MAXIMUM 16MBPS TOKEN-RING FRAME SIZE =18000 BYTES
```

UTILIZATION PERCENT	LENGTH OF QUEUE IN FRAMES	BUFFER REQUIREMENTS IN BYTES		
		ETHERNET	4MBPS T-R	16MBPS T-R
0.00	0.000	0	0	0
10.00	0.011	17	50	200
20.00	0.050	75	225	900
30.00	0.129	193	579	2315
40.00	0.267	400	1200	4800
50.00	0.500	750	2250	9000
60.00	0.900	1350	4050	16200
70.00	1.633	2450	7350	29400
80.00	3.200	4800	14400	57601
91.00	9.201	13802	41406	165621
92.00	10.580	15870	47611	190441
93.00	12.356	18534	55601	222403
94.00	14.727	22090	66270	265080
95.00	18.050	27075	81225	324900
96.00	23.040	34560	103680	414720
97.00	31.363	47045	141135	564540
98.00	48.020	72030	216090	864359
99.00	98.009	147015	441043	1764171

Figure 4.17 Execution results of program QVU.BAS

Figure 4.17 illustrates the results obtained from the execution of QVU.BAS. In examining the data in Figure 4.17 note that the length of the queue in terms of frames is relatively small until the server's utilization level exceeds 70%. Thereafter, it rapidly increases and will approach infinity as the utilization level approaches 100%. Thus, you can use the data in Figure 4.17 to determine if you really need to continue further and compute $P(N > K)$ or if you can simply estimate that at the level of server utilization the buffer requirements are so small that just about every bridge and router should have a sufficient amount of buffer memory. For example, suppose that your server's utilization level was 50% and your organization operates a 4 Mbps Token-Ring LAN. Figure 4.17 indicates an average buffer storage requirement of 2250 bytes, infinitesimally small in comparison to the 32 or 64 kbytes of buffer storage included in most remote bridges and routers. Thus, without further analysis to compute $P(N > K)$ you could safely conclude that a 32 kbyte buffer area should be sufficient for $P(N > 99.9)$. However, since many readers will probably feel more comfortable in selecting a probability level and performing the six-step sequence previously listed, Appendix A summarizes values of $P(N)$ and $P(N > K)$ for different server utilization levels ranging from $P = 10\%$ to $P = 95\%$ in increments of 5%.

4.4.5 Summary

Although a variety of queuing concepts have been examined in this chapter, it is most important to remember several concepts which govern the application of queuing theory to networking. One concept is that as the level of utilization of a server increases, its queue length increases. A second concept worth remembering is the fact that as the level of utilization for a single server system exceeds 50%, queues become more observable to whatever process you are performing. A third concept worth noting is the fact that as the level of utilization of a server approaches 100%, the length of a queue increases dramatically and will eventually approach infinity.

Table 4.2 gives the queue length for different utilization levels of a single-phase, single-channel system. Note that at a 50% utilization level, the mean queue length is 0.5; however, at a 70% level of utilization, the queue length is more than three times the 50% figure. Also note that an increase in utilization from 70 to 80% results in a doubling of the mean queue length, and an increase in utilization from 80 to 91% results in the length of the

Table 4.2   Queue length versus server utilization

Utilization (%)	Length of queue
0	0.000
10	0.011
20	0.050
30	0.129
40	0.267
50	0.500
60	0.900
70	1.633
80	3.200
91	9.201
92	10.580
93	12.356
94	14.727
95	18.050
96	23.040
97	31.363
98	48.020
99	98.009

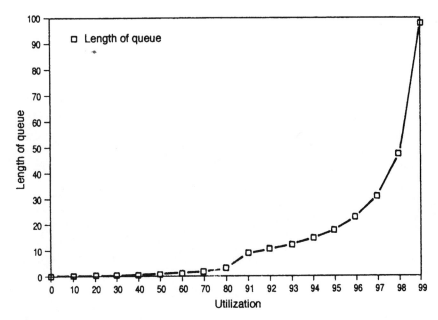

Figure 4.18   Queue length versus server utilization for a single-channel, single-phase system

queue nearly tripling. Figure 4.18 graphically illustrates the same data. In examining Figure 4.18, it is important to remember that the mean queue length is directly related to the mean waiting time, and this explains why most network managers, analysts, and designers should consider modifying a network facility when its utilization level exceeds 50%.

5

USING THE AVAILABILITY LEVEL AS A DECISION CRITERION

In Chapter 4 the application of queuing theory to determining transmission delays through remote bridges and routers was examined. As noted in that chapter, you can use queuing theory to compare the use of single versus multiple circuits used to connect remote bridges and routers. In doing so, the use of single and multiple circuits were examined from a performance perspective, leaving until this chapter a discussion of availability issues.

One of the more important decisions that network managers face is in determining whether to install single or multiple port devices such as remote bridges and routers. By understanding how availability is computed one can obtain the knowledge necessary to determine whether or not the cost of additional bridge ports, communications equipment, and transmission facilities is worthwhile with respect to the additional level of network availability obtained through the use of different communications configurations.

In this chapter we focus our attention on the use of the availability level of different network configurations as a decision criterion. That decision criterion can range from the direct selection of one configuration over another based on their level of availability, to the use of several selection parameters, including such additional parameters as performance and cost.

5.1 AVAILABILITY

In the same way that 'one person's passion is another person's poison', there are different ways in which you can look at and define availability. Thus, to alleviate any possibility of confusion, let us first define the term as it relates to both components and systems. Once this has been accomplished, we can examine its applicability to different local area network communications configurations.

5.1.1 Component availability

The availability of an individual component can be expressed in two ways which are directly related to one another. First, as a percentage, availability can be defined as the operational time of a device divided by the total time, with the result multiplied by 100. This is indicated by the following equation:

$$A\% = \frac{\text{operational time}}{\text{total time}} \times 100$$

where $A\%$ is availability expressed as a percentage.

For example, consider a leased line modem which normally operates continuously 24 hours per day. Over a one-year period of time let us assume that the modem failed once and required eight hours to repair. During the year the modem was available for use for 365 days × 24 hours/day less 8 hours, or 8752 hours. Thus, the modem was operational for 8752 hours during a period of 8760 hours. Using our availability formula we obtain

$$A\% = \frac{8752}{8760} \times 100 = 99.9\%$$

MTBF and MTTR

Now let us define two commonly used terms and discuss their relationship to operational time and total time. The first term, Mean Time Before Failure (MTBF), is the average operational time of a device prior to its failure. Thus, MTBF is equivalent to the operational time of a device.

Once a device has failed, you must effect its repair. The interval from the time the device fails until the time the device is repaired is known as the time to repair, and the average of each repair time is known as the Mean Time To Repair (MTTR). Since the total time is MTBF + MTTR, we can rewrite our availability formula as follows:

$$A\% = \frac{\text{MTBF}}{\text{MTBF} + \text{MTTR}} \times 100$$

It is important to remember the M in MTBF and MTTR, as you must use the average or mean time before failure and average or mean time to repair. Otherwise, your calculations are subject to error. For example, if your modem failure occurred halfway through the year, you might be tempted to assign 4380 hours to the MTBF. Then you would compute availability as

$$A\% = \frac{4380}{4380 + 8} \times 100 = 99.91\%$$

The problem with the above computation is the fact that only one failure occurred, which results in the MTBF not actually representing a mean. Although the computed MTBF is correct for one particular modem, as sure as the sun rises in the East, the MTBF would be different for a second modem, different again for a third modem, and so on. Thus, if you are attempting to obtain an availability level for a number of devices installed or to be installed you, in effect, will compute an average level of availability through the use of an average MTBF. Thus, the next logical question is how to obtain average MTBF information for a communications device. Fortunately, many vendors provide MTBF information for the products they manufacture that you can use instead of waiting for a significant period of time to obtain appropriate information. Although many published MTBF statistics can be used as is, certain statistics may represent extrapolations that deserve a degree of elaboration. When vendors introduce a new product and quote an MTBF of 50 000, 100 000 or more hours, they obviously have not operated that device for that length of time. Instead, they either extrapolated MTBF statistics based on the improvements made to a previously manufactured product, or base their statistics on the MTBF values of individual components.

If you notice an asterisk next to an MTBF figure and the footnote indicates extrapolation, you should probably question the MTBF value. After all, if the MTBF of some device is indicated as 100 000 hours, or almost 12 years, why is the warranty period typically one or two years? In such situations you might wish to consider using the warranty period as the MTBF value instead of an extrapolated MTBF value. Concerning the MTTR, this interval is also provided by the manufacturer, but it normally requires a degree of modification to be realistic.

Most manufacturers quote a MTTR figure based upon the time required to repair a device once a repair person is on site. Thus, you must consider the location where your equipment is to be installed and the travel time from a vendor's location to your location. If your organization has a maintenance contract which guarantees a service call within a predefined period after notification of an equipment failure, you can use that time period and add it to the MTTR. For example, assume that the specification sheet for a vendor's modem listed a MTBF of 16 500 hours and a MTTR of two hours. If you anticipate installing the modem in Macon, Georgia, and the nearest vendor service office is located in the northern suburbs of Atlanta, you would probably add four to six hours to the MTTR time. This addition would reflect the time required for a repair person in Atlanta to receive notification that he or she should service a failed device in Macon, complete his or her work in Atlanta, and travel to the site in Macon. Although this may not be significant when a MTBF exceeds one year, suppose your equipment location was Boise, Idaho, and the modem vendor used next-day delivery to ship a replacement modem, in effect, repairing by replacement. In this situation you may have to add 24 hours or more to the time required to swap modems to obtain a more realistic MTTR value.

5.1.2 System availability

In communications a system is considered to represent a collection of devices connected by the use of one or more transmission facilities which form a given topology. Thus, to determine the availability of a system you must consider the availability of each device and transmission facility as well as the overall topology of the system. Concerning the latter, the structure of the system in which components are connected in serial or in parallel will affect the overall availability of a system. To illustrate the effect of topology upon system availability, several basic local area network structures in which devices are connected in series and in parallel will be examined.

Devices connected in series

The top part of Figure 5.1 illustrates the connection of n components in series. In this and subsequent illustrations a

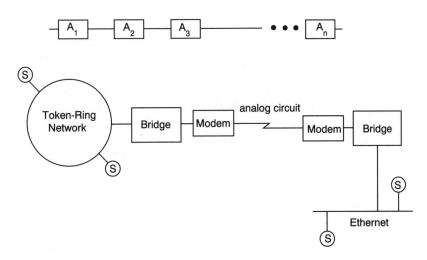

Figure 5.1 Network components in series. The availability of a system in which components are connected in series is obtained by multiplying together the availabilities of each of the individual components

component will be considered to represent either a physical network device or a transmission facility connecting two devices. Thus, the boxes labeled A_1, A_2, and A_3 could represent the availability of a modem (A_1), the availability of a leased line (A_2), and the availability of a second modem (A_3).

The availability of n components connected in series is computed by multiplying together the availabilities of each of the n individual components. Mathematically, this is expressed as follows for n components:

$$A = \prod_{i=1}^{n} A_i$$

To illustrate the computation of a system in which components are arranged in series, consider the Token-Ring network connected to an Ethernet LAN via the use of two remote bridges and a pair of analog modems. This networking system is illustrated in the lower portion of Figure 5.1.

Let us assume that each remote bridge has a MTBF of one year, or 8760 hours, and any failure would be corrected by the manufacturer shipping a replacement unit to each location where a bridge is installed. Thus, we might assume a worst-case MTTR of 48 hours to allow for the time between reporting a failure and the arrival and installation of a replacement unit. Similarly, let us assume a MTBF of 8760 hours and a MTTR of 48 hours for each modem. For the transmission line most communications carriers specify a 99.5% level of availability for digital circuits, so using a slightly lower level of 99.4% for an analog circuit would appear to be reasonable. Based upon the preceding formula, the availability of the communications system, A_S, which enables a user on a Token-Ring network to access the Ethernet network and vice versa via a pair of single port bridges, then becomes

$$A_S\% = [(\text{Bridge}_A)^2 \times (\text{Modem}_A)^2 \times \text{Line}_A] \times 100$$

where:

Bridge_A is the availability level of each bridge
Modem_A is the availability level of each modem
Line_A is the availability level of the analog circuit connecting the two locations

Since the availability of each component equals the MTBF divided by the sum of the MTBF and the MTTR, we obtain

$$A_A\% = \left[\left(\frac{8760}{8808}\right)^2 \times \left(\frac{8760}{8808}\right)^2 \times 0.994 \right] \times 100 = 97.25\%$$

This means that for approximately 2.75% of the time $(100 - 97.25)$ in which an attempt is made to use the communications system, the failure of one or more components will render the system inoperative.

Devices connected in parallel

Figure 5.2a illustrates n devices connected in parallel. If only one device out of n is required to provide communications at any point in time, then the availability of the system as a percentage becomes

$$A_S\% = \left(1 - \prod_{i=1}^{n} (1 - A_i) \right) \times 100$$

For example, assume that two devices each having an availability level of 99% are operated in parallel. Then, the availability level of the resulting parallel system becomes

$$A_S\% = \left(1 - \prod_{i=1}^{2} (1 - A_i) \right) \times 100$$

(a) n components connected in parallel

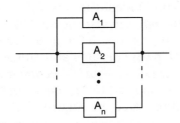

(b) Using dual single port bridges

(c) Using single dual port bridges

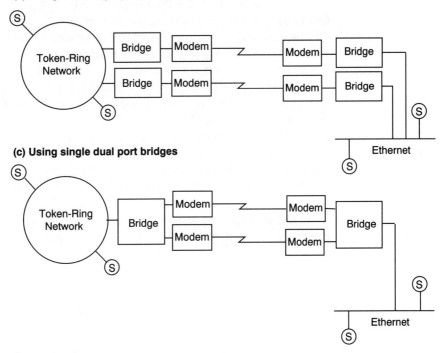

Figure 5.2 Connecting devices in parallel

Substituting, we obtain

$$A_A\% = [1 - (1 - 0.99) \times (1 - 0.99)] \times 100 = 99.99\%$$

Since communications within and between networks normally traverse multiple components, the use of parallel transmission paths normally involves multiple components on each path. Figures 5.2b and 5.2c illustrate two methods by which alternative paths could be provided to connect the Token-Ring and Ethernet networks together.

Readers should note that transparent bridging supported by Ethernet networks precludes the use of closed loops which physically occur through the use of dual bridges or multiport bridges illustrated in Figures 5.2b and 5.2c. However, if we assume that only one path operates at a single point in time, the use of two paths in which one only becomes active if the other becomes inactive is supported by transparent bridging.

In the topology illustrated in Figure 5.2b duplicate remote bridges, modems and transmission paths were assumed to be installed. In Figure 5.2c it was assumed that your organization could obtain a very reliable remote bridge and preferred to expend funds on parallel communications circuits and modems, because the failure rate of long-distance communications facilities normally exceeds the failure rate of equipment.

For simplicity, let us assume that the availability level of each component illustrated in Figure 5.2b is 0.9. For each parallel path you can consider the traversal of the path to encounter five components: two bridges, two modems, and the communications line. Thus, the upper path containing five devices in series would have an availability level of $0.9 \times 0.9 \times 0.9 \times 0.9 \times 0.9$ or 0.59049. Similarly, the lower path would have a level of availability of 0.59049. Thus, you have now reduced the network structure to two parallel paths, each having an availability level of 0.59049. If A_1 is the availability level of path 1 and A_2 is the availability level of the second path, the system availability A_S becomes

$$A_S\% = \left(1 - \prod_{i=1}^{2} (1 - A_i)\right) \times 100$$

Thus:

$$A_S\% = [1 - (1 - A_1)(1 - A_2)] \times 100$$

Simplifying the above equation by multiplying the terms and substituting 0.590 49 for A_1 and A_2, you obtain

$$A_S\% = [A_1 + A - (A_1 \times A_2)] \times 100 = 83.23\%$$

Mixed topologies

Now let us focus our attention upon the network configuration illustrated in Figure 5.2c in which a common bridge at each LAN location provides access to duplicate transmission facilities. To compute the availability of this communications system, you can

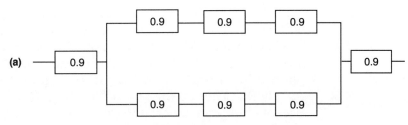

Availability of three serial devices = 0.9* 0.9* 0.9* = 0.729

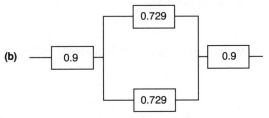

Availability of two parallel devices = 0.729 + 0.729 − 0.729 * 0.729 = 0.926

Availability of three serial devices = 0.9* 0.926* 0.9 = 0.75

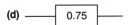

Figure 5.3 Computing the availability of a mixed serial and parallel transmission system

treat each bridge as a serial element, and the two modems and the communications line between each modem represent parallel routes of three serial devices.

Figure 5.3 illustrates how you can consider the communications system previously illustrated in Figure 5.2c as a sequence of serial and parallel elements. By combining groups of serial and parallel elements you can easily compute the overall level of availability for the communications system as indicated in the four parts of Figure 5.3. In Figure 5.3a the three serial elements of each parallel circuit are combined, including the two modems and communications line, to obtain a serial availability level of 0.9 × 0.9 × 0.9, or 0.729. Next, in Figure 5.3b the two parallel paths are combined to obtain a joint availability of 0.729 + 0.729 − (0.729 × 0.729), or 0.926. Finally, in Figure 5.3c the joint availability of the parallel transmission paths is treated as a serial element with the two bridges, obtaining a system availability of 0.75 (Figure 5.3d). Note that at a uniform 90% level of availability for each device the use of single bridges in place of dual bridges lowers the system availability by approximately 8%. That is, the system availability obtained through the use of dual single-port bridges illustrated in Figure 5.2b was computed to be 83.23%; in comparison, the system availability obtained from the use of single dual-port bridges illustrated in Figure 5.2c was determined to be 75%.

5.1.3 Dual hardware versus dual transmission facilities

In the above calculations, assuming a uniform component availability of 0.9 (90%), the system availability of the dual network illustrated in Figure 5.2b was computed to be 83.23%, and the availability of the network illustrated in Figure 5.2c was computed to be 75%. Although the difference in availability of over 8% could probably justify the extra cost associated with dual bridges for organizations with critical applications, what happens to the difference in the availability of each network as the availability level of each component increases?

Table 5.1 compares the system availability for the use of single multiport and parallel single port bridge networks as component

Table 5.1 System availability comparison

Component availability	System availability	
	Single multiport bridge	Parallel single-port bridges
0.90	0.7505	0.8323
0.91	0.7778	0.8586
0.92	0.8049	0.8838
0.93	0.8318	0.9073
0.94	0.8582	0.9292
0.95	0.8841	0.9488
0.96	0.9094	0.9659
0.97	0.9337	0.9800
0.98	0.9571	0.9908
0.99	0.9792	0.9976
0.999	0.9980	0.9999

availability increases from 0.9 to 0.999. In examining the entries in Table 5.1 you will note that the difference between the availability level of each network decreases as component availability increases. In fact, the 8% difference at a component availability level of 0.9 decreases to under 4% at a component availability level of 0.98 and to under 2% at a component availability level of 0.99. Since most modern communications devices have a component availability level close to 0.999, which, by the way, usually exceeds the availability level of a transmission facility by 0.005, the use of dual bridges instead of multiport bridges may be limited to increasing network availability by 0.1%. Thus, you must balance the gain in availability against the cost of redundant bridges.

Concerning cost, although bridges vary considerably with respect to features and price, at the end of 1996 their average price was approximately $1500. In comparison, the incremental cost of a dual port bridge over that of a single port bridge was typically less than $500. Since you require two bridges to link geographically separated networks, the cost difference between the use of dual single-port bridges and single dual-port bridges is approximately $(1500 - 500) \times 2$, or $2000. Thus, in this example you would have to decide if an increase in network availability by approximately 0.1% is worth $2000.

If your organization operates a reservation system in which a minute of downtime could result in the loss of thousands of dollars of revenue, the additional cost would probably be most acceptable. If your organization uses your network for interoffice electronic mail transmission, you might prefer to save the $2000 and use single dual-port bridges instead of dual single-port bridges. This is because a gain of 0.1% of availability based upon an eight-hour workday with 22 workdays per month would only provide 2.1 additional hours of availability per year. At a cost of approximately $1000 per hour for the additional availability, it might be more economical to simply delay non-urgent mail and use the telephone for urgent communications.

If you apply the preceding economic analysis to routers, the cost disparity between different network configurations becomes more pronounced. For example, a middle-range router might cost $5000, whereas the incremental cost of a dual-port router can be expected to add approximately $750 to the cost of the device. Then the cost difference between dual single-port routers and single dual-port routers becomes $(5000 - 750) \times 2$ or $8500. Thus when routers are used, your decision criteria could be one of deciding if an increase in network availability of approximately 0.1% is worth $8500.

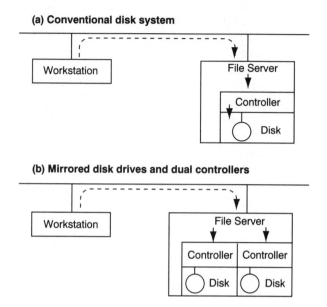

Figure 5.4   Comparing data flow using conventional and mirrored disk systems on a file server

5.1.4 Evaluating disk mirroring

Another area where the use of availability computations can be valuable with respect to LAN performance is in evaluating the advantage associated with a disk mirroring system. To illustrate the use of availability in evaluating the practicality of a disk mirroring system let us compare different file server equipment structures.

The top portion of Figure 5.4a illustrates the use of a conventional disk subsystem installed in a file server. In this example data transmitted from a workstation flow across the network media into the file server and through its controller onto the disk. Thus, the conventional disk subsystem from the perspective of availability can be schematically represented as three components in series: the file server, controller and disk. The rationale for including the file server when computing the availability level of a disk system is the fact that the failure of the server terminates access to the disk. Although you might be tempted to compare availability levels of different disk systems without considering the availability level of the file server, by including the server you obtain a more realistic real-life comparison.

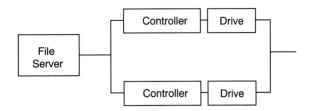

Figure 5.5 A schematic representation of a fully mirrored disk subsystem from the perspective of its availability

Figure 5.4b illustrates the data flow when a file server has dual controllers and dual disks installed, a configuration commonly referred to as a fully mirrored disk subsystem.

A schematic representation, from the perspective of availability, for the mirrored disk drives and dual controllers is shown in Figure 5.5. Note that the file server can be considered to be placed in series with two pairs of parallel arranged devices: the controller and disk drive. Thus, if the file server fails, access to either drive is blocked which represents reality.

Since we need availability levels of the file server, controller and disk to compare single and mirrored disk systems, let us make some assumptions. Let us assume that the file server is expected to fail once every three years and will require replacement via Express Mail, UPS or another service within a 48 hour notification period. Thus, the availability of the file server becomes

$$A\% = \frac{8760 \times 3}{8760 \times 3 + 48} \times 100 = 99.82$$

For the disk controller, let us assume that it is very reliable, and might fail once in a five year period and its replacement will require 24 hours. Thus, the availability of the disk controller becomes

$$A\% = \frac{8760 \times 5}{8760 \times 5 + 24} \times 100 = 99.95$$

Although disk vendors commonly quote a MTBF of 100 000 hours or more, from practical experience my file server disks seem to need replacement on average once every $2\frac{1}{2}$ years. When they fail, their replacement involves more than installing new hardware, as the last backup must be moved onto the disk. Again, from this author's experience the ordering of a replacement disk, its arrival and installation accompanied by a full restoral can require an average MTTR of 36 hours. Thus, I would compute the availability of the disks that I use as follows:

$$A\% = \frac{8760 \times 2.5}{8760 \times 2.5 + 36} \times 100 = 99.84$$

Now that we have an availability level for each component, let us compare the availability level of the single and fully mirrored disk systems.

Single disk system

The single disk system can be represented by three components in series. Hence, its availability becomes

$$A_s\% = (0.9982) \times (0.9995) \times (0.9984) \times 100 = 99.61$$

Mirrored disk system

For the fully mirrored disk system the availability of a controller and disk in series becomes

$$A\% = (0.9995) \times (0.9984) \times 100 = 99.79$$

The fully mirrored system consists of two parallel paths of a controller and disk in series. Thus, the availability of each of those parallel paths becomes

$$A\% = [0.9979 + 0.9979 - (0.9979)(0.9979)] \times 100 = 99.99956$$

When we consider the availability of the file server, the availability of the fully mirrored disk subsystem, including the computer that its components reside in, becomes

$$A_s\% = (0.9982)(0.9999956) \times 100 = 99.82$$

In comparing the availability level of a single disk subsystem with fully redundant mirrored disks with dual controllers, note that the availability has increased from 99.61% to 99.82%. By itself this increase of 0.21% may not be meaningful, so let us attempt to consider it from an operational perspective. Over a three year period, not considering a leap year in that period, there are 8760×3 or 26 280 hours. By increasing availability by 0.21% we can expect to gain $26\,280 \times 0.0021$ or 55.2 hours of equipment life prior to a failure occurring which terminates access to data. Whether the additional operational time is worth the additional cost associated with installing a fully mirrored disk subsystem obviously depends on its additional cost as well as the actual MTBF and MTTR values that you would use in your computations. However, the preceding information provides you with a methodology that you can easily alter to analyze the equipment you may be considering.

5.2 AUTOMATING AVAILABILITY COMPUTATIONS

As we noted in the first section of this chapter, the computation of system availability can be reduced to a series of computations for devices in series and in parallel. To facilitate the computations involved in determining serial and parallel component availability, the program AVAIL.BAS was developed. Figure 5.6 lists the statements in that BASIC language program.

5.2.1 Program AVAIL.BAS

The program AVAIL.BAS can be used to compute the availability levels for components connected in series or in parallel. In fact, by selecting the program's BOTH option, the program will first compute the availability level of components connected in series and then compute the availability level of components connected in parallel.

To facilitate data entry the program permits you to enter data in either of two ways. You can enter data concerning the availability level of individual components as a percentage value or you can enter MTBF and MTTR values. For either data entry method the program accepts a maximum of 10 component availability level values which should be more than sufficient for essentially all network configurations. In the event that you require the computation of more than 10 component availability level values, you can easily modify AVAIL.BAS. To do so you would simply add a DIM statement at the beginning of the program which would contain a value for each array used in the program that reflects the highest number of components that you intend to analyze. Since BASIC automatically dimensions all arrays to 10 elements, no DIM statement was required in AVAIL.BAS.

```
REM PROGRAM AVAIL.BAS
CLS
PRINT "PROGRAM AVAIL.BAS TO COMPUTE AVAILABILITY LEVELS"
PRINT
PRINT "INDICATE COMPUTATIONS DESIRED "
PRINT "     S)ERIAL"
PRINT "     P)ARALLEL"
PRINT "     B)OTH SERIAL AND PARALLEL"
AGN:    INPUT "ENTER THE TYPE OF COMPUTATIONS DESIRED          : ", COMP$
IF COMP$ <> "S" AND COMP$ <> "P" AND COMP$ <> "B" THEN GOTO AGN:
IF COMP$ = "B" THEN TRY$ = "A"
IF COMP$ = "B" THEN COMP$ = "S"
GOSUB DENTER
IF COMP$ = "S" THEN GOSUB SCOMPUTE
IF COMP$ = "P" THEN GOSUB PCOMPUTE
IF TRY$ = "A" THEN COMP$ = "P"
IF TRY$ = "A" THEN GOSUB DENTER
IF TRY$ = "A" THEN GOSUB PCOMPUTE
STOP
DENTER:
        IF COMP$ = "P" THEN GOTO PAR
        INPUT "ENTER NUMBER OF COMPONENTS IN SERIAL -MAX 10    : ", C
        IF COMP$ = "S" THEN GOTO SER
PAR:    INPUT "ENTER NUMBER OF COMPONENTS IN PARALLEL - MAX 10 : ", C
SER:    PRINT
        PRINT "HOW DO YOU WANT TO ENTER DATA ?"
        PRINT "AS  P)ERCENT E.G. 12.5"
        PRINT "AS  M)TBF AND MTTR"
        INPUT "ENTER DATA ENTRY METHOD -P OR M                 : ", D$
        IF D$ <> "P" AND D$ <> "M" THEN GOTO DENTER
        IF D$ = "M" GOTO MENTRY
        FOR I = 1 TO C
        PRINT "FOR COMPONENT"; I;
        INPUT "ENTER PERCENT AVAILABILITY      : ", A(I)
        A(I) = A(I) / 100
        NEXT I
        RETURN
MENTRY:
        FOR I = 1 TO C
        PRINT "FOR COMPONENT"; I;
        INPUT "ENTER MTBF AND MTTR VALUES      : ", MTBF(I), MTTR(I)
        A(I) = MTBF(I) / (MTBF(I) + MTTR(I))
        NEXT I
        RETURN
SCOMPUTE:
        IF COMP$ = "P" GOTO PCOMPUTE
        PROD = 1
        FOR I = 1 TO C
        PROD = PROD * A(I)
        NEXT I
        PRINT USING "AVAILABILITY OF ## "; C;
        PRINT USING " DEVICES IN SERIES = ##.#####"; PROD * 100
        RETURN
PCOMPUTE:
        PROD = 1
        FOR I = 1 TO C
        PROD(I) = (1 - A(I))
        PROD = PROD * PROD(I)
        NEXT I
        AVAIL = 1 - PROD
        PRINT USING "AVAILABILITY OF ##"; C;
        PRINT USING " DEVICES IN PARALLEL = ##.#####"; AVAIL * 100
        RETURN
END
```

Figure 5.6   Program listing of AVAIL.BAS

5.2.2 Program execution

Because the best way to illustrate the use of a computer program is to execute the program, let us do so. In doing so, let us assume our network configuration consists of two sets of five components connected in series, with each set routed parallel to the other set of components. Let us also assume that we have component availability expressed as a percentage for one set of components and as MTBF and MTTR data for the second set of components.

Figure 5.7 illustrates the execution of AVAIL.BAS to compute the availability of five serially connected components when the availability for each component is specified as a percentage. In this example it was assumed that four components each had an availability level of 99.9%, and one component had an availability level of 99.85%. As noted at the bottom of Figure 5.7, the availability level of the five devices in series was computed to be 99.45%.

Figure 5.8 illustrates the execution of the program AVAIL.BAS to compute the availability of five serially connected components when you wish to use and have available MTBF and MTTR data. In this example it was assumed that four components each had an MTBF of 8000 hours and an MTTR of 24 hours. Concerning the latter, it was assumed that repair is accomplished by replacement and that your organization uses Express Mail, Federal

```
PROGRAM AVAIL.BAS TO COMPUTE AVAILABILITY LEVELS

INDICATE COMPUTATIONS DESIRED
        S)ERIAL
        P)ARALLEL
        B)OTH SERIAL AND PARALLEL
    ENTER THE TYPE OF COMPUTATIONS DESIRED       : S
    ENTER NUMBER OF COMPONENTS IN SERIAL -MAX 10  : 5

    HOW DO YOU WANT TO ENTER DATA ?
    AS  P)ERCENT E.G. 12.5
    AS  M)TBF AND MTTR
    ENTER DATA ENTRY METHOD -P OR M              : P
    FOR COMPONENT 1 ENTER PERCENT AVAILABILITY   : 99.9
    FOR COMPONENT 2 ENTER PERCENT AVAILABILITY   : 99.9
    FOR COMPONENT 3 ENTER PERCENT AVAILABILITY   : 99.85
    FOR COMPONENT 4 ENTER PERCENT AVAILABILITY   : 99.9
    FOR COMPONENT 5 ENTER PERCENT AVAILABILITY   : 99.9
    AVAILABILITY OF  5  DEVICES IN SERIES = 99.45120
```

Figure 5.7 Execution of program AVAIL.BAS to compute availability of serially connected devices using the percent availability method of data entry

```
PROGRAM AVAIL.BAS TO COMPUTE AVAILABILITY LEVELS

INDICATE COMPUTATIONS DESIRED
      S)ERIAL
      P)ARALLEL
      B)OTH SERIAL AND PARALLEL
ENTER THE TYPE OF COMPUTATIONS DESIRED       : S
ENTER NUMBER OF COMPONENTS IN SERIAL -MAX 10 : 5

HOW DO YOU WANT TO ENTER DATA ?
AS  P)ERCENT E.G. 12.5
AS  M)TBF AND MTTR
ENTER DATA ENTRY METHOD -P OR M              : M
FOR COMPONENT 1 ENTER MTBF AND MTTR VALUES   : 8000,24
FOR COMPONENT 2 ENTER MTBF AND MTTR VALUES   : 8000,24
FOR COMPONENT 3 ENTER MTBF AND MTTR VALUES   : 720,2
FOR COMPONENT 4 ENTER MTBF AND MTTR VALUES   : 8000,48
FOR COMPONENT 5 ENTER MTBF AND MTTR VALUES   : 8000,48
AVAILABILITY OF  5  DEVICES IN SERIES = 97.94843
```

Figure 5.8 Execution of program AVAIL.BAS to compute availability of serially connected devices using the MTBF and MTTR method of data entry

Express, or a similar overnight service to deliver a new device which will be used to replace a failed device. Since your presumed experience is that the average time from failure notification to the replacement of the failed device is 24 hours, you used 24 for each of four MTTR values. For one component you used an MTBF of 720 hours and an MTBR of two hours. This availability setting is representative of many digital transmission lines, since there are 24×30, or 720 hours in a 'typical' month, and one two-hour failure provides an approximate 99.7% level of line availability. As indicated at the bottom of Figure 5.8, the availability level of this second set of five devices connected in series was computed to be 97.95%.

Now that you have determined the availability level of each set of serially connected devices you can compute system availability by treating each resulting computed value as two devices in parallel. Thus, you can use AVAIL.BAS one more time to compute the system availability level of your two sets of five serially connected devices. To do so you will execute AVAIL.BAS and select the parallel computation option.

Figure 5.9 illustrates the execution of AVAIL.BAS in which the parallel option was selected. Since your previous executions of AVAIL.BAS resulted in two availability levels expressed as a percentage, you will now select the percent data entry method for the parallel component computations. As indicated in Figure 5.9, entering the results of the previous serial availability levels

```
PROGRAM AVAIL.BAS TO COMPUTE AVAILABILITY LEVELS

INDICATE COMPUTATIONS DESIRED
      S)ERIAL
      P)ARALLEL
      B)OTH SERIAL AND PARALLEL
ENTER THE TYPE OF COMPUTATIONS DESIRED          : P
ENTER NUMBER OF COMPONENTS IN PARALLEL - MAX 10 : 2

HOW DO YOU WANT TO ENTER DATA ?
AS   P)ERCENT E.G. 12.5
AS   M)TBF AND MTTR
ENTER DATA ENTRY METHOD -P OR M                 : P
FOR COMPONENT 1 ENTER PERCENT AVAILABILITY      : 99.4512
FOR COMPONENT 2 ENTER PERCENT AVAILABILITY      : 97.94843
AVAILABILITY OF  2 DEVICES IN PARALLEL = 99.98874
```

Figure 5.9   Execution of program AVAIL.BAS to compute availability of parallel connected devices

results in an availability level of 99.98874%. This represents the system availability level of the two sets of five serially connected components whose individual availability levels were previously specified. As indicated by this short example, you can use the program AVAIL.BAS to simplify the computations associated with different network structures, since those structures can be considered to represent a mixture of devices connected in series or in parallel.

ESTIMATING ETHERNET NETWORK PERFORMANCE

In Chapters 4 and 5 several models were developed and exercised to compute transmission delays, buffer memory requirements, and availability levels associated with the use of remote bridges and routers as well as single and mirrored disk systems.

In Chapter 4 you did not have to consider the types of local area networks to be connected, other than noting that transmission delays and buffer memory requirement computations were based upon several average frame sizes assumed to be flowing on a network. This enabled us to develop general models that can be tailored to a specific network environment by exercising a model with the appropriate frame size monitored or estimated to be carried by a network.

In Chapter 5, it was noted that the availability levels of different network configurations are independent of the types of local area networks to be connected. In this chapter we will begin to focus our attention upon the performance requirements of specific types of local area networks by examining the CSMA/CD access protocol. This will enable us to construct a model which reflects the transfer of frames on Ethernet and Fast Ethernet networks at different levels of network utilization. This in turn will provide us with a foundation for computing the maximum frame forwarding rate required to be supported by a bridge or router connected to different types of Ethernet network to ensure the device is fully capable of supporting the maximum level of Ethernet transmission. As in preceding chapters, a BASIC language program will be developed and executed to facilitate exercising the mathematical models developed in this chapter.

6.1 CSMA/CD NETWORK PERFORMANCE

Ethernet is a carrier sense multiple access with collision detection (CSMA/CD) network. Each station on the network listens for a carrier and attempts to transmit data when it senses the absence of that signal. Unfortunately, two stations may attempt to transmit data simultaneously, resulting in the occurrence of a collision. Even when one station thinks there is no carrier, it is quite possible that a carrier signal is propagating down the transmission path. Thus, a station transmitting data when its sampling of the line indicates the absence of a carrier may also result in a collision.

Because of the random nature of collisions, Ethernet bus performance is not deterministic, and performance characteristics and message transmission delays are not predictable. However, over a period of time you can determine average and peak utilization, data elements which you may use to split one Ethernet LAN into two or more LANs via the use of bridges to increase individual network performance.

6.1.1 Determining the network frame rate

In this section we will compute the frame rate on Ethernet and 100BASE-TX Fast Ethernet networks. Because the frame flow on 100BASE-TX is ten times that of the 10BASE-T Ethernet network operating at 10 Mbps we will first focus our computations on the lower speed network. Once we have computed the frame rate on 10 Mbps, Ethernet we will simple multiply the result by 10 to determine the frame rate on Fast Ethernet.

The top portion of Figure 6.1 illustrates the IEEE 802.3 (Ethernet) frame format. In this illustration the seven byte preamble field and the one-byte start of frame delimiter field are combined into a common eight-byte preamble field for simplicity. In actuality, the preamble field used by Ethernet is an eight-byte sequence of alternating 1s and 0s, the IEEE 802.3 frame format uses a seven-byte preamble field of alternating 1s and 0s. The one-byte start of frame delimiter field used in IEEE 802.3 frames follows a seven-byte preamble field, using the sequence of alternating 1s and 0s but ends with two set bits instead of the 1 and 0 used in the Ethernet preamble field. Since computations required to estimate Ethernet network and bridge and router performance are based upon frame length and not frame composition, the use of a common eight-byte preamble field, although not technically

Preamble	Destination Address	Source Address	Length or Type	Data	Frame Check Sequence
8	6	6	2	46≤n≤1500	4

Frame Size (bytes)

Field	Maximum Size Frame	Maximum Size Frame
Preamble	8	8
Destination Address	6	6
Source Address	6	6
Length or Type	2	2
Data	46	1500
Frame Check Sequence	4	4
Total Size	72	1526

Figure 6.1 IEEE 802.3 (Ethernet) frame format

correct from a frame composition basis, does not affect our computations. As indicated by the tabulation of frame field lengths in the lower portion of Figure 6.1, the frame size can vary from a minimum of 72 to a maximum of 1526 bytes.

Under Ethernet and 802.3 standards there is a dead time of 9.6 μs between frames. Using the frame size and dead time between frames you can compute the maximum number of frames per second that can flow on an Ethernet network. For our example, let us assume that we have a 10 Mbps LAN, such as a 10BASE-2, 10BASE-5 or 10BASE-T network. Here the bit time then becomes $1/10^7$ seconds or 100 ns.

Now let us assume that all frames are at the maximum length of 1526 bytes. Then the time per frame becomes

$$9.6\,\mu\text{s} + 1526 \text{ bytes} \times \frac{8 \text{ bits}}{\text{byte}} \times \frac{100\,\text{ns}}{\text{bit}} = 1.23\,\text{ms}$$

Since one 1526 byte frame requires 1.23 ms, then in one second there can be 1/1.23 ms or approximately 812 maximum-sized frames. Thus, the maximum transmission rate on an Ethernet network is 812 frames per second when information is transferred in 1500 byte units within a sequence of frames. One example of a situation in which data would be transferred in 1500 byte units is when a workstation downloads a file from a server or transfers a file to another workstation or to a server. When this type of data transfer occurs, the data fields of a large number of sequential frames would be filled to their maximum size of 1500 bytes. If the last portion of the file being transferred is less than 1500 bytes, then the data field of the last frame used to transport the file would be less than 1500 bytes in length.

Now that the maximum number of frames that can traverse an Ethernet network when the data field is at its maximum size has been determined, let us compute the frame rate when the data field is at its minimum length. When that occurs the data field contains up to 46 characters of information, since pad characters are required to fill the data field to a minimum length of 46 characters. This results in a minimum size Ethernet frame being 72 characters in length.

For a minimum frame length of 72 bytes, the time per frame is $9.6\,\mu s + 72$ bytes $\times 8$ bits/byte $\times 100\,ns/bit$, or 67.2×10^{-6} seconds. Thus, in one second there can be a maximum of $1/67.2 \times 10^{-6}$, or 14 880 minimum-size 72 byte frames.

Table 6.1 summarizes the frame processing requirements for 10 Mbps Ethernet and 100 Mbps Fast Ethernet networks under 50% and 100% load conditions based upon minimum and maximum frame sizes. Note that those frame processing requirements define the frame examination (filtering) operating rate of a bridge connected to an Ethernet. That rate indicates the number of frames per second that a bridge connected to a 10 Mbps or 100 Mbps Ethernet local area network must be capable of examining under heavy (50% load) and full (100% load) traffic conditions. Those frame processing requirements also define the maximum frame forwarding rate for a bridge or router connected to a single network, because if all frames were routed off the network the forwarding rate would equal the filtering rate.

As an example of the potential utilization of information contained in Table 6.1, assume that you are considering the acquisition of a two port 10BASE-T bridge. That bridge must have a filtering capability at or above 29 780 72 byte frames per second to ensure that it is capable of examining each frame that can flow on a 10BASE-T network connected to each port. Similarly, in a worst-case operational scenario the bridge must be capable of forwarding 29 780 72 byte frames per second through the bridge to ensure that no frames that require forwarding are lost.

Table 6.1 Ethernet frame processing capability (Frames per second)

Network type	Average frame size (bytes)	Frames per second	
		50% load	100% load
Ethernet	1526	406	812
	72	7 440	14 880
Fast Ethernet	1526	4 060	8 120
	72	74 400	148 800

Program EPERFORM.BAS

From the two sets of computations already performed in this section, Ethernet bridge and router processing requirements and 50% and 100% network load conditions were determined. To facilitate performing additional computations, a general model of Ethernet bridge and router processing requirements will be developed which will be incorporated into a BASIC language program. That program, which we will appropriately name EPERFORM.BAS, will be exercised by varying the Ethernet frame size from its minimum frame length of 72 bytes to its maximum frame length of 1526 bytes.

To develop a general model which provides the maximum number of frames that can be transmitted on an Ethernet network, we can simply replace the specific frame length used in prior computations by the variable FLENGTH. Then, we obtain the maximum frame rate in frames per second (FPS) under a 100% network load using the following equation:

Ethernet 100% load frame rate

$$= \frac{1}{9.6\,\mu s + \text{FLENGTH} \times 8 \text{ bits/byte} \times 100\,\text{ns/bit}}$$

Figure 6.2 lists the contents of the program EPERFORM.BAS developed to exercise the previously developed Ethernet frame rate model for frame lengths varying from 72 to 1526 bytes in length under 50% and 100% load conditions. In this program the

```
REM PROGRAM EPERFORM.BAS
LPRINT "THIS PROGRAM COMPUTES ETHERNET BRIDGE FRAME PROCESSING REQUIREMENTS"
LPRINT "        BASED UPON VARYING AVERAGE ETHERNET FRAME LENGTHS"
LPRINT
LPRINT "AVERAGE FRAME LENGTH        FRAME PROCESSING REQUIREMENT"
LPRINT "                            50% LOAD      100% LOAD"
LPRINT
FOR J = 1 TO 12 STEP 3
READ A, B, C
DATA 72,72,1,80,100,20,125,1500,25,1526,1526,1
FOR FLENGTH = A TO B STEP C
FPS = 1 / (.0000096 + FLENGTH * 8 * .0000001)
LPRINT USING "   #####     "; FLENGTH;
LPRINT USING "                     ######.##   ######.##"; FPS / 2; FPS
NEXT FLENGTH
NEXT J
END
```

Figure 6.2 Program listing of EPERFORM.BAS

FOR J loop is used to define four sets of variables for use by the FOR FLENGTH loop which performs the computations required to determine Ethernet frame processing requirements based upon different frame lengths. The variable FPS computes the frame per second rate based on a bit duration of 100 ns (0.0000001), which represents the bit duration of a 10 Mbps Ethernet network. You can either lower the bit duration by a factor of 10 and change the interframe gap from 0.0000096 to 0.00000096 to compute a table of frame rates for Fast Ethernet or multiply the results obtained from the execution of the unmodified program by ten.

The first iteration of the J loop simply sets FLENGTH to compute the frame processing requirements for a frame length of 72 bytes. The second iteration of the J loop results in the FLENGTH loop computing the frame processing requirement for frame lengths from 80 to 100 bytes in increments of 20 bytes. The third iteration of the J loop results in the FLENGTH loop computing the frame processing requirements for frame lengths from 125 to 1500 bytes in increments of 25 bytes. Finally, the fourth iteration completes the computations for the maximum frame length of 1526 bytes.

Figure 6.3 lists the results obtained from the execution of the program EPERFORM.BAS. By using monitoring equipment, such as a protocol analyzer, you can determine the average frame length transmitted on your network. Then you can use those data in conjunction with the frame processing requirement columns listed in Figure 6.3 to determine the frame processing requirements for your specific network environment. As indicated in the footnote of Figure 6.3, by multiplying an entry in either frame processing column by 10 you can obtain the frame processing requirement for a 100BASE-TX Fast Ethernet network.

Due to improvements in bridge and router frame processing resulting from the incorporation of low-cost, high-performance microprocessors, such as the Intel 80486 and Pentium, today you should be able to obtain bridges and routers with a processing capability that exceeds the frame processing requirements for all Ethernet frame lengths. Thus, the data listed in Figure 6.3 are primarily of value if you are using a 10 Mbps Ethernet network to decide whether or not you should continue to use older bridges and routers as your network operation changes. If you are using or considering the installation of Fast Ethernet the frame processing requirements listed in Figure 6.3 increase by a factor of ten. In such circumstances, many bridges or routers may not be capable of supporting a 100% load requirement. This is especially true if you anticipate adding a new adapter card and driver to support 100BASE-T operations in an existing PC based

THIS PROGRAM COMPUTES ETHERNET BRIDGE FRAME PROCESSING REQUIREMENTS
BASED UPON VARYING AVERAGE ETHERNET FRAME LENGTHS

AVERAGE FRAME LENGTH	FRAME PROCESSING REQUIREMENT	
	50% LOAD	100% LOAD
72	7440.48	14880.95
80	6793.48	13586.96
100	5580.36	11160.71
125	4562.04	9124.09
150	3858.02	7716.05
175	3342.25	6684.49
200	2948.11	5896.23
225	2637.13	5274.26
250	2385.50	4770.99
275	2177.70	4355.40
300	2003.21	4006.41
325	1854.60	3709.20
350	1726.52	3453.04
375	1614.99	3229.97
400	1516.99	3033.98
425	1430.21	2860.41
450	1352.81	2705.63
475	1283.37	2566.74
500	1220.70	2441.41
525	1163.87	2327.75
550	1112.10	2224.20
575	1064.74	2129.47
600	1021.24	2042.48
625	981.16	1962.32
650	944.11	1888.22
675	909.75	1819.51
700	877.81	1755.62
725	848.03	1696.07
750	820.21	1640.42
775	794.16	1588.31
800	769.70	1539.41
825	746.71	1493.43
850	725.06	1450.12
875	704.62	1409.24
900	685.31	1370.61
925	667.02	1334.04
950	649.69	1299.38
975	633.23	1266.46
1000	617.59	1235.18
1025	602.70	1205.40
1050	588.51	1177.02
1075	574.98	1149.95
1100	562.05	1124.10
1125	549.69	1099.38
1150	537.87	1075.73
1175	526.54	1053.07
1200	515.68	1031.35
1225	505.25	1010.51
1250	495.25	990.49
1275	485.63	971.25
1300	476.37	952.74
1325	467.46	934.93
1350	458.88	917.77
1375	450.61	901.23
1400	442.63	885.27
1425	434.93	869.87
1450	427.50	854.99
1475	420.31	840.62
1500	413.36	826.72
1526	406.37	812.74

Figure 6.3 Execution results of program EPERFORM.BAS

Note: Multiply a frame processing requirement entry by 10 to obtain the requirement for 100BASE-TX Fast Ethernet.

bridge. Thus, you should carefully examine the frame processing capability of bridges and routers prior to using them for Fast Ethernet applications.

Another area in which the data presented in Figure 6.3 can be extremely valuable is in evaluating bridges and routers. Suppose that you are evaluating two bridges manufactured by the well-known vendors X and Y. Let us assume that vendor X's sales literature lists an Ethernet frame processing capability of 15 000 frames per second without specifying the average frame length, and vendor Y's sales literature lists an Ethernet frame processing capability of 20 000 frames per second, also without specifying the average frame length. Which vendor product provides a higher level of capability?

Since each vendor's frame processing rate exceeds 14 880 frames per second, both have the ability to process a fully loaded Ethernet network. Thus, the higher processing capability of vendor Y is irrelevant and you should consider both products to be equivalent with respect to their frame processing capability.

6.1.2 The actual Ethernet operating rate

Now that the maximum number of frames per second that can be carried on 10 Mbps and 100 Mbps Ethernet LANs has been determined, that information can be used to determine the utilization of the LAN. To do so we must recognize that the actual number of bits per second that can be carried on an Ethernet LAN will always be less than its operating rate due to the dead time between frames. For example, to compute the actual number of bits transmitted in one second using the maximum length frame, you must subtract the number of bits that cannot be transmitted during the 812 slots of dead time (9.6 μs for a 10 Mbps Ethernet) from the LAN operating rate. Then, when 1526 byte frames are transmitted, the actual maximum 10 Mbps Ethernet network data transfer operating rate becomes

$$10\,\text{Mbps} - \frac{9.6\,\mu\text{s}}{100\,\text{ns}} \times 812 = 9\,922\,048\,\text{bps}$$

Thus, for 100% utilization of a 10 Mbps Ethernet when a maximum frame size of 1526 bytes is used, 9.922 Mbps must be transmitted. For a Fast Ethernet LAN idle characters are transmitted between frames, which in effect result in a dead time between frames. That dead time is $\frac{1}{10}$th that of a 10 Mbps Ethernet, or 0.96 μs, and the bit duration is reduced to 10 ns.

Thus, the actual maximum 100 Mbps Fast Ethernet data transfer operating rate when 1526 byte frames are transmitted becomes

$$100\,\text{Mbps} - \frac{0.96\,\mu\text{s}}{10\,\text{ns}} \times 8127 = 99\,220\,480\,\text{bps}$$

Since many inexpensive test devices are capable of counting frames, or bits, or both frames and bits, using such equipment with knowledge of the maximum achievable data transfer rate on the network provides us with the ability to compute its utilization. In addition, you may be able to defer the purchase of a more expensive LAN performance analyzer, which, due to the prices of such equipment, may result in a considerable saving.

Network utilization

To illustrate the computations required to determine the level of 10 Mbps Ethernet network utilization, let us assume that the monitoring of an Ethernet LAN indicates that during 10 minutes of monitoring, a total of 280 000 frames with an average data field length of 100 bytes were counted. The average frame length, including 100 data bytes, would be 126 bytes due to the 26 overhead bytes required to transport each frame. Then the average number of frames per second would be computed as follows:

280 000 frames/10 minutes = 466.67 frames per second

The number of bits per second flowing on the network is computed by multiplying the frame size by 8 bits/byte and then multiplying the result by the frame rate. Thus, 126 bytes/ frame × 8 bits/byte × 466.67 frames/second is 470 403 bits per second. Then, the level of utilization would be (470 403/ 9 922 048) × 100%, or 4.74%.

Based upon readily available performance statistics, a 100 node 10 Mbps Ethernet can normally be expected to have an average utilization level under 2%, with worst second, minute, and hour utilization levels of 40%, 15–20% and 3–5%, respectively. Similar utilization levels may not be applicable to 100 Mbps Fast Ethernet networks, because such networks operate at ten times the rate of 10BASE-T LANs. This means that they can support a significant increase in traffic prior to reaching a higher level of utilization. These performance statistics represent the activity on a typical Ethernet network in that at any particular time many network users are performing local processing, such as composing a memorandum or electronic message. Other network users may be reading a manual, talking on the telephone, or performing an activity completely unrelated to network usage. Thus, only a few users are actually transmitting or receiving information using the network. Concerning those users, one may be transmitting a short electronic mail message of a few hundred characters, while another might be downloading a file from the server or accessing a server facility. Thus, a typical 2% level of network utilization on a 10 Mbps Ethernet network equates to a data transfer rate of $9\,922\,048 \times 0.02$, or approximately 198 kbps. At this data transfer rate many users can be sending electronic messages, interacting with the file server, and performing file transfer operations. On a Fast Ethernet network a 2% level of network utilization means a data transfer rate ten times that of a 10 Mbps Ethernet network, or approximately 1.98 Mbps. To put this number in perspective, let us assume that the typical length of an electronic mail message is 1000 characters or 8000 bits. This means that at a 2% level of network utilization a 100 Mbps Fast Ethernet network could support the transfer of almost 250 one-thousand character electronic mail messages per second!

When a number of network users initiate file transfers you can expect a short peak level of utilization to approach or surpass 40% on a 10 Mbps Ethernet network. Since a 640 kbyte file transfer will require less than 0.7 seconds at 10 Mbps, many file transfers will rapidly be completed, which eliminates the potential for one file transfer to overlap another if two users initiate a file transfer just a second or two apart from one another. This explains why the worst-minute utilization level of a 10 Mbps Ethernet network is typically reduced to 15–20% in comparison to a worst second utilization level of 40%. Since our previous computation is much better than the typical worst-minute utilization, it would appear that the monitored LAN is not overloaded. However, an extension of monitoring of several hours of activity during peak periods should be considered to ensure that utilization peaks are not inadvertently missed.

Information transfer rate

Although knowledge concerning the average frame length and frame rate is important, by themselves they do not provide definitive information concerning the rate at which information can be transferred on a network. This is because a portion of an Ethernet frame represents overhead and does not carry actual data. Thus, to obtain a more realistic indication of the ability of an Ethernet network to transfer information, you must compute the information transfer rate in bps. This calculation is performed by first subtracting 26 bytes from the frame length for frames with a data field of 46 or more bytes, as there are 26 overhead bytes in each frame. Next, you would multiply the frame rate by the adjusted frame length and then multiply the result by eight to obtain the information transfer rate in bps.

Figure 6.4 lists the statements contained in a program named EITR.BAS. This program was developed to compute the information transfer rate in bps for a 10 Mbps Ethernet network based upon 16 average frame lengths and their corresponding frame transfer rates. Readers will note that the program EITR.BAS represents a simple modification to the previously developed program EPERFORM.BAS. Similarly to the method noted for modifying the program EPERFORM.BAS for computing Fast Ethernet statistics, you can modify the program listing contained in Figure 6.4. That is, you would change the computation for the variable FPS (frames per second) by modifying the interframe gap time and bit duration as indicated earlier in this chapter when the coding for the program EPERFORM.BAS was described. The results of the execution of EITR.BAS are listed in Table 6.2. To obtain the frames/second and information transfer rate for Fast Ethernet you can multiply the entries in the second and third columns of Table 6.2 by ten.

In examining the data contained in Table 6.2, let us focus our attention upon the information transfer rate in the third column.

```
CLS
REM PROGRAM EITR.BAS
PRINT "INFORMATION TRANSFER RATE VERSUS AVERAGE FRAME LENGTH"
PRINT
PRINT "AVERAGE FRAME    100% LOAD    INFORMATION TRANSFER"
PRINT "  LENGTH         FRAMES/SEC    RATE IN BPS          "
FOR J = 1 TO 12 STEP 3
READ A, B, C
DATA 72,72,1,80,100,20,125,1500,125,1526,1526,1
FOR FLENGTH = A TO B STEP C
FPS = 1 / (.0000096 + FLENGTH * 8 * .0000001)
PRINT USING "#####          ######"; FLENGTH; FPS;
PRINT USING "            ########"; FPS * (FLENGTH - 26) * 8
NEXT FLENGTH
NEXT J
END
```

Figure 6.4 Program listing of EITR.BAS. This program computes the 10 Mbps Ethernet information transfer rate based upon an average frame length and resulting 100% frame rate

Table 6.2 Execution results from program EITR.BAS

Average frame length	100% load frames/second	Information transfer rate (bps)
72	14 881	5 476 191
80	13 587	5 869 565
100	11 161	6 607 143
125	9 124	7 226 278
250	4 771	8 549 618
375	3 230	9 018 088
500	2 441	9 257 812
625	1 962	9 403 454
750	1 640	9 501 312
875	1 409	9 571 590
1000	1 235	9 624 506
1125	1 099	9 665 787
1250	990	9 698 891
1375	901	9 726 027
1500	827	9 748 677
1526	813	9 752 926

Note that at an average frame length of 72 bytes the information transfer rate is approximately 5.48 Mbps, or slightly more than half the Ethernet 10 Mbps operating rate. At an average frame length of 1526 bytes in which all frames are of the maximum length, the information transfer rate increases to approximately 9.75 Mbps. This explains why a large 10 Mbps Ethernet network can safely handle many simultaneous file transfer operations without degradation, because a file transfer increases the average frame length, which increases the ability of an Ethernet network to transport information.

To illustrate how the information transfer rate depends upon the average frame length, the results obtained from the execution of EITR.BAS are plotted as a line graph in Figure 6.5. In examining the entries in the y-axis of Figure 6.5 note that they range up to 10 Mbps, representing the information transfer rate on a 10 Mbps Ethernet network. Since Figure 6.5 is based on the plot of column 3 versus column 1 from Table 6.2, you can simply multiply the y-axis values by 10 to obtain a plot of the frame length versus the information transfer rate for 100 Mbps Fast Ethernet.

In our examination of the overhead associated with the composition of Ethernet frames in Chapter 2, we noted that relatively short frames have a relatively large overhead owing to the necessity to use pad characters to fill a data field to a

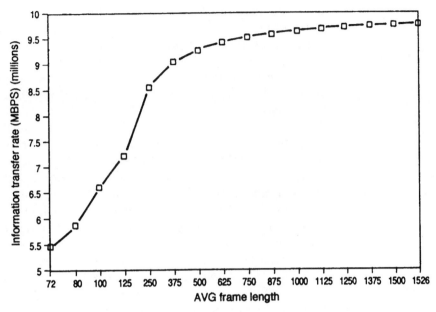

Figure 6.5 Frame length versus information transfer rate

minimum of 46 characters. At that time we noted that by composing a client screen to accept several items of information rather than perform separate queries we could enhance the efficiency of Ethernet frames as they would transport larger data fields. At that time we did not note an optimum data field size other than the fact that a maximum data field of 1500 characters is the most efficient.

In examining Figure 6.5 note that for a frame length between 375 and 625 characters, including frame overhead characters, you can achieve an information transfer rate between 9 and 9.5 Mbps. This indicates that by attempting to keep your client queries to that range you can significantly increase the network information transfer rate to over 90% of that obtainable by a maximum length frame. Thus, a frame length between 375 and 625 characters would be an appropriate range to make programmers developing client–server applications aware of as a design goal to increase the transmission efficiency of client–server applications.

6.2 USING BRIDGES TO ADJUST THE NETWORK

One of the most valuable indicators of poor network response time other than user complaints is a high level of utilization.

When Ethernet utilization climbs above 25–35% for long periods of time, either a large number of file transfers are hogging the network, or network traffic has grown to the point where you may wish to modify the LAN to increase its performance. One of the most common methods used to improve LAN performance is to split the network into smaller segments through the use of one or more bridges.

Figure 6.6 illustrates the potential use of a local bridge to split an Ethernet into two smaller segments, thereby reducing the traffic on each of the resulting subnets. The maximum number of devices placed on each subnet depends upon the traffic generated by each device, with a higher level of device traffic resulting in a lower limit on the number of devices per segment prior to network performance becoming unacceptable. By using a LAN protocol analyzer, you can obtain an accurate measurement of traffic per device that can assist you in determining both when and where to subdivide the LAN. However, once a decision has been made to employ the use of one or more local bridges, you should estimate their performance requirements to ensure that the equipment you acquire does not become a bottleneck. To do so you should ensure that the filtering and forwarding rate of a bridge under consideration at a minimum exceeds the frame processing rate associated with the average frame length monitored or estimated to be carried on your linked networks. As previously discussed in this chapter, most modern 10 Mbps Ethernet bridges fabricated using high performance Intel 80486 or Pentium microprocessors or similar hardware will provide a level of frame processing which provides the ability to filter and forward frames under 100%

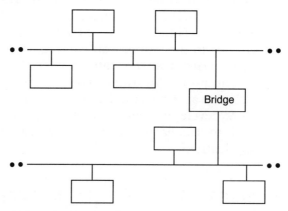

Figure 6.6 Using a bridge to improve Ethernet LAN performance. By using one or more bridges, a single LAN can be subdivided, reducing the traffic on each of the resulting subnets

loading without becoming a bottleneck. However, if you are using or considering the use of 100 Mbps Fast Ethernet, you should carefully check the filtering and forwarding rates of bridges against the 100% frame load that a Fast Ethernet, network can provide. With a load rate ten times that of 10 Mbps Ethernet, many bridges are only capable of supporting a percentage of the maximum frame rate of a Fast Ethernet network.

6.2.1 Predicting throughput

Until now it has been assumed that the operating rate of each LAN linked by a bridge is the same. However, in many organizations, this may not be true, owing to the implementation of LANs at different times using different technologies. Thus, Accounting could be using a 10 Mbps Ethernet 10BASE-T LAN, and the personnel department might be using an AT&T StarLAN CSMA/CD network operating at 1 Mbps.

Linked LANs

Suppose that you wanted to interconnect the two LANs using a local bridge. To predict throughput between LANs, let us use the network configuration illustrated in Figure 6.7. Here the operating rate of LAN A is assumed to be R_1 bps, and the operating rate of LAN B is assumed to be R_2 bps.

In one second R_1 bits can be transferred on LAN A and R_2 bits can be transferred on LAN B. Similarly, it takes $1/R_1$ seconds to transfer one bit on LAN A and $1/R_2$ seconds to transfer one bit on LAN B. Thus the time, $1/R_T$, to transfer one bit across the bridge from LAN A to LAN B, ignoring the transfer time at the bridge, is given by

$$\frac{1}{R_T} = \frac{1}{R_1} + \frac{1}{R_2}$$

or

$$R_T = \frac{1}{\dfrac{1}{R_1} + \dfrac{1}{R_2}}$$

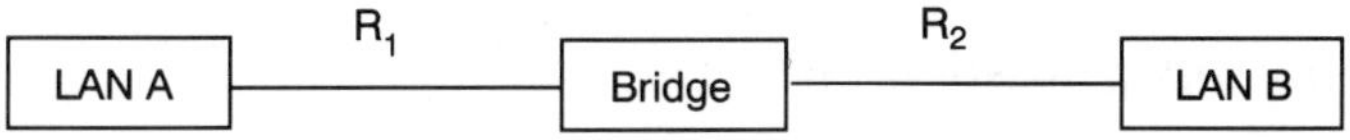

Figure 6.7   Linking LANs with different operating rates. When LANs with different operating rates $(R_1$ and $R_2)$ are connected via a bridge, access of files across the bridge may result in an unacceptable level of performance

Previously we computed that a 10 Mbps Ethernet would support a maximum transfer rate of 812 maximum-sized frames per second. If we assume that the second LAN, operating at 1 Mbps, is also an Ethernet, we would compute its transfer rate to be approximately 81 maximum-sized frames per second. Thus, the throughput in frames per second would become

$$R_T = \frac{1}{\dfrac{1}{812} + \dfrac{1}{81}} = 73 \text{ frames per second}$$

It should be noted that the preceding computation represents a best-case scenario in which it is assumed that one station has full access to the bandwidth of each network as well as to the resources of the bridge. Unfortunately, this is usually the exception rather than the rule, unless some inter-LAN activity is performed at 3 a.m.! Thus, you will want to adjust this frame transfer rate and the key question becomes how to do so. Fortunately, there are a number of low-cost LAN monitoring software products, such as Triticom Corporation's EtherVision and TokenVision software programs, which were described in the author's books *Token-Ring Networks* and *Ethernet Networks 2 ed*, published by John Wiley & Sons. By using those products you can determine the average number of stations active on a network.

Suppose that there were three users on LAN A transmitting data at any given time and two users on LAN B. Then you would adjust the previous computations to reflect the fact that several users share the bandwidth of each linked network. To do so the maximum transfer rate on LAN A would become 812/3, or about 271 frames per second, and the maximum transfer rate on LAN B would become 81/2, or approximately 41 frames per second. Then, the expected throughput which considers the fact that the bandwidth on each network is shared becomes

$$R_T = \frac{1}{\dfrac{1}{271} + \dfrac{1}{41}} = 36 \text{ frames per second}$$

Estimating data transfer time

Knowing the transfer rate between LANs can help us answer many common questions, as well as providing us with a mechanism for determining whether or not the location of application programs on different servers should be altered. For example, suppose that a program was located on a server on LAN B which suddenly became popular for use by workstations on LAN A. If the program required 320 kbytes of storage, we could estimate the minimum transfer time required to load that program and, depending upon the results of our calculation, we might want to move the program onto a server on LAN A. For this example, the data transfer rate would be 73 frames/second × 1500 bytes/frame, or 109 500 bytes per second. Dividing the data to be transferred by the data transfer rate, we obtain

$$\frac{320 \text{ kbytes} \times 1024 \text{ bytes/K}}{109\,500 \text{ bytes/second}} = 2.99 \text{ seconds}$$

Similar to our prior notation concerning the computation of the frame rate between linked LANs, the above transfer time computation represents a best-case scenario. That is, it would take 2.99 seconds to transfer the 320 kbyte file if no other users required the bandwidth of each LAN during the file transfer activity. However, as previously noted, it was assumed that the use of a software monitoring program indicated that three users were actively performing network-related activities on LAN A and two users were performing network-related activities on LAN B. Thus, a more realistic transfer time computation would use a frame rate of 36 frames per second. In modifying our computations, the transfer rate would be 36 frames/second × 1500 bytes/frame, or 54 000 bytes per second. By dividing the data to be transferred by the data transfer rate, we obtain

$$\frac{320 \text{ kbytes} \times 1024 \text{ bytes/K}}{54\,000 \text{ bytes/second}} = 6.07 \text{ seconds}$$

Here, the 6.07 seconds represents the average transfer time between networks, and the 2.99 seconds transfer time represents the optimum transfer time.

Considering remote connections

We can extend our analysis of Ethernet frames and the process by which we can estimate data transfer time by considering the frame rate supported by different link speeds. For example, let us consider a pair of remote bridges connected by a 9.6 kbps line. The time per frame for a 72 byte frame at 9.6 kbps is

$9.6 \times 10^{-6} + 72 \times 8 \times 0.000\,1041$ seconds/bit, or $0.059\,9712$ seconds per frame. Thus, in one second the number of frames is $1/0.059\,9712$, or 16.67 frames per second. Table 6.3 compares the frame per second rate supported by different link speeds for minimum and maximum size Ethernet frames. As expected, the frame transmission rate supported by a 10 Mbps link for minimum and maximum size frames is exactly the same as the frame processing requirements under 100% loading as previously indicated in Table 6.1.

In examining Table 6.3 readers should note that the entries in this table do not consider the effect of the overhead of a protocol used to transport frames between two networks. Thus, readers should decrease the frame per second rate by approximately 20% for all link speeds through 1.536 Mbps. The reason why the 10 Mbps rate should not be adjusted is that it represents a local bridge connection that does not require the use of a wide area network protocol to transport frames. Readers should also note that the link speed of 1.536 Mbps represents a T1 transmission facility that operates at 1.544 Mbps. However, since the framing bits on a T1 circuit use 8 kbps, the effective line speed available for the transmission of data is 1.536 Mbps.

Once you have determined the frame transfer rate supported by a remote connection, you can use a precise value based upon knowledge of the average frame rate monitored or estimated to be carried by the network only if that rate falls between the frame rate range noted in Table 6.3. Otherwise, you would use the range of frame rates listed in Table 6.3 in your computations to obtain a range of transfer times. For example, assume that you wish to link two LANs using remote bridges as illustrated in Figure 6.8a. If the DSUs operate at 56 kbps they are able to support a frame transmission rate between 4.6 and 97.44 frames per second prior to adjusting the rate downward by 20% to account for the wide

Table 6.3 Link versus frame rate

Link speed	Frames per second	
	Minimum	Maximum
9.6 kbps	16.67	0.79
19.2 kbps	33.38	1.58
56.0 kbps	97.44	4.60
64.0 kbps	111.17	5.25
1.536 Mbps	2 815.31	136.34
10 Mbps	14 880	812

(a) Topology

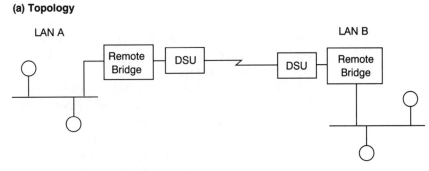

(b) Operating Rate Model Components

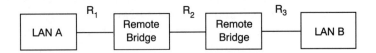

Legend: DSU = digital service unit

Figure 6.8   Linking remote networks

area network protocol overhead. If you monitored LAN A and determined the average frame rate to be 250 frames per second, you could not use that value as the potential frame rate between LANs as it would exceed the transmission capacity of the circuit. Without prior knowledge obtained from monitoring the circuit, you would also use the range of frame rates listed in Table 6.3 and adjust them downward by 20% to account for the wide area network protocol overhead. For either situation you would then estimate the data transfer time between stations on one network from that on another by considering the operating rate of each network and the remote connection. Figure 6.8b illustrates the operating rate components for the network topology shown in Figure 6.8a.

To determine the frame transfer rate between remotely connected networks you would then solve the following equation:

$$\frac{1}{R_T} = \frac{1}{R_1} + \frac{1}{R_2} + \frac{1}{R_3}$$

Solving for R_T, we obtain

$$R_T = \frac{R_1 R_2 R_3}{R_2 R_3 + R_1 R_3 + R_2 R_3}$$

By using specific values for R_1, R_2, and R_3 we would determine R_T, which would provide us with the frame transfer rate between networks. Then, knowing the file size and average frame rate, you could compute the transfer time in the same manner as previously computed.

As indicated in this chapter, you can use your knowledge of the structure and operation of Ethernet LANs to compute a number of performance measurements. Some of those measurements provide you with a basis for selecting an appropriately performing bridge or router, and other calculations provide you with the ability to estimate the time required to load programs across a bridge connecting LANs operating at different data rates. These calculations also provide you with the tools necessary to adjust the configuration of LANs and recognize requirements to move application programs to different servers to increase network performance.

7

ESTIMATING TOKEN-RING NETWORK PERFORMANCE

In Chapter 6 our attention was focused upon Ethernet network performance, and we developed a mathematical model to determine the frame rate based upon different frame lengths. The results of that model were then used to determine the information transfer capability of a 10 Mbps Ethernet network based upon different frame sizes. As you might intuitively expect, the use of larger frames provided a higher information transfer capability because each Ethernet frame is separated from preceding and succeeding frames by a uniform time gap. Thus, longer frames were expected to be more efficient and this was determined to be true.

In this chapter our attention will turn to Token-Ring network performance in a similar manner to our method of examining Ethernet performance. That is, we will first develop a model which is representative of the flow of data on a Token-Ring network. Then we will exercise the model manually as well as through the use of a BASIC language program to determine the frame rate as a function of the number of stations on the network and the ring length, as well as several other variables. In doing so we will note that the performance models for CSMA/CD and Token-Ring networks differ considerably due to the basic differences between each network access protocol.

In a CSMA/CD network the transmission of a frame is read by all stations without one station's reading activity delaying another station's reading activity. In a Token-Ring network the opposite is true, because station n must process a token or frame prior to passing it onto station $n + 1$ on the network. Thus, the Token-Ring model that will be developed in this chapter will considerably differ from the previously developed Ethernet model presented in Chapter 6. A second area of difference concerns the cabling structure of Ethernet and Token-Ring networks. Most Ethernet bus-based networks use a fraction of the cabling used in the star-bus topology of a Token-Ring. Thus, propagation delay time assumes a much more meaningful role in determining network performance, and it results in the inclusion of the speed in which tokens and frames traverse the cable in the Token-Ring model that we will develop in this chapter.

7.1 TOKEN-RING TRAFFIC MODELING

In comparison with Ethernet the modeling of a Token-Ring network can be much more complex. This is because the frame rate depends upon the number of nodes in a network, the token holding time per node, the type of wire used for cabling and ring length, and the type of adapter used as a ring interface unit.

The number of nodes and their cabling govern both token propagation time and holding time as a token flows around the ring. The type of adapter used governs the maximum frame rate supported. This rate can vary between vendors as well as within a vendor's product line. For example, Texas Instruments' original MAC code permitted a maximum transmission of 2200 64 kbyte frames per second. New software from that vendor raised the frame rate to 3300 and a more recent release known as Turbo MAC 2.1 increased it to 4000 frames per second.

The type of cabling and ring length govern the propagation delay associated with the flow of tokens and frames around the ring. Although the data rate around a ring is consistent at either 4 Mbps or 16 Mbps, tokens and frames do not flow instantaneously around the ring and are delayed, depending upon the distance they must traverse and the type of cabling used. In addition, a slight delay is encountered at each node because the token must be examined to determine its status.

7.1.1 Model development

In developing a model to determine Token-Ring frame rates let us assume that there are N stations on the network. Then, on average a token will travel $N/2$ stations until it is grabbed and converted into a frame. Similarly, a frame can be expected to travel $N/2$ stations until it reaches its destination and another $N/2$ stations until it returns to the origination station and is reconverted back into a token.

As mentioned at the beginning of this chapter, performance of a Token-Ring network is typically more dependent upon the total network cable length than that of an Ethernet network. Thus, in developing a model of Token-Ring network performance a mechanism is required to equate cable length to the propagation delay of electrons flowing on the cable. To do so let us start with the well-known velocity of light.

Propagation delay

In free space the velocity of light is 186 000 miles per second. In a twisted pair cable the speed of electrons is approximately 62% of the velocity of light in free space. Thus, electrons will travel at approximately $186\,000 \times 0.62$, or $115\,320$ miles per second. Since there are 5280 feet in a mile, this rate is equivalent to $608\,889\,600$ feet per second or approximately 609 feet per microsecond. Then to traverse 1000 feet of cable would require $1000/609 \times 10^6$, or approximately 1.64×10^{-6} seconds.

At a Token-Ring operating rate of 4 Mbps, the bit duration is $1/4\,000\,000$, or 2.5×10^{-7} seconds. At a network operating rate of 16 Mbps, the bit duration is $1/16\,000\,000$, or 0.625×10^{-7} seconds. Since the time required for electrons to traverse 1000 feet of cable is 1.64×10^{-6} seconds, the cable propagation delay time per 1000 feet of cable can be converted into a bit time delay to simplify computations. At a Token-Ring operating rate of 4 Mbps the bit time delay per 1000 feet of cable becomes $1.64 \times 10^{-6}/2.5 \times 10^{-7}$, or 6.56 bit times. When the Token-Ring network operates at 16 Mbps the bit time delay per 1000 feet of cable becomes $1.64 \times 10^{-6}/0.625 \times 10^{-7}$, or 26.24 bit times.

4 Mbps model

In developing a Token-Ring performance model, let us commence our effort by assuming that the network operates at 4 Mbps. Once we have developed this model and use it to perform a series of manual calculations, we will then construct a general model applicable to both 4 and 16 Mbps networks. That model will then be used as a basis for developing a BASIC language program that will be used to generate a comprehensive series of tables contained in Appendix B, as well as two tables in this chapter whose entries we will examine in detail. The tables contained in Appendix B can be used to facilitate determining the frame flow on a Token-Ring network since they enable the frame flow computations to be supplemented by a table lookup process. The tables in this chapter can be considered to represent extracts from Appendix B and their use serves as a guide to the use of the tables contained in Appendix B.

For the development of a 4 Mbps Token-Ring performance model let us start with the flow of a token as indicated by the following steps in the model development process.

1. Given a Token-Ring network with N stations, a free token travels on the average $N/2$ stations until it is grabbed and converted into a frame.

2. Each station adds a 2.5 bit time delay to examine the token. At a 4 Mbps ring operating rate a bit time equals 2.5×10^{-7} seconds. Thus, each station induces a delay of $2.5 \times 2.5 \times 10^{-7}$, or 6.25×10^{-7} seconds.

3. The token consists of three bytes or 24 bits. The time required for the token to be placed onto the ring is

$$24 \times 2.5 \times 10^{-7} \text{ seconds/bit} = 60 \times 10^{-7} \text{ seconds}$$

4. The time for the token to be placed onto the ring and to flow around half the ring until it is grabbed is the sum of the times of step 2 and step 3. This time then becomes

$$N/2 \times 6.25 \times 10^{-7} + 60 \times 10^{-7}$$

5. Once a token has been grabbed it is converted into a frame. On the average the frame will travel $N/2$ stations to its destination. A frame containing 64 bytes of information consists of 85 bytes, since 21 bytes of overhead, including starting and ending delimiters, source and destination addresses, and other control information, must be included in the frame. Thus, the time required to place the frame on the ring becomes

$$85 \text{ bytes} \times 8 \text{ bits/byte} \times 2.5 \times 10^{-7} \text{ seconds/bit}$$
$$= 1.7 \times 10^{-4} \text{ seconds}$$

6. If the network contains N stations the frame must traverse on average $N/2$ stations to reach its destination. Thus, the time required for the frame to be placed onto the ring, and to traverse half the ring, becomes

$$1.7 \times 10^{-4} + N/2 \times 6.25 \times 10^{-7} \text{ seconds}$$

7. The total token and frame time from steps 4 and 6 above is

$$N/2 \times 6.25 \times 10^{-7} + 60 \times 10^{-7} + N/2 \times 6.25 \times 10^{-7} + 1.7 \times 10^{-4}$$
$$\text{or} \quad N \times 6.25 \times 10^{-7} + 60 \times 10^{-7} + 1.7 \times 10^{-4} \text{ seconds}$$

8. Once the frame has reached its destination it must traverse another $N/2$ stations on average to return to its originating station which then removes it from the network. When this occurs the originating station generates a new token onto the network and the previously described process is repeated. The time for the frame to again traverse half of the network becomes

$$N/2 \times 6.25 \times 10^{-7} \text{ seconds}$$

This time must be added to the time in step 7. Doing so we obtain

$$N \times 9.375 \times 10^{-7} + 60 \times 10^{-7} + 1.7 \times 10^{-4} \text{ seconds}$$

9. To consider the effect of propagation delay time as tokens and frames flow in the cable we must consider the sum of the ring length and twice the sum of all lobe distances. Here we must double the lobe distances because the token will flow to and from each workstation on the lobe. If we let C be the number of thousands of feet of cable, we obtain the time in seconds to traverse the ring as

$$N \times 9.375 \times 10^{-7} + 60 \times 10^{-7} + 1.7 \times 10^{-4} + 1.64 \times 10^{-6} \times C$$

which equals

$$N \times 9.375 \times 10^{-7} + 1.76 \times 10^{-4} + 1.64 \times 10^{-6} \times C$$

where

    $N =$ number of stations
    $C =$ thousands of feet of cable

7.1.2 Exercising the model

To illustrate the use of the above Token-Ring performance model, let us assume that a Token-Ring network of 50 stations has 8000 feet of cable. Then, with $N = 50$ and $C = 8$, the time for a token and frame to circulate the ring becomes

$$50 \times 9.375 \times 10^{-7} + 1.76 \times 10^{-4} + 1.64 \times 10^{-6} \times 8$$
$$= 468.75 \times 10^{-7} + 1.76 \times 10^{-4} + 13.12 \times 10^{-6}$$
$$= 0.46875 \times 10^{-4} + 1.76 \times 10^{-4} + 0.1312 \times 10^{-4}$$
$$= 2.36 \times 10^{-4} \text{ seconds}$$

Thus, in one second there will be on average $1/2.36 \times 10^{-4}$, or 4237, 64 byte information frames that can flow on a Token-Ring network containing 50 stations and a total of 8000 feet of cable.

Network modification

To illustrate the use of the previously developed model in determining the effect of cabling and network stations upon the frame rate, let us now consider what happens when the network is reduced in size. Suppose that the number of workstations is halved to 25 and the total cable distance reduced to 4000 feet. Then, with $N = 25$ and $C = 4$, the time for a token and frame to flow around the ring becomes

$$25 \times 9.375 \times 10^{-7} + 1.76 \times 10^{-4} + 1.64 \times 10^{-6} \times 4$$
$$= 0.234375 \times 10^{-4} + 1.76 \times 10^{-4} + 0.0656 \times 10^{-4}$$
$$= 2.06 \times 10^{-4} \text{ seconds}$$

Thus, in one second there will be on average $1/2.06 \times 10^{-4}$, or 4854, 64 byte information frames. As we would intuitively expect, as the number of stations and cable distance decrease the transmission capacity of the ring increases.

Varying the frame size

Now let us examine the effect of transmitting larger information frames. Suppose that we transmit 4000 byte information frames. Here a total of 4021 bytes is required. Thus, the time required for the frame to be placed on the ring becomes

$$4021 \times 8 \times 2.5 \times 10^{-7} = 80.42 \times 10^{-4} \text{ seconds}$$

Then, the total token and frame time becomes

$$N \times 9.375 \times 10^{-7} + 60 \times 10^{-7} + 80.42 \times 10^{-4} + 1.64 \times 10^{-6} \times C$$

Again, let us assume the number of stations N is 50, and the cabling distance is 8000 feet. Thus, we obtain the token and frame revolution time as follows:

$$50 \times 9.375 \times 10^{-7} + 60 \times 10^{-7} + 80.42 \times 10^{-4} + 1.6 \times 10^{-6} \times 8$$
$$= 0.46875 \times 10^{-4} + 0.06 \times 10^{-4} + 80.42 \times 10^{-4}$$
$$+ 0.1312 \times 10^{-4}$$
$$= 81.08 \times 10^{-4} \text{ seconds}$$

Thus, in one second there will be $1/81.08 \times 10^{-4}$ or 123.3 frames. Since each frame contains 4000 bytes of information, the effective operating rate becomes $123.3 \times 4000 \times 8$, or 3.946 Mbps for a 50 station Token-Ring network with 8000 feet of cable using 4000 character information frames. In comparison, a similar Token-Ring network using 64 byte information frames would have a frame rate of 4237 frames per second. However, this rate would be equivalent to an information transfer rate of $4237 \times 64 \times 8$, or 2.169 Mbps. Thus, larger frame sizes provide a more efficient data transportation capability.

The preceding computations which represent the use of a simplified model of a 4 Mbps Token-Ring network, indicate an important concept. That is, the frame length, cabling distance, and number of network stations govern the maximum frame rate that can flow on a Token-Ring network. This tells us that when a network becomes saturated due to heavy usage you should consider breaking larger networks into subnetworks interconnected by bridges to improve Token-Ring network performance. The model presented above is simplified owing to the fact that it does not include the effect of the flow of network management frames which, when they flow on the network, preclude the transfer of data. For example, every seven seconds the active monitor transmits an Active Monitor Present frame for which all other stations respond with a Standby Monitor Present frame. Since the frame rate on a Token-Ring network will range from over 100 frames per second when the frame length approaches the maximum-size frame length on a 4 Mbps network, to many thousands of frames per second when the minimum-length frame is transmitted, the effect of the Active Monitor Present frames and responding Standby Monitor Present frame every seven seconds, is negligible upon network performance. This is because those two frames are relatively short and would result in a maximum of 260 frames every seven seconds, during which approximately 15 000 or more similar length frames could be transported on the network. Thus, the use of a simplified model does not materially affect our model.

Adapter card considerations

One of the more interesting aspects of Token-Ring frame rates is that the majority of adapter cards from different vendors which use the Texas Instrument chip set support a maximum frame rate of 4000 frames per second. This indicates that a further constraint on the number of nodes and cable length is the adapter cards used in a network. In 1991 Madge Systems introduced an adapter card which was capable of transmitting approximately 12 000 64 byte frames per second. Thus, using that firm's adapter card or other higher performance adapter cards manufactured by other vendors can significantly improve the performance of a Token-Ring network. However, the use of such high performance adapter cards is irrelevant when a network grows in size in terms of the number of network stations and cable distance. In such situations the capability of high performance network adapter cards cannot be effectively used.

Now that we have developed and exercised a mathematical model to determine the frame rate on a 4 Mbps Token-Ring network, we will use our prior effort to develop a general model for 4 and 16 Mbps networks. In doing so let us use BASIC language variables so that we can exercise our model through its incorporation into a BASIC language program.

7.1.3 General model development

To denote the difference between 4 and 16 Mbps networks, let us use the array variable BITTIME(I). Then, we can assign the value 1/4000 000 to BITTIME(1) to represent the bit time duration on a 4 Mbps Token-Ring network and the value 1/16 000 000 to BITTIME(2) to represent the bit time duration on a 16 Mbps network.

Referring to our previous nine-step approach used in the development of a 4 Mbps Token-Ring performance model, step 2 computed the station delay. Using the variable S.DELAY to represent the station delay, we obtain

$$S.DELAY = 2.5 \times BITTIME(I)$$

In step 3 we determined the time to place a token on the ring. Using the variable T.PLACEMENT to represent the token placement time, we obtain

$$T.PLACEMENT = 24 \times BITTIME(I)$$

Then, using the variable H.TRINGFLOW to represent the time for a token to be placed on the network and traverse half the ring (step 4 in our earlier model), we obtain

$$H.TRINGFLOW = (N/2) \times S.DELAY + T.PLACEMENT$$

Once a token has been grabbed it is converted into a frame. Because the time required to place the frame onto the ring depends upon the length of the frame, let us use the array variable FRAMELENGTH(F) to denote different frame lengths. In actuality, let us assign different information field values to each FRAMELENGTH(F) value and add 21 bytes to represent the overhead per frame. Then, if we use the variable FRAMETIME to denote the time required to place a frame on the ring, we obtain

$$FRAMETIME = (FRAMELENGTH(F) + 21) \times 8 \times BITTIME(I)$$

As noted in step 6 in our prior model, the frame must traverse $N/2$ stations on the average to reach its destination. If we denote the variable H.FRAMEFLOW to represent the time required for the frame to be placed on the ring and flow $N/2$ stations down the ring, we obtain

$$H.FRAMEFLOW = (N/2) \times S.DELAY + FRAMETIME$$

If we use the variable C to denote the cable length (ring plus twice each lobe distance) in 1000 foot increments and the variable C.PROPTIME to denote the propagation delay time, we obtain

$$C.PROPTIME = C \times 1.64E - 06$$

Then to compute the frame rate using the variable FPS, we obtain

$$FPS = 1/(TOTAL.TIME + C.PROPTIME)$$

Program TPERFORM.BAS

To facilitate the execution of our general Token-Ring performance model, the program TPERFORM.BAS was developed. This program, whose statements are listed in Figure 7.1, can be used to generate a series of tables which indicates the frame rate based upon the network operating rate, number of stations on the network, average frame length, and network cable length in 1000 foot increments. As previously noted, the frame length is specified in terms of the information field to which 21 bytes representing frame overhead are added.

In examining the program listing of TPERFORM.BAS, note that the FOR–NEXT loops which vary the number of stations, frame length, and cable length would result in 910 frame rate computations for each ring operating rate. Rather than place a large set of tables in this chapter, the results obtained from the execution of TPERFORM.BAS are placed in Appendix B. In addition, readers can modify the entries in the DATA statement to initialize a specific frame length more applicable to their network or change the FOR–NEXT loop variable values for N and/ or C to obtain information concerning the frame rate for a specific number of stations or cable length that is not included in Appendix B.

To provide readers with an example of the ease with which TPERFORM.BAS can be modified, as well as data that we can use to further discuss Token-Ring performance, let us modify the program. By changing the FOR N loop parameters to 40 TO 50 STEP 5 and the FOR F loop parameters to 1 TO 2 STEP 1, the printed output contained in Tables 7.1 and 7.2 is obtained.

General observations

In reviewing the results of the frame rate computations presented in Table 7.1, let us first examine the effect of a change in the average frame length compared with a change in the cable length of a network. This will enable us to determine the relative effects of average frame length and cable distance for a network with a given number of stations. Next, we will observe the effect on the frame rate of an increase in the number of network stations.

For a 40 station network with an average frame length of 64 bytes, note that each increase in network cabling by 2000 feet results in a decrease in the frame rate ranging from 69 (4613 – 4544) to 63 (4413 – 4350) frames per second. Note that a 40 station network with an average frame length of

```
REM PROGRAM TPERFORM.BAS
        CLS
REM THIS PROGRAM GENERATES A SERIES OF TABLES INDICATING THE FRAME RATE
REM ON A TOKEN-RING NETWORK BASED UPON THE NETWORK OPERATING RATE, NUMBER
REM OF STATIONS, AVERAGE FRAME LENGTH AND TOTAL NETWORK CABLE LENGTH
        FOR K = 1 TO 7                         ' initialize frame lenghts
        READ FRAMELENGTH(K)
        NEXT K
        DATA 64,128,256,512,1024,2048,4096
        BITTIME(1) = 1 / 4000000               ' initialize bit duration
        BITTIME(2) = 1 / 16000000
        RATE$(1) = "4MBPS"                      ' initialize network rate
        RATE$(2) = "16MBPS"
START:

        LCOUNT = 0                             ' initialize line count
        FOR I = 1 TO 2                         ' vary network operating rate
        IF I = 1 THEN GOTO NXT
        FOR LC = 1 TO 50 - LCOUNT: LPRINT : NEXT LC: LCOUNT = 0
NXT:    GOSUB HOUTPT                           ' print page header
        FOR N = 10 TO 260 STEP 10              ' vary number of stations
        FOR F = 1 TO 7 STEP 1                  ' vary frame length (bytes)
        FOR C = 2 TO 10 STEP 2                 ' vary cable length (per 1000 feet)
        S.DELAY = 2.5 * BITTIME(I)
        T.PLACEMENT = 24 * BITTIME(I)
        H.TRINGFLOW = (N / 2) * S.DELAY + T.PLACEMENT
        FRAMETIME = (FRAMELENGTH(F) + 21) * 8 * BITTIME(I)
        H.FRAMEFLOW = (N / 2) * S.DELAY + FRAMETIME
        TOTAL.TIME = H.TRINGFLOW + H.FRAMEFLOW + (N / 2) * S.DELAY
        C.PROPTIME = C * .00000164#
        FPS = 1 / (TOTAL.TIME + C.PROPTIME)
        GOSUB DOUTPT
        NEXT C
        NEXT F
        NEXT N
        NEXT I
        END
HOUTPT:
        LPRINT "FRAME RATE OF A "; RATE$(I); " TOKEN-RING NETWORK"
        LPRINT "BASED UPON THE NETWORK OPERATING RATE, NUMBER OF"
        LPRINT "STATIONS, FRAME LENGTH AND TOTAL CABLE LENGTH "
        LPRINT
        LPRINT "NUMBER OF  AVG FRAME    CABLE LENGTH   FRAME RATE"
        LPRINT "STATIONS    LENGTH       X000 FEET      IN FPS"
        RETURN
DOUTPT:
        IF LCOUNT < 50 THEN GOTO SKIP
        FOR LC = 1 TO 10                       ' move to top of next page
        LPRINT
        NEXT LC
        LCOUNT = 0
        GOSUB HOUTPT
SKIP:   LPRINT USING "  ####      ######"; N; FRAMELENGTH(F);
        LPRINT USING "        ###"; C;
        LPRINT USING "      ######## "; FPS
        LCOUNT = LCOUNT + 1
        RETURN
```

Figure 7.1 Program listing of TPERFORM.BAS

Table 7.1 Frame rate of a 4 Mbps Token-Ring network based upon the network operating rate, number of stations, frame length and total cable length

Number of stations	Avg frame length	Cable length × 000 feet	Frame rate in FPS
40	64	2	4613
40	64	4	4544
40	64	6	4477
40	64	8	4413
40	64	10	4350
40	128	2	2900
40	128	4	2873
40	128	6	2846
40	128	8	2820
40	128	10	2794
45	64	2	4515
45	64	4	4449
45	64	6	4385
45	64	8	4323
45	64	10	4263
45	128	2	2861
45	128	4	2835
45	128	6	2809
45	128	8	2783
45	128	10	2758
50	64	2	4422
50	64	4	4359
50	64	6	4297
50	64	8	4237
50	64	10	4179
50	128	2	2824
50	128	4	2798
50	128	6	2772
50	128	8	2747
50	128	10	2723

128 bytes has a decrease in the frame rate ranging from 27 (2900 − 2873) to 26 (2820 − 2794) frames per second as the cable length increases in 2000 foot increments from 2000 to 10 000 feet. When the average frame length is 64 bytes, a decrease in frame flow of 64 frames per second per 2000 foot cable length increase is equivalent to a decrease of $64 \times 64 \times 8$, or 32 768 bits per second in the information flow capability of the network. When the average frame length is 128 bytes, a decrease in frame flow of 26 frames per second due to a cable length increase of 2000 feet results in a decrease of $128 \times 26 \times 8$, or

Table 7.2 Frame rate of a 16 Mbps Token-Ring network based upon the network operating rate, number of stations, frame length and total cable length

Number of stations	Avg frame length	Cable length × 000 feet	Frame rate in FPS
40	64	2	17 651
40	64	4	16 685
40	64	6	15 819
40	64	8	15 039
40	64	10	14 332
40	128	2	11 280
40	128	4	10 877
40	128	6	10 503
40	128	8	10 153
40	128	10	9 826
45	64	2	17 293
45	64	4	16 365
45	64	6	15 531
45	64	8	14 778
45	64	10	14 095
45	128	2	11 133
45	128	4	10 740
45	128	6	10 375
45	128	8	10 033
45	128	10	9 714
50	64	2	16 950
50	64	4	16 057
50	64	6	15 253
50	64	8	14 527
50	64	10	13 866
50	128	2	10 989
50	128	4	10 607
50	128	6	10 250
50	128	8	9 917
50	128	10	9 604

26 624 bits per second in the flow of information. Thus, as the average frame length increases, the effect of an increase in the amount of cabling used in the network slightly decreases.

Now let us examine the frame rate as the average frame length increases and the number of stations remains fixed. Note that for a 40 station network, an increase in the average frame rate from 64 to 128 bytes for a cable length of 2000 feet results in a decrease in the frame rate of 1713 (4613 − 2900) frames per second. For a cable length of 10 000 feet, an increase in the average frame length from 64 to 128 bytes for a 40 station network results in a decrease in the frame rate of 1556 (4350 − 2794) frames per second. Thus, the effect of the frame length upon the frame rate exceeds the effect of the cable length.

Now let us turn our attention to observing the effect of an increase in the number of network stations with a fixed average frame length and cable length. For a 40 station network that has an average frame length of 64 bytes and a cable length of 2000 feet, the frame rate is 4613 frames per second. When the number of stations is increased to 45 the frame rate drops to 4515, a decrease of almost 100 frames per second. On a per-station-increase basis, this results in a decrease of approximately 20 frames per second when the average frame length is 64 bytes. Note that this decrease in the frame rate is slightly less than the decrease in the frame rate as the network cable distance increases in 800-foot steps from 2000 to 10 000 feet. This means that each increase in the number of stations has a lesser effect upon network performance than an increase of 800 feet in the cabling used in a network. Although these figures slightly differ as the number of stations on a network increases, you can use the preceding as a general guide for configuring and expanding Token-Ring networks. That is, by limiting your network cabling distance you may be able to alleviate the effect of an increase in the number of network stations on network performance.

Station effect upon network performance

To obtain a more detailed understanding of the effect of an increase in the number of network stations upon network performance, the comprehensive series of tables contained in Appendix B was used to extract data. In doing so the frame rate for 4 and 16 Mbps Token-Ring networks was extracted for 64 byte frame lengths and 10 000 feet of cable as the number of network stations varied from 10 to 260 in increments of 10 stations. Table 7.3 contains the frame rate information extracted from Appendix B.

In examining the frame rates for 4 and 16 Mbps networks listed in Table 7.3, note that the number of stations has a considerable effect upon the information flow on a Token-Ring network. For example, a 10 station 4 Mbps network supports a frame rate of 4956 frames per second, which is equivalent to an information transfer rate of 4956 frames/second × 64 bytes/frame × 8 bits/byte, or 2.537 Mbps. For a 260 station network, the frame rate is reduced to 2293 frames per second, which is equivalent to an

Table 7.3 Frame rate versus number of network stations (based upon a 64 byte average frame length and 10 000 feet of network cabling)

Number of stations	Frames per second	
	4 Mbps	16 Mbps
10	4956	15 938
20	4736	15 364
30	4535	14 830
40	4350	14 332
50	4179	13 866
60	4022	13 430
70	3876	13 020
80	3740	12 634
90	3613	12 271
100	3495	11 928
110	3384	11 603
120	3280	11 296
130	3182	11 005
140	3090	10 728
150	3003	10 465
160	2921	10 215
170	2843	9 976
180	2769	9 748
190	2699	9 530
200	2632	9 322
210	2659	9 123
220	2508	8 932
230	2451	8 748
240	2396	8 573
250	2343	8 404
260	2293	8 241

information transfer rate of 2293 frames/second × 64 bytes/frame × 8 bits/byte, or 1.174 Mbps. Turning our attention to the frame rates listed in Table 7.3 for a 16 Mbps Token-Ring, note that a 10 station network supports an information flow of 15 938 frames/second × 64 bytes/frame × 8 bits/byte, or 8.16 Mbps. When the number of stations is increased to 260, the information rate decreases to 8241 frames/second × 64 bytes/frame × 8 bits/byte, or 4.219 Mbps. Although the primary reason why a Token-Ring network supports a maximum of 260 network stations is based upon 'jitter' of the bits flowing on the network, the approximate halving of the information transfer capability is another important consideration to limit the number of stations on a network.

7.2 BRIDGE AND ROUTER PERFORMANCE REQUIREMENTS

In the first section in this chapter we focused our attention upon the development of mathematical models to estimate the flow of data on 4 and 16 Mbps Token-Ring networks. In this section we will use our previously obtained knowledge about Token-Ring performance to examine the flow of data between networks when bridges are used. In doing so we will obtain answers to such questions as 'What is the forwarding and filtering rate required to be supported by a Token-Ring bridge or router prior to that device becoming a potential internet bottleneck?' and 'What effect does the use of different types of wide area network transmission facilities have upon the data transfer capability of Token-Ring remote bridges and routers?' Because the use of wide area network transmission facilities is only applicable to remote bridges and routers, let us first examine the required level of performance of a local bridge and then turn our attention to the use of remote bridges and routers.

7.2.1 Local bridges

Figure 7.2 illustrates the use of a local bridge to connect two Token-Ring networks. Here, each Token-Ring network can operate at either 4 or 16 Mbps, resulting in three distinct mixtures of network operating speeds that the bridge must support: 4 and 4 Mbps, 4 and 16 Mbps, and 16 and 16 Mbps. Thus, the level of performance required by a local bridge linking Token-Ring networks will depend upon the average frame length, the total cable length, the number of stations, and the operating rate of

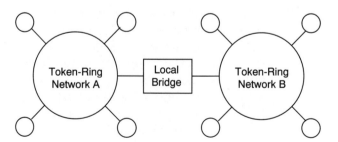

Figure 7.2 Using a local Token-Ring bridge. The performance required by a local Token-Ring bridge is primarily dependent upon the operating rate of each network to be connected, the number of stations on each network, the average frame length on each network, and the total length of cabling used on each network

each network. Obtaining this information will provide you with the frame rate in frames per second that you can expect each network to carry. Then, the frame processing capability of the local bridge should equal the sum of the frame rate expected to be carried by each Token-Ring network or the bridge will become a network bottleneck.

Considering a performance range

Because the average frame length carried on a network varies with time and the number of stations on a network expands and contracts in tandem with personnel changes and corporate policy, instead of determining one number you may prefer to work with a range of values. As an alternative, you may wish to select a network situation in which a bridge meeting the frame rate requirements of a certain networking scenario can be expected to satisfy a large variance in future changes to each Token-Ring network to be interconnected. For example, assume that you have a 4 Mbps and a 16 Mbps Token-Ring network that you wish to locally connect, and through monitoring you have determined that the average frame length on each network was 128 bytes. Assuming that the 4 Mbps network has 50 stations and the 16 Mbps network has 80 stations and each network uses 6000 feet of cable, you would use Appendix B to determine that the expected frame rate on the 4 Mbps network is 2772 fps whereas the expected frame rate on the 16 Mbps network is 9561 fps. Then, the local bridge should have a frame filtering capability equal to the sum of each network expected frame rate, or 12 333 fps. However, what happens if either network changes?

Considering the effect of network changes

If the number of stations and length of network cabling increase, the frame rate on the network decreases. Thus, an increase in either or both of those variables has no effect upon a bridge acquired to support the frame rate of smaller networks. Similarly, an increase in the average frame length results in a decrease in the frame rate on each network. Because the most variable factor is the average frame length, you may wish to consider selecting a lower average frame length which in effect increases the network frame rate. In doing so you are adding a margin of safety to the processing requirements of a local Token-Ring bridge. For example, lowering the average frame length to 64 bytes while keeping the number of stations and cable length of the network constant results in the 4 Mbps network being projected to have a frame rate of 4297 fps, whereas the 16 Mbps network has its frame rate projection increased to 13 776 fps. Then the local bridge that you would use to connect the two networks should have the capability to process 18 073 64 byte frames per second. Concerning the bridge forwarding rate, under a worst case scenario assume that each frame on each network for a short period of time is routed to the other network. Then the forwarding rate of the local bridge should equal its filtering rate to ensure that the bridge will not become a network bottleneck and cannot congest the flow of data between networks.

7.2.2 Remote bridges and routers

As previously noted, the performance requirement for a local bridge is simply the sum of the frame rate on each connected network. That aggregate number of frames per second provides you with the overall frame processing rate that a local bridge must exceed prior to it becoming a potential network bottleneck. In turning our attention to remote bridges and routers used to connect two geographically dispersed Token-Ring networks, we must consider the operating rate of the wide area network transmission facility used to connect networks. Unless that transmission facility operates at the network operating rate, a condition which essentially occurs only when a local bridge is used, the transmission facility functions as a filter which reduces the maximum potential forwarding rate of frames routed from one network to the other network.

Wide area network operating rate

There are three key variables which govern the frame rate that can be achieved on a wide area transmission facility used to interconnect remotely located Token-Ring networks. Those variables include the frame lengths, the WAN operating rate, and the overhead of the transmission protocol used to transport frames between networks. Since the protocol overhead can vary, depending upon the type of protocol used by a bridge or router manufacturer as well as by their use of data compression, we will first examine the maximum frame rate for different frame lengths without considering the effect of the protocol or presence or absence of data compression.

Program TRWAN.BAS

To facilitate the computation of frame rates for different average frame lengths, the BASIC language program TRWAN.BAS was developed. Figure 7.3 lists the statements in that program which computes the frame rate for average frame lengths of 64, 128, 256, 512, 1024, 2048 and 4096 bytes. In actuality, the program adds 21 bytes to each frame length to correspond to the overhead bytes which are wrapped around the information field. Thus, the average frame length actually represents the length of the information field. The WAN operating rates, which vary from 4800 bps to 1.536 Mbps, represent commonly available analog leased line operating rates (through 19 200 bps) and commonly available digital leased line operating rates. Figure 7.4 illustrates the table generated from the execution of that program.

In examining the entries in Figure 7.4 note that the T1 operating rate of 1.536 Mbps represents the T1 speed of 1.544 Mbps less 8000 bps used for T1 framing. Also note that at the 1.536 Mbps rate and an average frame length of 64 bytes, the maximum frame rate of 2259 fps is less than the frame rate of 2293 fps for a 260 station 4 Mbps Token-Ring network

```
REM PROGRAM TRWAN.BAS
REM THIS PROGRAM COMPUTES THE MAXIMUM FRAME RATE THAT A WIDE AREA
REM NETWORK TRANSMISSION FACILITY CAN CARRY BETWEEN TWO REMOTE BRIDGES
CLS
DIM MFPS(9, 7)                                    'max frames per sec
FOR I = 1 TO 9
READ RATE(I)
NEXT I
DATA 4800,9600,19200,56000,64000,128000,256000,512000,1536000
FOR I = 1 TO 7
READ FLENGTH(I)
NEXT I
DATA 64,128,256,512,1024,2048,4096
FOR I = 1 TO 9
FOR J = 1 TO 7
MFPS(I, J) = (RATE(I) / 8) / (FLENGTH(J) + 21)
NEXT J
NEXT I
PRINT "WAN RATE        --------MAXIMUM FRAME RATE PER SECOND -----------"
PRINT "  BPS              BASED UPON AVERAGE FRAME LENGTH IN BYTES"
PRINT "                64      128     256     512    1024     2048    4096
PRINT
J = 1
FOR I = 1 TO 9
PRINT USING " ######## "; RATE(I);
PRINT USING " #####.## #####.## #####.##"; MFPS(I, 1); MFPS(I, 2); MFPS(I, 3);
PRINT USING " #####.## #####.##"; MFPS(I, 4); MFPS(I, 5);
PRINT USING " #####.## #####.##"; MFPS(I, 6); MFPS(I, 7)
NEXT I
END
```

Figure 7.3 Program TRWAN.BAS

WAN RATE BPS	--------MAXIMUM FRAME RATE PER SECOND ----------- BASED UPON AVERAGE FRAME LENGTH IN BYTES						
	64	128	256	512	1024	2048	4096
4800	7.06	4.03	2.17	1.13	0.57	0.29	0.15
9600	14.12	8.05	4.33	2.25	1.15	0.58	0.29
19200	28.24	16.11	8.66	4.50	2.30	1.16	0.58
56000	82.35	46.98	25.27	13.13	6.70	3.38	1.70
64000	94.12	53.69	28.88	15.01	7.66	3.87	1.94
128000	188.24	107.38	57.76	30.02	15.31	7.73	3.89
256000	376.47	214.77	115.52	60.04	30.62	15.47	7.77
512000	752.94	429.53	231.05	120.08	61.24	30.93	15.55
1536000	2258.82	1288.59	693.14	360.23	183.73	92.80	46.64

Figure 7.4 Execution results of program TRWAN.BAS

constructed using 10 000 feet of cable (see Appendix B). Thus, the WAN operating rate of a high-speed T1 circuit can be expected to function as a bottleneck for the transfer of data between Token-Ring networks without considering the effect of the overhead of the transmission protocol or the use of data compression to enhance transmission efficiency.

Protocol overhead

To illustrate the effect of a protocol's overhead upon the maximum frame rate supported by different WAN operating rates, let us revise the program TRWAN.BAS. If we assume the WAN protocol overhead is 20%, we change the computation of the two-dimensional array MFPS to

$$MFPS(I,J) = (RATE(I)/8)/((FLENGTH(J) + 21) \times 1.2)$$

If you want to examine the effect of a different overhead percentage, change the multiplier 1.2 to 1.15 to compute a 15% protocol overhead, to 1.1 for a 10% protocol overhead, and so on. Figure 7.5 lists the results obtained by executing the program TRWAN.BAS in which a protocol overhead of 20% was used for frame rate computations.

Data compression

Due to the ability of data compression to reduce redundancies contained within the information field of a Token-Ring frame, the use of this technology increases the efficiency of the wide area network transmission facility. Since 1990 several vendors, including Newport Systems and Magnalink

```
           ADJUSTED FRAME RATE BASED UPON 20 PERCENT WAN PROTOCOL OVERHEAD
WAN RATE          --------MAXIMUM FRAME RATE PER SECOND -----------
  BPS                 BASED UPON AVERAGE FRAME LENGTH IN BYTES
                64        128       256       512      1024      2048     4096

     4800      5.88      3.36      1.81      0.94      0.48      0.24     0.12
     9600     11.76      6.71      3.61      1.88      0.96      0.48     0.24
    19200     23.53     13.42      7.22      3.75      1.91      0.97     0.49
    56000     68.63     39.15     21.06     10.94      5.58      2.82     1.42
    64000     78.43     44.74     24.07     12.51      6.38      3.22     1.62
   128000    156.86     89.49     48.13     25.02     12.76      6.44     3.24
   256000    313.73    178.97     96.27     50.03     25.52     12.89     6.48
   512000    627.45    357.94    192.54    100.06     51.04     25.78    12.95
  1536000   1882.35   1073.83    577.62    300.19    153.11     77.33    38.86
```

Figure 7.5 Execution results of program TRWAN.BAS with a 20% protocol overhead

Communications, have introduced compression-performing remote bridges. Although the effect of compression depends upon the level of data redundancy which changes from frame to frame, most vendors advertise an average compression ratio of 2:1 for their products. What this means is that the logical data carried by the information field on the average is doubled within the physical information field. Thus, to consider the effect of data compression upon the frame rate transfer capability of the wide area network transmission facility you would modify the computation of MFPS(I,J) in the program TRWAN.BAS as follows:

$$MFPS(I,J) = (RATE(I)/8)/(FLENGTH(J) \times K + 21)$$

where K represents the reciprocal of the average data compression ratio. To consider the effect of both data compression and protocol overhead upon the frame transfer rate of the wide area network transmission facility, you would modify the computation of MFPS(I,J) as follows:

$$MFPS(I,J) = (RATE(I)/8)/((FLENGTH(J) \times K + 21) \times P)$$

where K represents the reciprocal of the average data compression ratio and P represents the average protocol overhead.

To illustrate the use of the revised computation of MFPS(I,J), let us assume that the average data compression ratio is 2 and the expected protocol overhead is 15%. Then, K has a value of 1/2 or 0.5, and P has a value of 1.15. Figure 7.6 illustrates the tabulation of frame rates obtained by modifying the computation of MFPS(I,J) as previously discussed and then executing the program TRWAN.BAS again. In comparing the tabulations contained in Figures 7.4 through 7.6, you will note that the key to reducing the potential of the wide area network transmission facility from functioning as a network bottleneck is obtained by the application of data compression. In fact, at certain operational rates the WAN transmission facility may no longer be a bottleneck. For example, from Figure 7.6 you will note that a T1 circuit is capable of transporting 3150 64 byte frames per second with a data compression ratio of 2 and a protocol overhead of 15%. In comparison, we previously noted that the frame rate on a 260 station 4 Mbps Token-Ring network constructed using 10 000 feet of cable is 2293 frames per second. Thus, this WAN link connected to compression performing remote bridges would have the capability to transfer a greater number of frames per second than the 4 Mbps Token-Ring network could generate. Readers can modify the program TRWAN.BAS and use it in conjunction with the entries in Appendix B to determine the most appropriate WAN operating rate based upon the topology, size, and operating rates of networks to be connected, as well as on the transmission protocol overhead and the expected gain in transmission efficiency due to the use of compression performing bridges or routers if this feature is included in the remote bridges or routers you are using or anticipate acquiring.

Internet traffic flow

Now that mathematical models have been developed to estimate the frame flow on individual Token-Ring networks and through the use of remote bridges and routers connected using different types of WAN transmission facilities, let us focus our attention upon the traffic flow between remotely located interconnected networks. In doing so we will use the model presented

WAN RATE BPS	--------MAXIMUM FRAME RATE PER SECOND ----------- BASED UPON AVERAGE FRAME LENGTH IN BYTES						
	64	128	256	512	1024	2048	4096
4800	9.84	6.14	3.50	1.88	0.98	0.50	0.25
9600	19.69	12.28	7.00	3.77	1.96	1.00	0.50
19200	39.38	24.55	14.01	7.53	3.92	2.00	1.01
56000	114.85	71.61	40.85	21.97	11.42	5.82	2.94
64000	131.26	81.84	46.69	25.11	13.05	6.66	3.36
128000	262.51	163.68	93.38	50.23	26.10	13.31	6.72
256000	525.02	327.37	186.75	100.46	52.21	26.63	13.45
512000	1050.04	654.73	373.50	200.91	104.41	53.26	26.90
1536000	3150.12	1964.19	1120.51	602.73	313.24	159.77	80.69

Figure 7.6 Execution results of program TRWAN.BAS using a data compression ratio of 2 and a protocol overhead of 15%

in Chapter 6 in which the total traffic flow, R_T, between networks has the following relationship to the frame rates on networks 1 (R_1) and 2 (R_2) and the wide area transmission facility frame transfer rate which we will denote as R_3:

$$\frac{1}{R_T} = \frac{1}{R_1} + \frac{1}{R_2} + \frac{1}{R_3}$$

or

$$R_T = \frac{R_1 R_2 R_3}{R_2 R_3 + R_1 R_3 + R_1 R_2}$$

To illustrate the use of this equation, let us assume that you wish to download a 640 kbyte file from a server located on a 16 Mbps Token-Ring network which has 200 stations and 10 000 feet of cable to a 4 Mbps Token-Ring which has 50 stations and 4000 feet of cable, and the remote bridges or routers connecting each network use a 56 kbps transmission facility. Since a file transfer uses the largest frame available for most of the transfer, the transfer would take place using 4500 byte frames which is the largest information field length supported by both 4 and 16 Mbps Token-Ring networks. From Appendix B the closest entries we can locate govern the frame rate for a frame length of 4096 bytes. From that appendix, the maximum frame rate supported by a 4 Mbps network with 50 stations and 4000 feet of cable is 121 fps, and the maximum frame rate on a 16 Mbps network with 200 stations and 10 000 feet of cable is 471 fps. From Figure 7.5 we note that the maximum frame rate supported by a 56 kbps digital circuit with a 20% protocol overhead is 1.42 fps when the average frame length is 4096 bytes. Using our formula to find the transfer rate, we obtain

$$R_T = \frac{121 \times 471 \times 1.42}{471 \times 1.42 + 121 \times 1.42 + 121 \times 471} = 1.399 \text{ fps}$$

As we noted in Chapter 6, this computed value of R_T represents a best-case scenario in that it assumes that the transfer of data from one network to another occurs without other stations on each network using the network or requesting internet transmission. Suppose that the use of a monitoring program on each network indicated that at any time an average of three workstations were using the transmission facilities of each network and two workstations were using internet transmission. Then you would adjust the values of R_1 and R_2 by dividing each by 3, and adjust the value of R_3 by dividing its value by 2. Doing so we obtain

$$R_T = \frac{(121/3)(471/3)(1.42/2)}{(471/3) \times (1.42/2) + (121/3) \times (1.42/2) + (121/3) \times (471/3)}$$

$$= 0.69\,\text{fps}$$

Based upon the preceding, you can expect a best-case frame flow between networks of 1.399 frames per second and an average frame flow between networks of 0.69 frames per second.

For an information field of 4096 bytes the maximum flow of information between networks is 4096 bytes/frame $\times$ 1.399 frames per second, or 5730 bytes per second. Then, the optimum transfer time of a 640 kbyte file would become

$$\frac{640\,\text{kbyte} \times 1024\,\text{bytes/K}}{4096\,\text{bytes/frame} \times 1.399\,\text{frames/second}} = 114\,\text{seconds}$$

To compute the average file transfer time we would use the average transfer rate of 0.69 frames per second. Using an information field of 4096 bytes and a frame rate of 0.69 fps, the average information transfer capability between networks becomes 4096 bytes/frame $\times$ 0.69 frames per second, i.e. 2826 bytes/second. Then, the average transfer time to move a 640 kbyte file between networks becomes

$$\frac{640\,\text{kbyte} \times 1024\,\text{bytes/K}}{2826\,\text{bytes/second}} = 232\,\text{seconds}$$

This indicates that the transmission time to move a 640 kbyte file between two Token-Ring networks connected by a pair of remote bridges or routers using a 56 kbps wide area network transmission facility can be expected on the average to be 232 seconds or slightly under four minutes. In a best-case scenario the transfer time will be 114 seconds or slightly under two minutes. Both timings are based upon the network characteristics previously discussed and will obviously change if either network or the wide area network transmission rate changes.

You can extend the previous computations to determine a peak transmission time by monitoring each network to determine the peak number of users performing network activity at a given period of time. Once you have obtained this information, you would then adjust the values for R_1, R_2 and R_3 in a manner similar to that in which those values were adjusted to determine the average frame transfer rate between networks. By considering the peak traffic on each network, your computation for R_T would result in a worst-case frame transfer rate which you could use to compute the maximum file transfer time.

Whether or not the optimum, average and peak transfer times are acceptable depends upon your organization and its need for speed. Although an increase in the WAN operating rate will have a significant effect upon the ability to transfer frames between networks, it is not without cost. Thus, you may wish to perform a cost analysis to determine if a reduction in file transfer time or an increase in the transfer capability of the WAN is worth the expense associated with obtaining a higher wide area network transmission capability. In addition, you should consider the relationship of file transfer activity in the form of programs and data files to the transfer of relatively short electronic messages in the form of files. For example, if the primary use of the internet is to transport short electronic mail files, would an additional expense of $1000 or more per month to reduce the transfer time of a message from three seconds to one second be worthwhile? Considering the fact that it may take a second or two for a person to move his or her hand to the keyboard and press a key to 'open the mail', I would probably defer the expense. However, the answers to such questions are for you to decide. In doing so you can use the models provided in this book to determine transfer rates and transfer times and use that information in conjunction with the cost of communications equipment and transmission facilities as your decision criteria.

8

WORKING WITH IMAGES

Advances in the graphics capability of personal computers, coupled with low-cost digital cameras have resulted in a significant increase in the use of image-based applications. From photographs of employees being digitized and incorporated into personnel databases, to photographs of automobile accidents with a digital camera being uploaded by insurance agents to the home office, we are witnessing an explosion in the use of image-based applications. Since local area networks primarily support personal computer based applications it should come as no surprise that the transmission of images via LAN media is also increasing. In addition, the explosion in the growth of the World Wide Web has a considerable effect upon the transmission of images on both an inter- and an intra-LAN bases.

For LANs connected to the Internet, the 'surfing' of Web sites can considerably increase the flow of images on the corporate LAN. Even without connecting the corporate LAN to the Internet, the establishment of corporate Web server based help desks can result in an increase in the transport of images. Although the use of images a few years ago was basically a curiosity, today they are essentially a necessity.

In this chapter we will focus our attention on techniques to enhance the storage and transmission of images. To obtain an appreciation for the problems associated with the use of images we will briefly review their storage requirements, as their transmission time is proportional to their storage requirements. Once this has been accomplished we will compare and contrast the effect of transmitting images on LAN bandwidth to the use of text-based applications. Doing so will provide information which not only explains the bandwidth problems associated with transmitting images on a LAN, but also provides a foundation for discussing techniques that you may consider to minimize the effect of images on LAN bandwidth and server storage capacity.

Thus, we will conclude this chapter by examining a variety of techniques that you may consider to enhance the use of images on a local area network while minimizing their effect on other network users.

8.1 IMAGE BASICS

Images can be categorized by the manner by which they are stored displayed and manipulated. There are two general categories of images: raster and vector.

8.1.1 Raster images

A raster image, perhaps more correctly termed an image stored in a raster format, is represented by a series of picture elements or pixels of equal size. The raster format breaks an image into a grid of pixels and records color information for each pixel.

The number of colors that can be represented by each pixel depends on the number of bits used to record each pixel, a term commonly referred to as the pixel color depth. Since each pixel in a file will have the same color depth, the term is also commonly used as a reference to a file's color representation.

Color depth

A raster image with a color depth of one bit per pixel is restricted to providing a black or white color representation, as only two choices are available per bit position. Most raster image formats support more than one bit per pixel, permitting more than one level of color per image. Table 8.1 lists some common bits-per-pixel values supported by popular raster image formats and the corresponding maximum number of colors.

In examining the entries in Table 8.1 several items are worth discussing which may influence the manner by which you use images. First, the capability of many personal computers, including most PCs manufactured before 1994, are limited to displaying a maximum of 256 colors. Secondly, a color depth of 24 bits is commonly referred to as 'true color', as human eyesight cannot normally distinguish colors beyond those supported by a 24 bit color depth. Although a few scanners now support a color depth of 32 bits per pixel, scanning at that color depth will more than likely

Table 8.1 Maximum color support versus bits per pixel

Bits per pixel	Maximum number of colors
1	2
2	4
4	16
8	256
16	32 768
24	16 777 216

result in a conversion to a lower color depth, as the most commonly used raster file formats support a lesser number of bits per pixel.

8.1.2 Vector images

A second category by which images are stored and displayed is based on the use of direct line segments in place of pixels. Those line segments are recorded as mathematical formulae, with the resulting shape referred to as a vector image. Although a vector image is scalable without distortion and normally results in significantly smaller files than raster-based files, vector data cannot reproduce realistic photographic images.

Photographs taken with a digital camera, scanned images and creative art drawn using a pixel-based 'paint' program are examples of raster images. In comparison, a series of algorithms that represent the positioning and placement of lines and arcs created using a computer-aided design (CAD) program would be stored as a vector image. Since employee pictures in personnel files, real estate applications which include photographs of interiors and exteriors of homes, and most World Wide Web pages are based on the use of raster images, the focus of this chapter is also upon this category of graphics representation. In addition, since the data storage requirements of raster-based images can exceed by several orders of magnitude the data storage requirements of vector-based images, it is the former type of image that can be expected to significantly consume LAN bandwidth. Thus, our focus on raster-based images will provide an understanding of where the majority of bandwidth-associated imaging problems arise, as well as enabling a description of methods that you can consider to alleviate those problems.

8.1.3 Why images are a problem

To understand the data storage problem associated with the use of raster images, let us assume that you have just returned from the store with the results of your latest camera operation, and have noted a photograph that could be useful for incorporation into a server-based application. Off you go to your friend down the hall who has a scanner connected to his PC.

Storage considerations

Let us assume that your friend sets the resolution of his scanner to 300 dots per inch for both horizontal and vertical resolution. If your color photograph measures $3\frac{1}{2}$ by 5 inches, the scanned image will require 300×300 bits/inch multiplied 17.5 square inches divided by 8 bits/byte for a total of 196 875 bytes of storage, without considering a color depth beyond 1 bit per pixel. If you select a 256 color resolution scan, 8 bits per pixel would be required, and for true color 24 bits per pixel would be required. Getting out your calculator, your computations would note that the data storage requirements to store the image with a 256 color resolution would be 1 575 000 bytes, and its true color storage would require 4 725 000 bytes. To place the previously described image storage requirements in perspective, consider a full screen of text in which each character could be displayed in one of 256 colors. That screen would consist of 80 by 25 characters for a total of 2000 bytes. Adding one color attribute byte to represent the color depth of each displayed character would result in a requirement to store 4000 bytes. Note that this is almost one four-hundredth of the data storage required for the previously described 256 color resolution image. Table 8.2 provides a comparison of the data storage requirements of the previously described image at three different color depths to a screen of text.

Table 8.2 Text versus image storage

Type of file*	Data storage (bytes)
Image with color depth of 1	196 875
Image with color depth of 8	1 575 000
Image with color depth of 24	4 725 000
Screen of text with color depth of 8	4 000

*Image is a 3.5 × 5 inch photograph scanned at 300 × 300 bits/inch.

Transmission delays

Although 10BASE-T Ethernet and Token-Ring LANs operate at 10 and 16 Mbps, respectively, in actuality their bandwidth is shared among network users. This means that a network consisting of 200 users, with an average of 10% of its workstations attempting to use the LAN at any particular point in time, results in a reduction of the average bandwidth to 10 Mbps/20 or 500 kbps per user on an Ethernet and 16 Mbps/20 or 800 kbps per user on a Token-Ring network. Of course, this quick calculation does not consider the effect of collisions on an Ethernet nor the flow of station management frames on a Token-Ring network, which would further reduce the average bandwidth obtainable by each user. This also means that downloading the previously described 256 color image on the Ethernet LAN could require 1.575 Mbytes/ 500 kbps or over three seconds. For the true color version of the image, the time would triple, because the data storage required for a true color raster image is three times that of a 256 color image.

Although you might be tempted to say 'so what' concerning a three or nine second delay, as other LAN users begin to work with applications that use images, the delays become cumulative. For example, as five users almost simultaneously query a visual database to retrieve the previously described 256 color image, the last person to press the Enter key or click on a Windows button could expect to encounter a delay exceeding 15 seconds. Just think what this does for time-sensitive frames, such as SNA data bound for a mainframe where delays of a few seconds can result in session timeouts. Fortunately, there are several methods that you can consider to reduce the effect of images upon LAN performance. Some methods, such as LAN segmentation, adding switching hubs and boosting servers to Fast Ethernet, ATM or another high-speed technology can result in a considerable expenditure of funds and may be ultimately necessary to implement. However, on occasion there are other possible solutions to the problems resulting from the transportation of images on LANs that can be performed through software, and in many instances may not require any additional expenditure of funds. Those possible solutions are based on the fact that scanning software as well as image viewing programs normally support multiple file formats. Some formats are limited to recording the image as is, on a pixel-by-pixel basis, whereas other formats support the use of one or more compression algorithms to reduce the quantity of data before its actual storage. Since a good LAN manager or network administrator, like a shopper, likes a bargain, we will first examine some of the more popular file formats used to store images, including their support of different types of compression. Once this has been accomplished we will describe and discuss several methods that can be used to adjust images which reduce their effect on network bandwidth. Although these methods may not be applicable to some applications, such as medical imaging where every pixel counts, for other applications the loss of a small amount of resolution may be an acceptable tradeoff for significantly reducing the storage required for an image, as well as decreasing the time required to transport the image on a network. After this has been accomplished we will turn our attention to other solutions that can be applicable to reducing the effect of transmitting images on other network users. Those solutions will involve the use of hardware, and, as you may surmise, they represent more expensive methods for supporting images than software-based solutions.

8.2 EXAMINING IMAGE FORMATS

Since images were first digitized and stored as files, over 50 formats have been developed to standardize their recording and viewing. Table 8.3 provides a summary of the file format extension, file format source and the support of different color depths for 30 commonly encountered raster images.

8.2.1 Common formats

Of those images listed in Table 8.3, a core set of five probably represents a large majority of the methods by which images are stored and viewed. Table 8.4 includes a list of five file formats, including a more descriptive explanation of each file format than contained in Table 8.3.

BMP

The Microsoft Windows bit map format (BMP) can store black and white and color images. Since one version of this format does not use any compression, the resulting files can be extremely large; however, they provide a mechanism for comparing the storage efficiency of other image formats. An option supported by the BMP image format includes the use of a Run Length Encoding (RLE)

Table 8.3 Common raster image file extensions, sources and color depth support

| File extension | Source | Color Depth Support | | | | |
		1 Grey	4 color	8 color	8 color	24 color
BMP	Microsoft Windows RGB encoded	×	×	×	×	×
BMP	Microsoft Windows RLE encoded	×	×		×	×
BMP	OS/2 RGB encoded	×	×		×	×
CLP	Windows Clipboard	×	×		×	×
CUT	Dr. Italo				×	
DCX	Multiple PCX images		×	×	×	×
GIF	CompuServe	×	×	×	×	
IMG	Gem Paint	×	×		×	
JPG	Joint Picture Experts Group			×		×
MAC	MacPaint	×				
PCD	Kodak Photo CD					×
PCX	ZSoft PaintBrush	×				
PCX	ZSoft PaintBrush Version 2	×	×			
PCX	ZSoft PaintBrush Version 3	×	×			
PCX	ZSoft PaintBrush Version 5	×	×		×	×
PGM	UNIX			×		
PIC	PC Paint	×	×		×	
PCT	QuickDraw Picture			×	×	
RLE	Microsoft Windows		×		×	
TGA	True Vision (Targa)			×	×	×
TIF	Aldus Corp Huffman Compressed	×				
TIF	Aldus Corp No Compression	×	×	×	×	×
TIF	Aldus Corp Packed bits	×	×		×	×
TIF	Aldus Corp LZW compression	×	×	×	×	×
TIF	Aldus Corp G3 compression	×				
TIF	Aldus Corp G4 compression	×				
WMF	Windows Metafile	×	×	×	×	×
WPG	WordPerfect Version 5.0	×	×		×	
WPG	WordPerfect Version 5.1	×	×		×	
WPG	WordPerfect Version 6.x	×	×		×	×

compression scheme. Under RLE repeated runs of pixels are compressed, which can result in a smaller BMP file. Although the use of RLE compression makes you expect that the resulting compressed image will be smaller than a non-compressed BMP image this is not always the case. A 'noisy' image which has many translations of color depth, object changes and other irregularities may well result in an expansion of storage when compressed using BMP's RLE compression option. This expansion results from characters required to denote the occurrence of compression

Table 8.4 Common image file formats

Extension	Description
BMP	The Microsoft Clipboard and file format which stores images in a bit map format and optionally supports RLE compression.
GIF	CompuServe's Graphical Interchange Format stores images using a 12 bit Lempel-Ziv-Welsh (LZW) lossless compression technique.
JPG	The Joint Picture Experts Group (JPEG) standardized the storage of images based on the ability of the user to specify the removal of details via a lossy compression method.
PCX	The ZSoft PaintBrush image format uses a run length limited (RLL) lossless compression method.
TIF	The Tag Image File Format (TIFF) represents a specification for the storage of images that was jointly written by Aldus Corporation and Microsoft. Although the copyright is held by Aldus, the specification is in the public domain. TIFF supports five compression methods: one lossy and four lossless.

adding to the size of the file when runs of the same pixel color depth are relatively short.

Because RLE compression is fully reversible, there is no loss of image quality when the compressed data is decompressed by a BMP viewer. The RLE compression method is referred to as lossless compression, because all pixels in the original image are restored upon decompression.

GIF

The CompuServe Graphical Interchange Format (GIF) was one of the earliest developed image storage and viewing formats; the first GIF standard was developed in 1987, and a downward compatible standard was developed during 1989. The GIF format is widely used by electronic bulletin board systems, as it was among the first to incorporate data compression, using a 12 bit Lempel-Ziv-Welsh (LZW) technique which typically provides a 2:1 or 3:1 reduction in the amount of data storage required to store an image in comparison to storing it in its original bit mapped format.

LZW is one of several string-based compression methods which is fully reversible. That is, the decompression algorithm when applied to a previously compressed file results in the recreation of the original file on a bit for bit basis without any loss of data. Due to this, this type of compression is also known as lossless compression.

JPG

The Joint Picture Experts Group (JPEG) standardized a method of image storage and viewing based on a series of compression methods. Although the technique is referred to as JPEG, the file extension resulting from an image stored using the JPEG technique is JPG, a carryover from the DOS and non-Windows 95 limitation of a three-character file extension.

JPEG image compression is based upon the transformation of 8 by 8 pixel blocks of a true color image into luminance and chrominance levels. Each block is processed by a two dimensional discrete cosine transformation to obtain 64 coefficients representing the block. Those coefficients are quantized by predefined tables for luminance and chrominance components, after which information about the block is packed into lower-frequency coefficients. This results in many coefficients being represented by 0s and 1s, which facilitates the compression of data representing the image.

Many imaging programs that support JPEG enable a user storing an image to adjust the quantization tables by defining a quality value. At the default of 75 used by most programs relatively little picture degradation occurs; however, a significant amount of compression may be obtainable. At lower quality values slightly better compression results are obtainable but a marked loss of image quality occurs when decompression occurs and the previously compressed image is viewed. Other imaging programs do not permit a user to directly alter the quantization tables by defining a quality value. Instead, they may internally define several quality values and associate those values with the terms 'least,' 'moderate' and 'highest' or similar meaning descriptors. Then, selecting a compression level descriptor results in the program using a predefined quality value.

The adjustment of JPEG quantization tables by specifying a quality value using a program compression descriptor, or using a program's default results in a permanent loss of image details. Thus, the method of compression used by JPEG is referred to as lossy because decompression does not result in the exact reconstruction of the original image. However, although lossless compression is extremely important when working with data files that can include financial information, word processing files and similar information, a small loss of image quality may not be perceptible to the human eye. Unlike the storage of data files which must be compressed using a lossless compression method, a degree of lossless compression is typically tolerable when working with most images. The trick when using a lossy compression method is similar to having self-control at an 'all you can eat' buffet. That is, do not overindulge, for an excessive amount of lossy compression will result in a bad visual feeling from a distorted image. If you are using an imaging program that directly supports the entry of a quality value, care should be taken when selecting values under 50. At or under a quality value of 50, depending on the image, you may begin to notice the 8-by-8 bit blocks as they begin to become more pronounced, due to excessive pixel loss. As we will shortly note, you can obtain a significant data reduction through the use of the default quality value of 75, resulting in an image that is essentially nondistinguishable from the original.

PCX

The PCX image format was developed for the ZSoft PC PaintBrush image editing program, and it represents one of the first graphics formats used with the IBM PC and compatible computers. The PCX format is supported by many DOS and Windows based programs and it supports color depths ranging from black and white to 24 bit true color.

PCX uses a run length compression method which results in a repetitive sequence of bits being replaced by a repeat count byte and a data byte. Run length compression is a lossless compression method which results in the recreation of an exact duplicate of the original image. The simplicity of the run length compression method results in coding and decoding operations occurring relatively fast; however, this compression method is in general inferior to the LZW compression method used in the GIF format and is supported as one of several compression methods by the TIFF image format described next.

TIF

The first Tag Image File Format (TIFF) specification was jointly developed by Aldus, Microsoft and several scanner manufacturers during 1986 as a mechanism to standardize a file format for images used in desktop publishing. Since then, a number of specification revisions have occurred which expanded TIFF support to digital video images and have increased the number of compression methods that can be used to reduce image storage requirements.

TIFF supports five compression methods, four lossless and one lossy. Lossless compression methods supported include two types of ITU-T (formerly CCITT) Group 3 and one method of Group 4 compression primarily associated with the use of fax, and LZW compression. A lossy JPEG compression method was added in TIFF specification revision 6.0. A TIFF compatible file generator program must support at least one compression method, whereas a reader should be capable of supporting all compression methods. Similarly to JPEG, TIFF files are commonly stored using a three character extension which explains why the second F is not used.

Although the TIFF specification is supported by a large number of popular programs there are a large number of options associated with the use of many programs, that requires some thought prior to clicking on a button or entering a command. Some programs use a default of no compression when the TIFF format is selected, which, as previously discussed, will result in a maximum amount of storage used for the image. Other programs provide support for a large number of patterns that can be used to store different types of images. Forgetting to set an appropriate compression method or the selection of an unnecessary pattern can result in a file storage size that warms the heart of a disk drive manufacturer, but when placed on a LAN can result in a minimum of some degraded performance being experienced by other network users. However, in some situations where large images or a large number of images are transmitted, the delays due to their transport can result in session timeouts as well as significantly degraded performance.

To obtain an appreciation of the effect of LAN-based images, as well as techniques that can be used to minimize the effect of their storage and transmission, requires an image to work with. Owing to the problems of copyright I decided not to use a picture of the Brooklyn Bridge, a famous museum or another object that might be difficult to obtain permission to use. Instead, I used a photograph of my daughter as a basis for reviewing key concepts that will facilitate the use of images on a network.

Figure 8.1 illustrates the scanned image of an approximate 8 by 10 inch photograph of the author's daughter, Jessica Held. When stored using a TIFF format without being compressed, the file required 2 494 045 bytes of storage.

Figure 8.1 An 8 × 10 inch photograph of the author's daughter stored as a non-compressed TIF file. This image will be used to illustrate the effect of changing image file formats upon the data storage requirements of an image

8.2.2 Comparing storage requirements

To illustrate the differences in data storage resulting from the use of other image formats, the author used the Image Manager program which is part of the Collage Complete image suite of programs from Inner Media, Inc. of Hollis, NH. Image Manager supports ten distinct file formats, permitting the original scan to be easily altered from its TIF format without having to rescan the photograph.

Figure 8.2 illustrates the Image Manager main screen after the previously scanned photograph was retrieved through the use of the program's File Open menu option. Because the photograph was scanned along its vertical axis, Figure 8.2 illustrates the initial selection of the program's Flip/Rotate option to reposition the image lengthwise to provide a more conventional view of the image. Figure 8.3 illustrates the result obtained by selecting a 90 degree clockwise rotation of the image. In the remainder of this

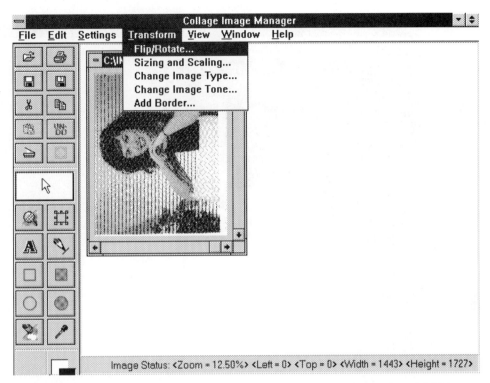

Figure 8.2 Using the Collage Image Manager to rotate the retrieved TIF image 90 degrees

chapter we will work with the image illustrated in Figure 8.3, transforming the TIF image format into other popular image formats so that we can examine the effect of different formats on their data storage requirements and transmission time on a network.

Figure 8.4 illustrates the Collage Image Manager program's 'Save Image As' window with its image format box selected to illustrate the file formats supported by the program. Although the program supports 10 distinct image file formats, it actually supports over 20 formats if you consider the fact that several formats include different subformats based on the program's support of one or more compression methods for several formats. Although this author used the Collage Image Manager program to perform his conversions it should be noted that there are numerous programs that provide this capability. Some programs, such as Paint Shop Pro can be obtained from many bulletin boards and Internet anonymous FTP archives and are available as shareware, requiring the payment of a nominal fee after a typical 30 day trial period, and other programs, such as the

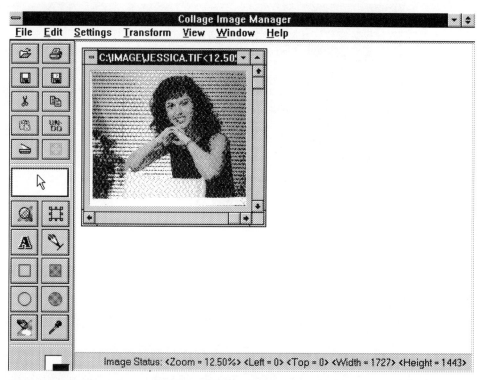

Figure 8.3 The resulting rotated image which will form the basis for performing several image conversions and image manipulation operations

Collage Complete suite or the popular Hijack suite, are well known commercial programs advertised for sale in many trade publications.

File format comparisons

Table 8.5 summarizes the storage requirements of different image file formats based on their conversion from the original scanned picture which was stored as a non-compressed TIF file. In examining the entries in Table 8.5 it should be noted that each image format was stored as a 256 level true gray 8 bit per pixel color type. Also, note that in comparing the data storage requirements of each image the presence or absence of compression as well as the type of compression used can have a considerable effect upon the data storage requirement of the image. For example, the non-compressed TIF image required 2 494 095 bytes of storage, whereas the same image stored using TIF's lossless LZW compression technique required 1 950 970 bytes of storage. Thus, simply changing the TIF file format to

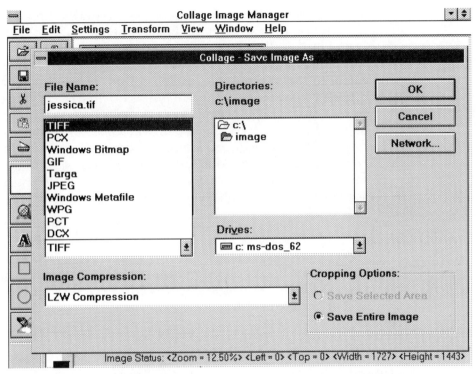

Figure 8.4 Through the Collage Image Manager's Save Image As option you can store a file in a different image format

Table 8.5 Comparing image format storage requirements

File format	Description	Data storage (bytes)
TIF	TIFF non-compressed	2 494 095
TIF	TIFF LZW-compressed	1 950 970
BMP	Windows Bitmap non-compressed	2 781 122
BMP	Windows Bitmap RLE compression	2 494 582
DCX	Multiple PCX color images: no compression	2 634 995
GIF	CompuServe Graphics Interchange LZW compression	1 803 744
JPG	JPEG Least Compression	1 365 036
JPG	JPEG Moderate Compression	163 888
JPG	JPEG Highest Compression	84 973
PCT	Quick Draw Picture no compression	2 571 200
PCX	PC PaintBrush no compression	2 634 591
TGA	Targa no compression	2 492 079
WMF	Windows Metafile	2 494 670

support its lossless compression method, which has absolutely no effect on the clarity of the image when it is decoded, results in (2 494 095 − 1 950 970)/2 494 095 (approximately 22% data storage reduction). Because transmission time is usually proportional to the size of a file, under normal network operating conditions you can reduce the transmission time of the image by 22% by storing it in a compressed form. As network utilization increases on an Ethernet LAN the additional effect of collisions will be reduced by transmitting images in their compressed format. In certain situations a reduction in the file size of an image by 20% might well result in a 100% or more reduction in the transmission time of an image on a heavily utilized local area network.

Examining visual image differences

To illustrate the visual differences between the original image and several converted images, Figures 8.5–8.8 represent the printout of four converted image formats.

Figure 8.5   The display of the GIF image format of the author's daughter

Figure 8.6   A printout of the image after its conversion to JPG using the Collage Image Manager's least compression specification

Figure 8.5 illustrates the display of the GIF image format of the author's daughter. Through the use of the lossless LZW compression technique the data storage requirement of the file was reduced to approximately 1.8 Mbytes, which although less than the non-compressed TIF file is significantly more than the storage required when the original TIF image was converted to several types of JPG image which are discussed later in this section. From Table 8.5 you will note that, other than the use of JPG file formats, GIF provides the best overall compression performance. Since the use of JPG can result in a considerable data reduction beyond that obtainable from lossless compression techniques let us focus our attention on the results obtained from converting the original TIF image to JPG using different quality values.

Considering JPG

Figures 8.6–8.8 illustrate the image after it was converted to JPG by specifying the least, moderate and highest compression. Those

Figure 8.7 The printout of the file stored using moderate JPG compression

three compression descriptors correspond to quality values of 97, 90 and 70, respectively. If you compare Figures 8.6–8.8 to the original TIF image in Figure 8.1, focusing on the facial features of each image, you may notice a very slight difference between the JPG and TIF images. The difference is slightly more pronounced when comparing Figure 8.8 and Figure 8.1.

In comparing Figures 8.6–8.8 to Figure 8.1, it is important to note that if your network user image operations are oriented to storing pictures of persons or places for a visual database application a slight degree of image distortion may be an acceptable price to pay for the significant reduction in data storage that becomes obtainable. For example, the data storage required for Figure 8.8 is 84 973 bytes, which as you will note from Table 8.5 is approximately $\frac{1}{30}$th of the data storage required by the non-compressed TIF file which was shown in Figure 8.1. In comparison, if the images is to be used in a desktop publishing application where clarity is of extreme importance, you would more than likely restrict compression to the lossless method. Similarly, when working with medical images, such as a chest X-ray, where the

Figure 8.8 The printout of the file stored using the highest JPG compression supported by the Collage Image Manager program

loss of even one pixel could result in a misdiagnosis, you should never consider the use of a lossy compression method.

8.2.3 Additional image management operations

Through the use of scanner software or an image management program you obtain the ability to perform a variety of functions which effect the storage and transmission time of images. In addition to selecting an appropriate file format, including the use of compression, you can consider such operations as image cropping and color reduction, as well as changing the resolution of a scanned image.

Image cropping

Image cropping provides you with the ability to eliminate unnecessary portions of an image, which obviously reduces its

Figure 8.9   The cropped TIF file using LZW compression requires 1 156 975 bytes of storage

storage requirements. To illustrate the effect of cropping, the compressed TIF and moderate compression JPG images were cropped. Figure 8.9 illustrates the cropped TIF image and Figure 8.10 illustrates the cropped JPG image. In comparing the cropped images to the original size images you will note that the background eliminated is more than likely unnecessary if the image is to be stored on a photo-ID database used to provide guards with pictures of employees or for similar applications. My cropping effort reduced the TIF file to 1 156 975 bytes and the moderately compressed JPG file was reduced to 98 153 bytes of storage.

Color reduction

Concerning color reduction, there are several questions that people working with images should be asked. First, do they really require a true color 24 bits per pixel image for applications that

Figure 8.10 The cropped moderately compressed JPG file has its data storage reduced to 98 153 bytes

never see a printed page? For example, does it make sense to scan photographs of employees using a 24 bit per pixel color depth? Perhaps 256 color (8 bits per pixel) or even a 16 level true gray using 4 bits per pixel might be sufficient. In fact, once an image is placed on a server you might wish to review its color depth with respect to its application through the use of an image management program. For example, returning to the Collage Image Manager program, Figure 8.11 illustrates the selection of the program's Change Image Type option window which was displayed by selecting the option from the program's Transform menu. In Figure 8.11 the New Type list was selected to provide readers with a visual indication of the color depth types supported by the program for TIF formatted files. Often you can significantly reduce the storage requirements of an image by changing its color depth. Now that we have an appreciation of the software-based techniques that we can consider to alter the storage requirements and network transmission time of images, let us turn our attention to hardware-based techniques.

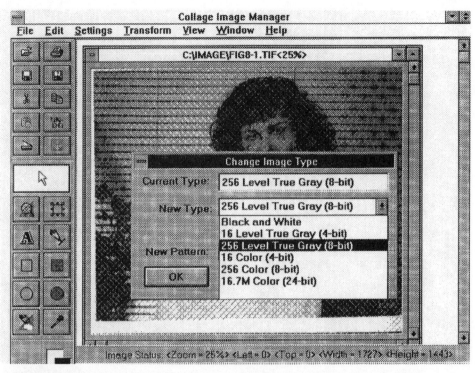

Figure 8.11 The Collage Image Manager Change Image Type window. Often you can significantly reduce the storage requirements of an image by changing its color depth.

8.3 HARDWARE CONSIDERATIONS

There are several hardware-based techniques that you can consider to minimize the effect of images on LAN performance. Those techniques include LAN segmentation, upgrading LAN adapter cards to obtain a higher throughput for servers storing images, upgrading your LAN infrastructure to a new and higher bandwidth capable network and using LAN switches. Since the use of LAN switches is the focus of Chapter 9 we will focus our attention on the first three hardware-based techniques in the remainder of this chapter.

8.3.1 LAN segmentation

A simple subdivision of a LAN into two or more segments connected by bridges may create more problems than it solves when working with images. To understand why this situation can

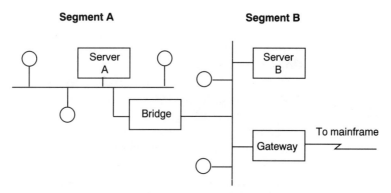

Figure 8.12 LAN segmentation. Network segmentation may not be a viable option when users on each segment work with image based applications

occur, consider Figure 8.12 which shows two LAN segments interconnected through the use of a bridge, with one segment connected to a gateway which provides access to a mainframe for users connected to both network segments.

If a user on either segment accesses an image application on server B, the transmission of the image can adversely effect users on both segments. In addition, depending on the size of the image and other user activity occurring on segment B, the additional bandwidth used by the image could delay an in-progress mainframe session to the point where it times out. If you can segregate images to server A and have a minimal number of users on segment B requiring access to server A, you can reduce and possibly eliminate the possibility of session timeouts. If you can place all users requiring access to image-based applications on one segment and interlan traffic is primarily time-insensitive electronic mail, you could minimize the effect of image applications on segment B users. However, since many if not most LAN users typically require access to a mixture of applications, it may not be possible to perform the previously mentioned segmentation. Instead, you may have to consider an alternative hardware approach, such as upgrading LAN adapter cards, upgrading your LAN infrastructure or acquiring LAN switches.

8.3.1 Upgrading adapter cards

One of the key bottlenecks that hinders network performance is the adapter card used in workstations and servers. For example, the data transfer capability of 10BASE-T Ethernet network interface cards can easily vary from 300 000 bytes/s to over

600 000 bytes/s. If you do not know the transfer rate of your adapter you can consider running a predefined test. To do so you should create a large file on your network server and download it to a workstation when you are the only user on the network. By clocking the transfer time and using that time as a divisor to the file size transferred, you can obtain a viable estimate of the NIC's maximum transfer rate. Then, if that rate appears low in comparison with the capability of other NICs you should consider replacing server and workstation NICs for users that work with images. Because the replacement of NICs is significantly less costly than other hardware alternatives you might consider placing this option at the top of your hardware list. Readers are referred to Section 6 of Chapter 10 for additional information concerning the performance of network adapter cards.

8.3.3 Upgrading the LAN infrastructure

Although the title of this section can be considered applicable to the previous sections in this chapter, I am using it here in the context of upgrading an existing LAN infrastructure to a new and higher bandwidth capable network. This hardware solution might involve replacing a 10BASE-T network by a 100BASE-T, or a Token-Ring by an ATM network, and it obviously represents the most costly method for handling images. In fact, due to the cost associated with upgrading an entire existing LAN it should normally be considered as a last resort, with the use of intelligent switching hubs normally providing a more economical method to support the effect of images being transported on LANs. Thus, readers are referred to Chapter 9 for detailed information concerning the operation and utilization of intelligent switches.

9

USING INTELLIGENT SWITCHES

The expansion of local area networks, both in terms of the number of network users supported and in the number and type of applications they use, typically results in a considerable increase in the use of network bandwidth. This in turn can result in the occurrence of problems ranging from sluggish network performance experienced by workstation users that marginally affects their productivity to the occurrence of session timeouts that terminate network-related work in progress, forcing users to redo previously performed operations or precluding users from performing certain types of network-related activity.

Until the early 1990s the primary method employed to overcome the effect of network congestion was segmentation, subdividing a network into two or more entities interconnected by a bridge or router. Today the network manager and administrator have several options, including the use of a higher operating rate network such as Fast Ethernet or ATM or the use of intelligent switches. In this chapter we will focus our attention on the latter, which are also referred to as switching hubs.

To obtain an appreciation for the role of intelligent switches we will first review the operation of conventional hubs, including bandwidth constraints associated with their use. Once this has been accomplished we will focus our attention on the different operational methods supported by intelligent switching hubs, including the basic switching methods supported by different products that fall into this class of networking device. Using this information as a foundation we will explore the use of both Ethernet and Token-Ring intelligent switching hubs, including obtaining an understanding of the key features built into many products, as well as why the presence of some features and the absence of other features can result in degraded performance instead of an expected improvement in performance. Owing to this, we will examine how the use of certain intelligent switch features can result in network problems and how those problems can be alleviated through the use of other device features. Since we will obtain a detailed understanding of the operational effect of a comprehensive set of intelligent switching hub features, the information presented in this chapter can also be used as a guide for the evaluation of switching hubs.

9.1 CONVENTIONAL HUB BOTTLENECKS

In this section we will examine why conventional hubs, which were developed to facilitate the cabling of network devices, also function as a bottleneck with respect to the use of network bandwidth. In doing so we will discuss the operation of both Ethernet and Token-Ring hubs, with the latter primarily referred to as a Multistation Access Unit (MAU).

9.1.1 Ethernet hub operation

In an Ethernet environment a single LAN is usually referred to as a segment, with large networks typically composed of multiple segments connected by a bridge or router. The early implementations of Ethernet in the form of 10BASE-5 and 10BASE-2 coaxial cable based networks resulted in the use of a common medium to which workstations are attached. This is illustrated in Figure 9.1 which shows the cabling structure of a coaxial-based Ethernet network.

Based on the fact that the bandwidth of the media is shared with only one user able to transmit at any given time, the

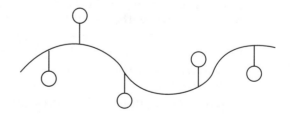

10BASE-5 and 10BASE-2 Etherent networks consist of
a coaxial run to which network devices are attached

Figure 9.1   A shared media, shared bandwidth Ethernet LAN segment

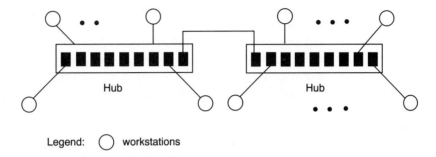

Figure 9.2 A two hub 10BASE-T Ethernet network

Ethernet LAN segment shown in Figure 9.1 is commonly referred to as a shared-media, shared-bandwidth network.

A change in the network topology and cabling structure of Ethernet resulted in the development of hub-centric 10BASE-T networks, in which cabling from individual network devices to dedicated ports on the hub resulted in a star-wiring configuration. When two or more hubs are interconnected to form a common network the wiring topology resembles a star-bus structure as illustrated in Figure 9.2. Although the wiring topology changed, the use of hubs did not alter the fact that the network remained a shared-media, shared-bandwidth network.

To illustrate the problem associated with the use of a shared-media, shared-bandwidth network, let us examine the operation of a conventional Ethernet hub. This type of hub simply duplicates nodes attached to the hub. Figure 9.3 illustrates the data flow when one workstation (node 1) transmits a frame to another workstation, file server, gateway or another network device, which is connected either to the same hub or to another hub which is connected to the hub that the data originator is

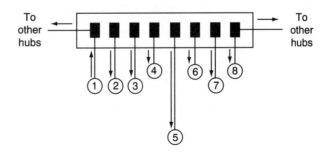

Figure 9.3 Conventional hub dataflow. A conventional hub functions as a data regenerator, outputting an incoming frame received on one port onto all other ports

connected to. Since the hub functions as a data regenerator, the frame is repeated onto each connection to the hub to include interconnections to other hubs. This restricts data flow to one workstation at a time, since collisions occur when two or more attempt to gain access to the media at the same time.

9.1.2 Token-Ring hub operation

Although data flow on a Token-Ring network is circular, this type of network is also a shared-media, shared-bandwidth network. In a Token-Ring network environment hubs, referred to as Multistation Access Units or MAUs, are connected via their Ring In and Ring Out ports to form a star-ring topology similar to that shown in Figure 9.4. The actual data flow of a frame is from one device to the next, including flowing down the cable, called a lobe, connecting the device to the MAU port

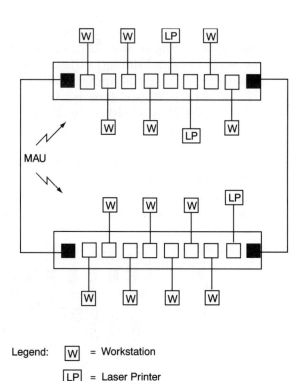

Legend: ⬚W = Workstation

ⳐLP = Laser Printer

■ = Ring In and Ring Out Ports

Figure 9.4　The connection of Token-Ring MAUs forms a star-ring topology

to an attached device and back to the port prior to flowing to the next port. Since only one frame can flow on the network at any point in time, access to the bandwidth is also shared. Thus, a Token-Ring network also represents a shared-media, shared-bandwidth network.

9.1.3 Bottleneck creation

Conventional Ethernet hubs create network bottlenecks because all traffic flows through a shared backplane in the hub. Thus, each device connected to an Ethernet hub competes for a slice of the bandwidth of the backplane. In a Token-Ring environment devices compete to acquire a token, resulting in the sharing of network bandwidth in a similar manner. The end result of this bandwidth sharing is an average transmission rate per device that is many times below the operating rate of the network. For example, consider a departmental 10BASE-T network operating at 10 Mbps consisting of 12 interconnected 8 port hubs that supports a total of 96 devices. Then the average slice of bandwidth available for each device is 10 Mbps/96 or approximately 104 kbps. Note that although each device transmits and receives data at the LAN operating rate of 10 Mbps, their average data transfer capability is approximately 104 kbps, because each device must compete with 95 other devices to obtain access to the network. Similarly, a 96 node Token-Ring network would result in each device attached to that network having an average data transfer capability of 4 Mbps or 16 Mbps divided by 96, depending on the operating rate of the network. This means that over a period of time the addition of network users, the introduction of one or more graphic-based applications or growth in the use of current applications can result in a severely taxed network. When this type of situation occurs, you may consider a variety of techniques to enhance network performance, including network segmentation through the use of a bridge or router, migrating your existing infrastructure to a different and higher operating rate technology, or employing intelligent switching hubs which is the focus of this chapter.

9.2 SWITCHING OPERATIONS

The development of intelligent switching hubs has its foundation, as with many other areas of modern communications, in telephone technology. Shortly after the telephone was invented the switchboard was developed to enable multiple simultaneous conversations to occur without requiring telephone wires to be installed in a complex matrix between subscribers. Later, telephone office switches were developed to route calls based on the telephone number dialed, followed in a similar manner by the development of bridges in a LAN environment. Bridges can be considered to represent an elementary type of switch owing to their limited number of ports and simplistic switching operation. That switching operation is based on whether the destination address in a frame 'read' on one port is known to reside on that port.

9.2.1 Bridge switching

Figure 9.5 illustrates the basic operation of a bridge. If you compare the operations performed by a bridge with respect to each port you will note that they are nearly identical, with the only

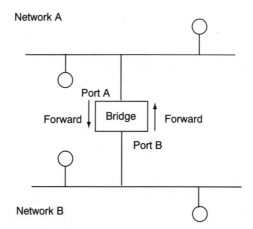

Port A operation

1. Read source address of frames on LAN A to construct a table of source addresses.
2. Read destination address in frames and compare to addresses in source address table.
3. If address not in table, forward onto Port B, otherwise, do nothing.

Port B operation

1. Read source address of frames on LAN B to construct a table of source addresses.
2. Read destination address in frames and compare to addresses in source address table.
3. If address not in table, forward onto Port A, otherwise, do nothing.

Figure 9.5   Bridge switching operation

difference between the two operations concerning the port they forward frames to when the destination address of a frame is compared to a table of source addresses and no match occurs. When this situation occurs the frame's destination is considered to reside on the network attached to the port other than the port it was read from, hence it is forwarded through the bridge to the other port and placed onto the network connected to that port. If n networks are connected in serial via the use of $n-1$ bridges, and a frame is transmitted on the network at one end of the interconnected group of networks to the network on the opposite end of the interconnected group of LANs, each bridge would perform a similar forwarding operation until the frame has traversed n bridges and is placed on the last network in the interconnected series. The simplicity associated with the operation of bridges makes them a popular networking device. However, most bridges are limited to forwarding or 'switching' frames on a serial basis, from one port to another. This restricts the forwarding rate to the lowest network operating rate. For example, the connection of a 10 Mbps Ethernet network to a 16 Mbps Token-Ring network via the use of a local bridge would reduce internetwork communications to a maximum operating rate of 10 Mbps, creating another network bottleneck.

9.2.2 The switching hub

Recognizing the limitations associated with the operation of bridges vendors incorporated parallel switching technology into devices known as intelligent switching hubs. This device was based on matrix switches which for decades have been successfully employed in telecommunications operations. By adding buffer memory to store address tables, frames flowing on LANs connected to different ports could be simultaneously read and forwarded via the switch fabric to ports connected to other networks.

Basic components

Figure 9.6 illustrates the basic components of a four-port intelligent switch. Unlike a bridge that reads frames flowing on a network to construct a table of source addresses, the tables in an intelligent switch are normally pre-configured. This allows the destination address to be compared to a table of destination

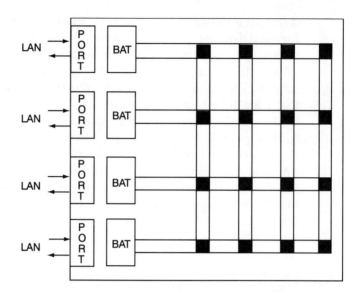

Figure 9.6 Basic components of an intelligent switch. An intelligent switch consists of buffers and address tables (BAT), logic and a switching fabric which permits frames entering one port to be routed to any port in the switch. The destination address in a frame is used to determine the associated port with that address via a search of the address table, with the port address used by the switching fabric for establishing the cross connection

addresses and associated port numbers. When a match occurs between the destination address of a frame flowing on a network connected to a port and the address in the port's address table, the frame is copied into the switch and routed through the switch fabric to the destination port, where it is placed onto the network connected to that port. If the destination port is in use due to a previously established cross-connection between ports, the frame is maintained in the buffer until it can be switched to its destination.

Delay times

Switching occurs on a frame-by-frame basis, with the cross-connection torn down after being established for routing one frame. Thus, frames can be interleaved from two or more ports to a common destination port with a minimum of delay. For example, consider a maximum length Ethernet frame of 1526 bytes to include a 1500 byte data field and 26 overhead bytes. At a 10 Mbps operating rate each bit time is $1/10^7$ seconds or 100 ns.

For a 1526 byte frame, the minimum delay time if one frame precedes it in attempting to be routed to a common destination becomes

$$1526 \text{ bytes} \times \frac{8 \text{ bits}}{\text{byte}} \times \frac{100 \text{ ns}}{\text{bit}} = 1.22 \text{ ms}$$

The previously computed delay time represents blocking resulting from frames on two service ports with a common destination, and should not be confused with another delay time referred to as latency. Latency represents the delay associated with the physical transfer of a frame from one port via the switch to another port and is fixed based on the architecture of the switch. In comparison, blocking delay depends on the number of frames from different ports attempting to access a common destination port and the method by which the switch is designed to respond to blocking. Some switches simply have large buffers for each port and service ports in a round-robin fashion when frames on two or more ports attempt to access a common destination port. This method of service is not similar to politics, as it does not show favoritism; however, it also does not consider the fact that some attached networks may have operating rates different from other attached networks. Other switch designs recognize that port buffers are filled based on both the number of frames having a destination address of a different network and the operating rate of the network. Such switch designs use a priority service scheme based on the occupancy of the port buffers in the switch.

Key advantages of use

A key advantage associated with the use of intelligent switching hubs results from their ability to support parallel switching, permitting multiple cross-connections between source and destination to occur simultaneously. For example, if four 10BASE-T networks were connected to the four port switch shown in Figure 9.6 two simultaneous cross-connections, each at 10 Mbps, could occur, resulting in an increase in bandwidth to 20 Mbps. Here each cross-connection represents a dedicated 10 Mbps bandwidth for the duration of a frame. Thus, from a theoretical perspective, an N-port switching hub supporting a 10 Mbps operating rate on each port provides a throughput of up to $N/2 \times 10$ Mbps. For example, a 128 port switching hub would support a throughput of up to $(128/2) \times 10$ Mbps or 640 Mbps, whereas a network constructed using a series of conventional hubs connected to one another would be limited to an operating rate of 10 Mbps, with each workstation on that network having an average bandwidth of 10 Mbps/128 or 78 kbps.

Through the use of intelligent switching hubs you can overcome the operating rate limitation of a local area network. In an Ethernet environment, the cross-connection through a switching hub represents a dedicated connection so there will never be a collision. This fact enabled many switching hub vendors to use the collision wire-pair from conventional Ethernet to support simultaneous transmission in both directions between a connected node and hub port, resulting in a full-duplex transmission capability that will be discussed in more detail later in this chapter. In fact, a similar development permits Token-Ring switching hubs to provide full-duplex transmission since if there is only one station on a port there is no need to pass tokens and repeat frames, raising the maximum bi-directional throughput between a Token-Ring device and a switching hub port to 32 Mbps. Thus, the ability to support parallel switching as well as initiate dedicated cross-connections on a frame by frame basis can be considered the key advantages associated with the use of intelligent switching hubs. Both parallel switching and dedicated cross-connections permit higher bandwidth operations. Now that we have an appreciation for the general operation of switching hubs, let us focus our attention on the different switching techniques that can be incorporated into this category of communications equipment.

9.2.3 Switching techniques

Three switching techniques are used by intelligent switching hubs: cross-point, also referred to as cut-through or 'on the fly'; store-and-forward; and a hybrid method which alternates between the first two methods based on the frame error rate. As we will soon note, each technique has one or more advantages and disadvantages associated with its operation.

Cross-point switching

The operation of a cross-point switch is based on an examination of the destination of frames as they enter a port on the switching hub. The switch uses the destination address as a decision criterion to obtain a port destination from a look-up table. Once a port destination has been obtained a cross-connection through the switch is initiated, resulting in the frame being routed to a destination port where it is placed onto a network for which its frame destination address resides. In actuality there are usually two look-up tables in a switch. The first table, which is usually constructed dynamically, consists of source addresses of frames flowing on the network connected to the port. This enables the switch to construct a table of known devices. Then the first comparison using the destination address in a frame is with the table of known source addresses. If the destination address matches an address in the table of known source addresses, this indicates that the frame's destination is on the current network and no switching operation is required. If the frame's destination address does not match an address in the table of known source addresses this indicates that the frame is to be routed through the switch onto a different network. Then the switch will search a destination look-up table to obtain a port destination and initiate a cross-connection through the switch, routing the frame to a destination port where it is placed onto a network where a node with the indicated destination address resides. Some switches use a single look-up table, with the destination address of each frame compared to the addresses in that table to determine whether or not switching is required, and other switches use two tables, as previously described. Another variation between switch designs concerns the number and location of look-up tables. Some switch designs result in each port having its own look-up table or set of tables, with a fixed amount of memory subdivided into a buffer area and look-up table similar to the buffer and address tables illustrated in Figure 9.6. Another switch design uses a common memory area which is logically subdivided for use by each port. Although this design makes more economical use of memory, the use of shared memory introduces delays that are avoided when memory is used with individual ports. However, from an upgrade perspective it is easier to upgrade one memory area than a series of memory areas. Thus, you may wish to consider differences in upgradability versus very slight differences in latency.

In the remainder of this chapter we will focus our attention on the operation of switching hubs by assuming that only one look-up table is used as it provides an easier mechanism to describe the basic operation of different switching methods. In addition, we will not differentiate performances based on the type and location of look-up tables, because the overall switch design, including the operation of custom-designed integrated circuits, has a more pronounced effect on switch performance than the type and location of look-up tables.

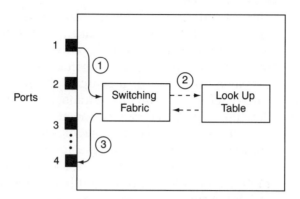

Figure 9.7 Cross-point/cut-through switching. A cross-point or cut-through operating switch reads the destination address in a frame prior to storing the entire frame (1). It forwards that address to a look-up table (2) to determine the port destination address which is used by the switching fabric to provide a cross-connection to the destination port (3)

Figure 9.7 illustrates the basic operation of cross-point or cut-through switching. Under this technique the destination address in a frame is read prior to the frame being stored (1). That address is forwarded to a look-up table (2) to determine the port destination address which is used by the switching fabric to initiate a cross-connection to the destination port (3). Because this switching method only requires the storage of a small portion of a frame until it is able to read the destination address and perform its table look-up operation to initiate switching to an appropriate output port, latency through the switch is minimized.

Latency functions as a brake on two-way frame exchanges. For example, in a client–server environment the transmission of a frame by a workstation results in a server response. Thus, the minimum wait time is $2 \times$ latency for each client–server exchange, lowering the effective throughput of the switch. Since a cross-point switching technique results in a minimal amount of latency, the effect on throughput of the delay attributable to a switching hub using this switching technique is minimal.

Store-and-forward

In comparison with a cut-through switching hub, a store-and-forward switching hub first stores an entire frame in memory prior to operating on the data fields within the frame. Once the frame has been stored, the switching hub checks the frame's integrity by performing a cyclic redundancy check (CRC) on the contents of the frame, comparing it's computed CRC against the CRC contained in the frame's Frame Check Sequence (FCS) field. If the two match, the frame is considered to be error-free and additional processing and switching will occur. Otherwise, the frame is considered to have one or more bits in error and will be discarded.

In addition to CRC checking, the storage of a frame permits filtering against various frame fields to occur. Although a few manufacturers of store-and-forward intelligent switching hubs support different types of filtering, the primary advantage advertised by such manufacturers is data integrity. Whether or not this is actually an advantage depends on how you view the additional latency introduced by the storage of a full frame in memory as well as the necessity for error checking. Concerning the latter, switches should operate error-free, so a store-and-forward switch only removes network errors, which should be negligible to start with.

When a switch removes an errored frame, the originator will retransmit the frame after a period of time. Since an errored frame arriving at its destination network address is also discarded, many persons question the necessity of error checking by a store-and-forward switching hub. However, filtering capability, if offered, may be far more useful, as you could use this capability, for example, to route protocols carried in frames to destination ports far easier than by frame destination address. This is especially true if you have hundreds or thousands of devices connected to a large switching hub. You might set up two or three filters instead of entering a large number of destination addresses into the switch.

Figure 9.8 illustrates the operation of a store-and-forward switching hub. Note that a common switch design is to use shared buffer memory to store entire frames which increases the latency associated with this type of switching hub. Since the minimum length of an Ethernet frame is 72 bytes, then the minimum one way delay or latency, not counting the switch overhead associated with the look-up table and switching fabric operation, becomes

$$96 \, \mu\text{s} + 72 \text{ bytes} \times 8 \text{ bits/byte} \times 100 \, \text{ns/bit}$$
$$\text{or} \quad 9.6 \times 10^{-6} + 576 \times 100 \times 10^{-9}$$
$$\text{or} \quad 67.2 \times 10^{-6} \text{ seconds}$$

Here 9.6 μs represents the Ethernet interframe gap, and 100 ns/ bit is the bit duration of a 10 Mbps Ethernet LAN. Thus, the minimum one-way latency of a store-and-forward Ethernet switching hub is 0.0000672 seconds, whereas a round trip minimum latency is twice that duration. For a maximum length Ethernet frame with a data field of 1500 bytes, the frame length becomes 1526 bytes. Thus, the one way maximum latency becomes

$$96\,\mu\text{s} + 1526 \text{ bytes} \times 8 \text{ bits/byte} \times 100 \text{ ns/bit}$$

or $9.6 \times 10^{-6} + 12\,208 \times 100 \times 10^{-9}$

or 0.012304 seconds

When considering the use of a Token-Ring store-and-forward switch, latency computations are more difficult as the time gap between frames, as noted in Chapter 7, depends on the number of stations on a ring connected to a switch on the port, the cable length of the ring including twice its sum of lobe cable runs, and the LAN operating rate. If only one station is connected to a port determining latency is simplified, as a ring is formed with the station and the port. Because the port acts as a participant on the ring, it can respond by passing the frame back to the originator with the delay essentially reduced to twice the latency through the

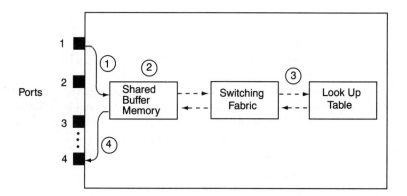

Figure 9.8 Store-and-forward switching. A store-and-forward switching hub reads the frame destination address (1) as it is placed in buffer memory (2). As the entire frame is being read into memory, a look up operation (3) is performed to obtain a destination port address. Once the entire frame is in memory a CRC check is performed, and one or more filtering operations may be performed. If the CRC check indicates that the frame is error-free, it is forwarded from memory to it's destination address (4), otherwise it is disregarded

switch. For example, a 2000 byte information field in a Token-Ring frame requires a total of 2021 bytes, including frame overhead. When received from a 16 Mbps Token-Ring network the frame would have a one way latency of

$$2021 \text{ bytes} \times \frac{8 \text{ bits}}{\text{byte}} \times \frac{1 \text{ s}}{16 \times 10^6 \text{ bit}}$$

or $\quad 16\,168 \text{ bits} \times 62.5 \, \frac{\text{ns}}{\text{bit}}$

or $\quad 0.0010105$ seconds

Hybrid

A hybrid switch supports both cut-through and store-and-forward switching, selecting the switching method based on monitoring the error rate encountered by reading the CRC at the end of each frame and comparing its value to a computed CRC performed 'on the fly' on the fields protected by the CRC. Initially the switch might set each port to a cut-through mode of operation. If too many bad frames are noted on the port, the switch will automatically set the frame processing mode to store-and-forward, permitting the CRC comparison to be performed prior to the frame being forwarded. This permits frames in error to be discarded without having them pass through the switch. Since the 'switch', no pun intended, between cut-through and store-and-forward modes of operation occurs adaptively, another term used to reference the operation of this type of switch is adaptive.

The major advantages of a hybrid switch are that it provides minimal latency when error rates are low, and discards frames by adapting to a store-and-forward switching method so that it can discard errored frames when the frame error rate rises. From an economic perspective, the hybrid switch can logically be expected to cost more than a cut-through or store-and-forward switch as its software development effort is more comprehensive. However, due to the competitive market for communications products, on occasion its price may be reduced below that of competitive switch technologies.

In addition to being categorized by their switching technique, switching hubs can be classified by their support of single or multiple addresses per port. The former method is referred to as port-based switching, whereas the latter switching method is referred to as segment-based switching.

Port-based switching

A switching hub which performs port-based switching only supports a single address per port. This restricts switching to one device per port; however, it results in a minimum amount of memory in the switch as well as provides for a relatively fast table look-up when the switch uses a destination address in a frame to obtain the port for initiating a cross-connect.

Figure 9.9 illustrates an example of the use of a port-based switching hub. In this example M user workstations use the switch to contend for the resources of N servers. If $M > N$, then a switching hub connected to Ethernet 10 Mbps LANs can support a maximum throughput of $N/2 \times 10$ Mbps, because up to $N/2$ simultaneous client–server frame flows can occur through the switch.

It is important to compare the maximum potential throughput through a switch to its rated backplane speed. If the maximum potential throughput is less than the rated backplane speed the switch will not cause delays based on the traffic being routed through the device. For example, consider a 64 port switch that has a backplane speed of 400 Mbps. If the maximum port rate is

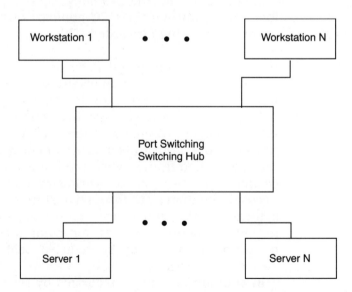

Figure 9.9 Port-based switching. A port-based switching hub associates one address with each port, minimizing the time required to match the destination address of a frame against a table of destination addresses and associated port numbers

10 Mbps, then the maximum throughput, assuming that 32 active cross-connections were simultaneously established, becomes 320 Mbps. In this example the switch has a backplane transfer capability sufficient to handle the worst-case data transfer scenario. Now let us assume that the maximum backplane data transfer capability is 200 Mbps. This would reduce the maximum number of simultaneous cross-connections capable of being serviced to 20 instead of 32, and adversely effect switch performance under certain operational conditions.

Since a port-based switching hub only has to store one address per port, search times are minimized. When combined with a pass-through or cut-through switching technique, this type of switch results in a minimal latency to include the overhead of the switch in determining the destination port of a frame.

Segment-based switching

A segment-based switching technique requires a switching hub to support multiple addresses per port. Through the use of this type of switch, you achieve additional networking flexibility because you can connect other hubs to a single segment-based switching hub port.

Figure 9.10 illustrates an example of the use of a segment-based switching hub in an Ethernet environment. Although two segments in the form of conventional hubs with multiple devices connected to each hub are shown in the lower portion of Figure 9.10, note that a segment can consist of a single device, resulting in the connection of one device to a port on a segment switching hub being similar to a connection on a port switching hub. However, unlike a port switching hub that is limited to supporting one address per port, the segment switching hub can, if necessary, support multiple devices connected to a port. Thus, the two servers connected to the switch at the top of Figure 9.10 could, if desired, be placed on a conventional hub or a high-speed hub, such as a 100BASE-T hub, which in turn would be connected to a single port on a segment switching hub.

In Figure 9.10 each conventional hub acts as a repeater, and it forwards each frame transmitted on that hub to the switching hub, regardless of whether or not the frame requires the resources of the switching hub. The segment switching hub examines the destination address of each frame against addresses in its look-up table, only forwarding those frames that warrant being forwarded. Otherwise, frames are discarded as they are local to the conventional hub. Through the use of a segment-based switching hub, you can maintain the use of local servers with respect to existing LAN segments, as well as install servers whose access is common to all network segments. The latter is illustrated in Figure 9.10 by the connection of two common servers shown at the top of the switching hub. If you obtain a store-and-forward segment switching hub which supports filtering, you could control access to common servers from individual workstations or by workstations on a particular segment. In addition, you can also use the filtering capability of a store-and-forward segment-based switching hub to control access from workstations located on one segment to workstations or servers located on another segment. Now that we have an appreciation of the general operation and utilization of switching hubs, let us examine those features which define their ability to provide different levels of operational capability. Once this has been accomplished we will turn our attention to Ethernet and Token-Ring networking techniques using different types of intelligent switches.

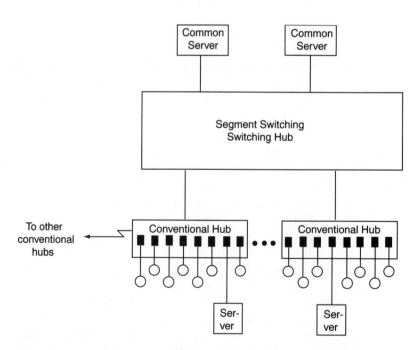

Figure 9.10 Segment-based switching. Through the use of a segment-based switching hub, you can maintain servers for use by workstations on a common network segment as well as provide access by all workstations to common servers

9.3 SWITCHING HUB FEATURES

Table 9.1 identifies eight groups of switching hub features and lists features in each group in a manner which facilitates a comparison of those features among vendor products. In examining the entries in Table 9.1 note that you can identify your organization's specific requirements for different switching hub features in the column labeled 'Requirements', and you can use the columns labeled 'Vendor A' and 'Vendor B' to compare the features of specific vendor products against your organization's requirements. Thus, you can consider Table 9.1 as a feature comparison worksheet. Although we previously obtained an overview of the switching technique and switching method, there are a few features within each of those groups that warrant an additional elaboration.

9.3.1 Switching technique

Since a store-and-forward switch physically stores an entire frame in memory, it can perform a number of operations on the frame to include CRC checking and filtering. Concerning the latter, some switch manufacturers support the ability to perform boolean comparisons of the contents of multiple fields with a frame, a capability necessary to identify protocols within certain types of frame, such as an Ethernet-SNAP frame.

Although you might be tempted to select a cut-through switch over a store-and-forward device based on present network operations, on occasion the establishment of a new network includes a new set of problems, including high frame error rates. Through the use of a hybrid switch that adapts to a switching technique based on the density of frame errors you can prepare for problems that you may not be experiencing.

9.3.2 Switching method

The addressing support provided by a segment-based switching hub has two limitations that you must consider: the maximum number of addresses supported per port and the maximum number of addresses supported by the hub. The second constraint also governs the first constraint and on occasion results in a degree of confusion when evaluating products from different manufacturers. For example, consider a 24-port

Table 9.1 Switching hub feature comparison

Feature	Requirement	Vendor A	Vendor B
Switching technique			
Cut-through	_____	_____	_____
Store-and-forward	_____	_____	_____
Error checking	_____	_____	_____
Filtering	_____	_____	_____
MAC address	_____	_____	_____
By protocol	_____	_____	_____
Hybrid	_____	_____	_____
Switching method			
Port-based switching	_____	_____	_____
Segment-based switching	_____	_____	_____
Maximum addresses per port	_____	_____	_____
Maximum addresses per unit	_____	_____	_____
Backplane throughput			
Simultaneous cross-connects	_____	_____	_____
Operating rate of cross-connects	_____	_____	_____
Maximum cross-connect throughput	_____	_____	_____
Backplane throughput (Mbps)	_____	_____	_____
Port support			
Ethernet			
Number of 10BASE-T ports	_____	_____	_____
Number of 10BASE-2 ports	_____	_____	_____
Number of 10BASE-F ports	_____	_____	_____
Number of AUI ports	_____	_____	_____
Token-Ring			
Number of Token-Ring ports	_____	_____	
High speed port operation			
Full-duplex transmission	_____	_____	_____
Fat pipe operation	_____	_____	_____
100BASE-T operation	_____	_____	_____
FDDI support	_____	_____	_____
ATM support	_____	_____	_____
Flow control support			
None	_____	_____	_____
Backpressure	_____	_____	_____
Server software module	_____	_____	_____
Statistics			
Peak/current utilizations	_____	_____	_____
Errors	_____	_____	_____
Virtual LAN creation support			
Number of stations/ports supported/group	_____	_____	_____
Number of groups supported	_____	_____	_____
Intra-group communications support	_____	_____	_____

10 Mbps/port Ethernet segment-based switching hub with a maximum address support of 8192 addresses for the hub and a maximum port address support of 1024. If you connect eight segments with 1024 workstations and servers to each hub port, you would reach the maximum address support of the switch. Then 16 ports would not be capable of being used. Owing to this pair of addressing constraints, you may wish to consider the segmentation of LAN segments to balance the addresses associated with each switch port as well as to improve the throughput of the switch. Concerning the latter, if you only use eight ports, the maximum number of simultaneous cross-connections would be four, resulting in a maximum throughput of 4×10 Mbps or 40 Mbps. If you were to re-segment your LAN segments and use all 24 ports of the switch, the maximum throughput that you could obtain would increase to 12×10 Mbps or 120 Mbps, a threefold increase. Of course, to obtain a given level of throughput based on a maximum number of cross-connections, the backplane transfer rate of the switch must equal or exceed the throughput obtained by the cross-connections.

9.3.3 Backplane throughput

The four entries in the backplane throughput group provide you with the ability to determine if and under what conditions the switching hub's architecture results in the switch becoming a bottleneck. To illustrate how you can use those entries, let us assume that we anticipate acquiring a 48-port 10BASE-T switch.

A 48-port switching hub will support a maximum of 24 simultaneous cross-connections. Because the operating rate of a 10BASE-T cross-connect is 10 Mbps, the maximum cross-connect throughput becomes 24×10 Mbps or 240 Mbps. If the rated backplane throughput of the switch is 240 Mbps or higher, its architecture will support its maximum cross-connect capability; however, if its backplane throughput is less than 240 Mbps this means that the design of the switch is not sufficient to support its maximum simultaneous cross-connection capability, and delays will occur as the number of active cross-connections through the switch increases. Those delays are proportional to the difference between the maximum cross-connect throughput and the backplane throughput, with an increase in the difference between the two resulting in an increase in frames being held in buffer areas within the switch.

9.3.4 Port support

The port support entries listed in Table 9.1 refer to the number and type of network connections that the switch supports. Because some hubs are designed as modular units, you may also wish to consider the expansion capability of the switch to add additional ports.

The types of port listed under the port support group purposely did not include high-speed connections which are listed in the next group. The rationale for this is twofold. First, switch manufacturers have different restrictions concerning the mixture of conventional and high-speed ports that are supported by their products. Secondly, although almost all hub manufacturers include at least three connectors on their conventional Ethernet ports (10BASE-T, 10BASE-2 and an Attachment Unit Interface), many hub manufacturers only support one method of high-speed port operation. Thus, it is normally clearer to focus our attention on high speed ports as a separate entity.

9.3.5 High-speed port operation

The cross-connection between the origination and destination port occurs on a frame-by-frame basis with the switching fabric in the switch building and removing each connection. When the connection has been established, other data sources routed to the same destination address are precluded by the switching fabric from interfering with the flow of data. Thus, this precludes the possibility of collisions occurring in an Ethernet environment. Recognizing this fact, switching hub designers were able to use the second wire pair of conventional Ethernet, previously used for collision recognition, as a path for the simultaneous transmission in the opposite direction, in effect obtaining a full-duplex transmission capability. In a Token-Ring environment if there is only one station on a port the need to pass tokens and repeat frames is eliminated, permitting full-duplex operations. Support for full-duplex Token-Ring operation is accomplished through the use of modified Token-Ring adapter cards. Such modified adapters do not include a repeater path, which is normally used to allow a frame appearing on the receive path of a lobe to be placed on its transmit path. Figure 9.11 compares the operation of conventional and full-duplex operating Token-Ring adapter cards.

In examining the illustration in the left part of Figure 9.11 note that although the title is 'conventional', in reality a conventional

Token-Ring adapter permits both reception and transmission of data to occur at the same time. Although this is indeed a full-duplex operation, only received data can be simultaneously placed on the lobe's transmit path. If a workstation is receiving a frame and has data to send, the frame must circulate back to the originator and be converted into a token. Then, on receipt of the token the workstation can transmit data. In comparison, when one Token-Ring station is connected to a port on a Token-Ring switch, as a frame is received the port can generate a new frame in the opposite direction, providing a true full-duplex operation in which different frames are simultaneously transmitted and received.

Although many vendors imply that the support of full-duplex transmission doubles the throughput of a 10BASE-T or Token-Ring port to 20 or 36 Mbps, in actuality your ability to increase the throughput through a port depends on the type of traffic supported by the port. For example, connecting a workstation to a full-duplex port would probably provide a negligible gain in throughput because most client–server communications are essentially half-duplex. However, the attachment of a server via a full-duplex port would enable the server to process query N while transmitting response $N - 1$ to query $N - 1$. Thus, you can obtain a degree of overlap of operations by using a server on a full-duplex switching hub port. Unfortunately, it is highly unlikely the

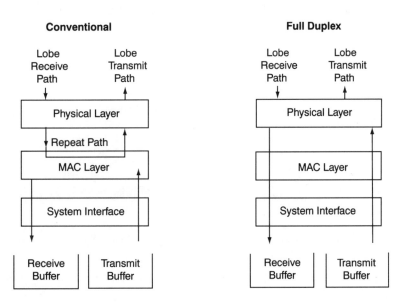

Figure 9.11 Comparing conventional and full-duplex Token-Ring adapter card operators

overlap of transmission and reception of data will occur for more than a small portion of time throughout the day. Thus, although throughput will increase through the use of a full-duplex port, the average transfer rate will be far less than double.

Fat pipe

A fat pipe is a term used by some vendors to represent a group of N ports that operate together as an entity, providing a throughput of $N \times$ (port operating rate) or $N \times 2 \times$ (port operating rate) if full duplex transmission is supported by each port in the fat pipe group of ports. For example, consider an Ethernet switch with a fat pipe that can be constructed through a grouping of five 10 Mbps ports. This will provide a maximum throughput of 50 Mbps or 100 Mbps if each port supports full-duplex data transfer. However, as previously noted, your ability to obtain anywhere near a sustained level of full-duplex data transfer is doubtful, and probably does not justify the purchase of full-duplex adapters to support workstations connected to switch ports.

Figure 9.12 illustrates a fat pipe formed by the grouping of five port connections which function as an entity. Note that in this example the fat pipe is used to provide a connection between a server and a switching hub which is the primary application for the use of a fat pipe, providing nodes with a higher level of throughput. This is because access to modern servers, as well as their ability to provide responses, are a typical constraint of heavily utilized 10 Mbps Ethernet and 16 Mbps Token-Ring networks.

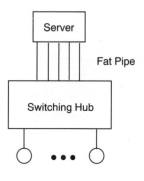

Legend: ◯ workstations and/or servers

Figure 9.12 Using a fat pipe. A fat pipe is a physical grouping of *n* ports that function as an entity

Once a frame destined for the server has been received by the switching hub, it is subdivided and transmitted over five physical connections. Because the server must reconstruct the frame, special software is required to operate on the server. Thus, the software must be compatible with the LAN operating system used by the server.

One of the problems associated with the use of fat pipes as well as the use of different types of high speed ports, such as 100BASE-T, FDDI, or ATM, is the situation in which a workstation query results in a lengthy response from the server. To illustrate this problem let us assume that we are using an Ethernet switching hub with a workstation connected to a port at 10 Mbps, whereas a server is connected to five 10 Mbps ports that form a fat pipe. Since the fat pipe response is at an operating rate of $n \times 10$ Mbps, whereas the workstation is connected to the hub at 10 Mbps, within a short period of time frames can be expected to overflow the port's receive buffer storage capacity, resulting in frame loss which requires the server to retransmit lost frames. To limit frame loss, vendors added buffer storage to their high-speed ports. However, no amount of buffer storage can prevent all frame loss, resulting in some vendors adding flow control support to their switches. Prior to discussing the methods commonly used to regulate traffic between high-speed and lower operating rate ports, let us examine other common methods used by intelligent switch vendors to provide a high-speed data transfer capability between a switch port and an attached device.

100BASE-T connection

The inclusion of 100BASE-T port support is similar to a fat pipe; however, an increase in throughput now occurs via the use of a single port connection instead of multiple port connections. Similar to the operation of a fat pipe, the use of a 100BASE-T connection can occur in either a half- or full-duplex operating mode. In addition, frame loss via a 100BASE-T connection is compensated for by buffer memory within the switching hub, but does not preclude the eventual loss of frames when a lengthy response to a query occurs.

FDDI and ATM connections

FDDI and ATM ports are incorporated into some intelligent switching hubs to provide a high-speed data transfer capability between the switch and an attached device. Although many users employ high-speed ports for use with servers, such ports can also be used to develop a hierarchical network of conventional hubs, switching hubs and high-speed backbone hubs. An example of the creation of a hub hierarchy is shown in Figure 9.13.

In the hub hierarchy illustrated in Figure 9.13, a FDDI hub is used to form a network consisting of three middle tier switching hubs. The switching hubs in turn support port switching or port and segment switching, with the connection of conventional hubs forming the lower tier in the three tier hub hierarchy. Through the use of one FDDI port on each switching hub, access is obtained to an FDDI ring constructed through the use of an FDDI hub. Assuming that each switching hub supports two different types of high-speed port, the second port might be a 100BASE-T port used to provide access at 100 Mbps between the switch and an attached server. Thus, this configuration allows users attached to a conventional hub to access servers on that hub, to access a server connected to the switching hub that their conventional hub is connected to, or to access a server connected to a different switching hub.

Although the FDDI operating rate is fixed at 100 Mbps there are two ATM LAN operating rates that you must consider. One rate is

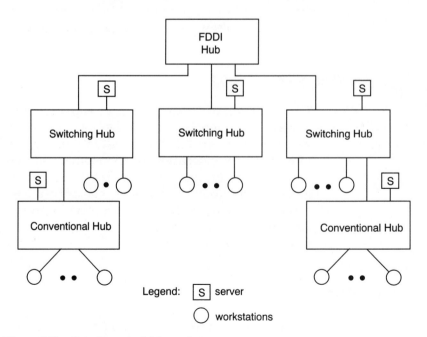

Figure 9.13 Creating a hub hierarchy

25 Mbps, whereas the second rate is approximately 155 Mbps. Because the lower rate may provide only a marginal improvement over full duplex 10BASE-T and full duplex 16 Mbps Token-Ring operations, it might be advisable to ignore that technology.

9.3.6 Flow control support

Flow control represents the orderly regulation of the transmission of information between devices, a necessity whenever there is a positive speed differential between the source and destination of information. Although some vendors include buffer storage to act as a temporary holding area until transmission ceases or the amount of data flow is reduced, no amount of buffer storage can guarantee data integrity. Thus, you can expect to lose frames if a switching hub does not provide flow control to regulate the flow of traffic between ports that have different operating rates.

The effect of frame loss depends on the overall traffic supported by the hub. If you have several servers connected to high-speed ports and short queries result in lengthy transmissions, the loss of frames is compensated for by server retransmissions. Under certain situations the additional retransmissions lock out responses to other workstation queries, and can actually result in a level of performance being less than that obtainable through the use of a conventional hub. For this reason the use of high-speed ports should normally be accompanied by the use of flow control, either the use of backpressure in an Ethernet environment or a server software module which works in tandem with the switch in both Ethernet and Token-Ring environments.

Backpressure

Backpressure is a term used to represent the generation of a false collision signal. Because a collision signal causes an Ethernet workstation or server to delay further transmission based on an exponential backoff algorithm, it provides a mechanism for implementing flow control. That is, once buffer storage in the hub has reached a predefined level of occupancy, the switch will generate a collision signal. As the transmitting device delays further transmission, the hub's destination port has the opportunity to empty the contents of it's buffer, precluding the occurrence of data loss.

Since backpressure requires the use of a second wire pair, it is mutually exclusive with full-duplex transmission. If you require full-duplex transmission on a high-speed port and want to preclude the loss of frames via flow control, you must turn to the use of a server software module.

Server software module

When this book was being prepared, switching hub vendors indicated they were developing software to operate under NetWare and Windows NT that would regulate the flow of data between hub ports and servers. Once such products become available, they will support full-duplex transmission, as well as precluding the occurrence of frame loss, something currently lacking in the switching hub marketplace.

9.3.7 Statistics

To assist network managers and administrators in performing their management functions, vendors have added a variety of statistical information that can be retrieved through a management port. Such statistics primarily fall into two areas: utilization statistics and error statistics. Utilization statistics commonly indicate data transfer between ports, as well as on a frame address basis and on a utilization level basis. Concerning error statistics, although they vary by the type of LAN supported some common errors have been reported for both Ethernet and Token-Ring connections, such as CRC errors and line coding violations. By noting the error density by port and frame addresses for frames in error, switch error statistics can provide a valuable mechanism for locating and correcting the conditions that cause frame errors.

9.3.8 Virtual LAN creation support

A virtual LAN represents a network segment created through software as opposed to the laying of a physical cable. Through the use of software you might create one or more virtual LANs based on organizational projects, or group persons based upon their job function or another activity.

The creation of a virtual LAN occurs through the coding of frame forwarding tables in an intelligent switching hub into logical segments based on a predefined criterion. Although that criterion is usually the station address on a switch port, if the switch supports filtering the criterion could be based on other factors, such as the network protocol being transported in a frame.

Figure 9.14 illustrates the creation of two virtual LANs on a four port Ethernet switching hub; however, readers should note that the software table creation concept is similarly performed by a Token-Ring switching hub that supports the creation of virtual LANs. In examining the virtual LAN table located in the lower portion of Figure 9.14, note that two virtual LANs were created by, in effect, cross-connecting, when necessary, ports 1 to 3 and 2 to 4. Then stations A, B, C and F are logically grouped into one network segment, and stations D, E, G and H are grouped into a different logically created network segment.

The previous example illustrated the creation of virtual LANs based on the port connection to a switching hub. More complex software permits the creation of virtual LANs based on the station MAC address. Although each station in Figure 9.14 was restricted to residing on a single virtual LAN, this is a current restriction based on available software. More advanced forms of virtual LAN support could support workstation and server membership of multiple virtual LANs. However, the ability to move from one virtual LAN to another represents a bridging or routing function which must then be added to the switch.

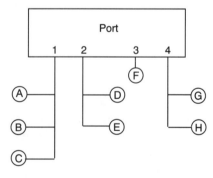

Virtual LAN Table

Station	Port Number	Virtual LAN Segment
A, B, C	1	1
D, E	2	2
F	3	1
G,H	4	2

Figure 9.14 Virtual LAN table entries for creating two virtual networks on a four port switch. Through the coding of frame forwarding tables, switch ports can be logically grouped to form virtual LANs

Returning to Table 9.1 and focusing our attention on the virtual LAN creation support group entries, note that the first entry, 'number of stations/ports per group', refer to the physical size of virtual LANs supported by a switching hub. In comparison, the second entry, 'number of groups supported', refer to the maximum number of virtual LANs that can be supported. The last entry, concerning intra-group communications, refer to the ability of the switch to permit a member of one virtual LAN to communicate with a member of another virtual LAN. As previously discussed, to do so requires the switch to support bridging or routing.

9.4 NETWORKING TECHNIQUES

In concluding this chapter on intelligent switches we will turn our attention to examining several networking techniques that take advantage of the switching capability of Ethernet and Token-Ring switching hubs. Perhaps the first place to start is by following up the reference in Chapter 8 concerning the use of switching hubs in alleviating network bottlenecks caused by the transmission of images on a network. In actuality, any user application that creates a bottleneck on a conventional hub should be considered for network redistribution through the use of a switching hub. Thus, the first network technique that we will examine is network redistribution.

9.4.1 Network redistribution

Network redistribution involves the movement of bandwidth-intensive workstations from conventional hubs, connecting them directly to ports on an intelligent switch. Figure 9.15 illustrates an example of network redistribution through the use of an intelligent switching hub.

In the left part of Figure 9.15 a conventional hub is shown providing support for n nodes to a common server. Assuming that two workstations require access to a visual database, transmit or receive large files, or perform other bandwidth intensive applications those workstations were redistributed onto an intelligent switch as shown in the right part of Figure 9.15. Note that only one server is shown in the 'after' network schematic, with the server relocated from the conventional hub to the intelligent switching hub, with the server connected to the intelligent switching hub by either a fat pipe or high-speed connection. If a

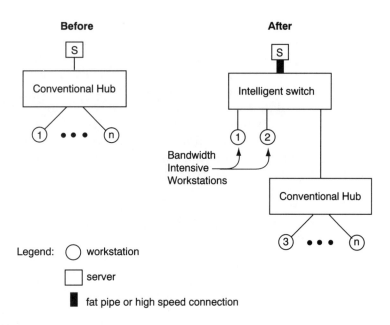

Figure 9.15 Network redistribution. Through the movement of bandwidth intensive workstations off conventional hubs, you can minimize the effect of bottlenecks they cause on other workstations remaining connected to conventional hubs

conventional connection were used the redistribution of workstations would have a negligible effect on performance, as access to the server would not increase, only enhancing any peer-to-peer communications that may occur.

9.4.2 Server segmentation

Because access to data on servers is normally the reason why network performance degrades, another technique commonly used is to segment servers. Figure 9.16 illustrates an example of server segmentation obtained through the use of an intelligent switching hub.

In the top part of Figure 9.16 two servers are shown on a network consisting of interconnected conventional hubs. In this example access to either server is constrained by the operating rate of the network. For example, if the top portion of Figure 9.16 were to represent a 10BASE-T network the maximum bandwidth to a server would be 10 Mbps, which is the operating rate of the LAN, whereas the average bandwidth would be 10 Mbps/n, where n represents the total number of nodes on the network.

Through the use of an intelligent switching, hub servers can be placed on their own network segment, as illustrated in the lower part of Figure 9.16. In addition, through the use of a fat pipe or high-speed connection between each server and the switch, you can enhance access to each server.

If you were simply to move each conventional hub onto a port on the switch your ability to enhance network access would be limited. This limitation would result from the fact that the simultaneous access of workstations on different conventional hubs to different servers only provides the ability to double bandwidth. Thus, you would probably want to consider connecting high-activity workstations directly to the switch which is shown in the lower part of Figure 9.16.

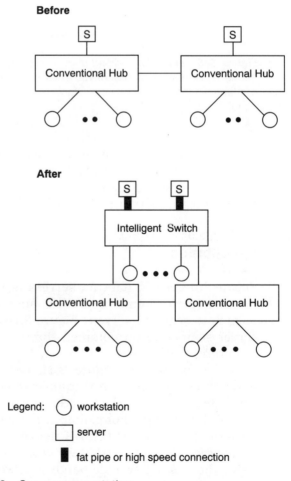

Figure 9.16   Server segmentation

9.4.3 Network segmentation

A third networking technique commonly associated with the use of intelligent switching hubs is network segmentation. Although the concept is similar to network segmentation performed by bridges and routers, the use of intelligent switches provides a significant increase in network configuration flexibility. To illustrate this increased flexibility consider Figure 9.17, in which one large Token-Ring network has been segmented into three via the use of a Token-Ring switch.

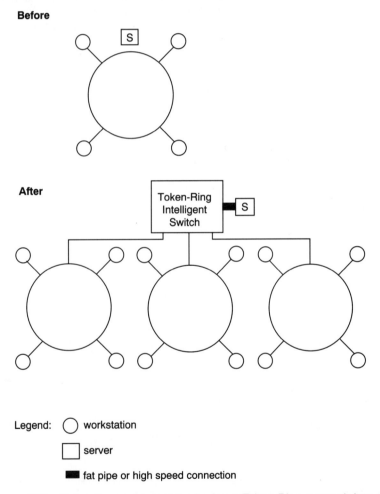

Before

After

Legend: ◯ workstation

☐ server

▬ fat pipe or high speed connection

Figure 9.17 Network segmentation of a large Token-Ring network into three networks. Network segmentation enables large networks to be subdivided into small networks. When a high speed connection to the server is used, overall performance is substantially enhanced

As indicated in our coverage of Token-Ring networks their performance in the form of their frame rate depends on the number of stations on the network, the total length of cabling used to form the network and the network operating rate. By reducing the size of the network you increase its frame transfer rate, in effect enhancing the performance of each subnetwork. In addition, through the use of a fat pipe or high-speed connection to the server operating at 100 Mbps the segmented network would triple the server access capability in comparison to the non-segmented network, and still have additional capability that you could use by adding additional network segments to the switch. Thus, network segmentation and the use of fat pipes or high-speed connections from a switch port to a server provides the capability to substantially enhance network performance.

10

TRANSMISSION OPTIMIZATION TECHNIQUES

Until now, the primary focus of this book has been upon the creation and use of mathematical models to predict the performance of different types of local area networks and internetworking devices. In this chapter we will turn our attention to the use of several optimization techniques which, when incorporated into bridges and routers, will enhance the efficiency of internet transmission. In addition, we will examine the use of different types of network interface cards or adapters, which when used in a workstation enhance its ability to transfer information onto and receive information from the network.

Techniques that we will examine in this chapter include the use of filtering, precedence and express queuing, data compression, frame truncation, and the switched telephone network to supplement the use of leased lines during peak transmission periods. Readers should note that most remote bridge and router manufacturers provide one or more of the techniques described in this chapter. However, readers should also note that the efficiency of the implementation of each technique varies between vendors. In addition, most vendors provide only a small subset of the techniques covered in this chapter. Since the value of each technique is based upon your specific networking requirements, you will have to compare the operational results of each technique against your specific communications environment to determine which techniques provide a higher level of networking capability, and you can then use this chapter as a guide in your equipment selection process.

In examining network interface cards our focus of attention will be upon different hardware design features, and the effect of those features upon the data transfer capability of the adapter. You can also use this information as a guide to facilitate your equipment selection process.

10.1 FILTERING

Filtering is the most common transmission optimization technique incorporated into remote bridges and routers. Although most devices support a predefined filtering capability in which source and/or destination frame addresses are entered into a filtering table during the equipment installation process, other devices permit an authorized administrator to dynamically change the filtering tables since few networks are static.

10.1.1 Local versus remote filtering

Through the use of filtering you can control the number and types of packets that are forwarded across a transmission circuit linking two remote bridges or routers. Although you can also use filtering to control the flow of data between two local area networks connected by a local bridge, we will focus our attention upon the application of filtering by devices interconnected via wide area transmission facilities. This is because the application of filtering by devices connected via wide area transmission facilities directly affects the required transmission rate linking the filtering devices. Because the monthly cost of a wide area transmission facility is proportional to its operating rate, the ability to lower the required operating rate through the use of filtering can be expected to reduce your organization's transmission cost. In comparison, the use of filtering by a local bridge has a less significant effect. First, it usually has no effect upon cost, because local cabling links each network at the common local bridge as illustrated at the top of Figure 10.1. Secondly, the use of filtering has a lesser effect upon performance when performed by a local bridge than when performed by a remote bridge. This is because the WAN link connecting two remote bridges or routers operates at a fraction of the operating rate of each network. Thus, the removal of frames via filtering as illustrated in the lower part of Figure 10.1 has a more pronounced effect upon a lower operating rate circuit than local cable connecting two higher operating rate local area networks.

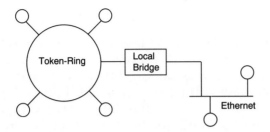

Filtering has no effect upon the cabling used to connect local networks. Since both networks operate at Mbps rates the removal of frames based on filtering usually has a negligible effect upon network performance

Remote bridging

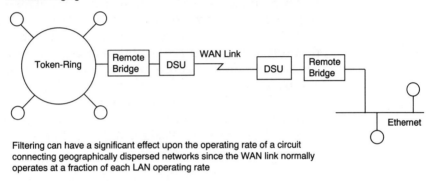

Filtering can have a significant effect upon the operating rate of a circuit connecting geographically dispersed networks since the WAN link normally operates at a fraction of each LAN operating rate

Figure 10.1 Effect of local versus remote bridge filtering

10.1.2 Filtering methods

Several types of filtering are supported by bridges and routers. Two of the most common methods of filtering frames are based upon the use of address and service fields in a frame.

Address field filtering

The most basic type of filtering is performed by bridges which operate at the MAC sublayer of the OSI Reference Model's data link layer. Operating at this layer, bridges are transparent to high-level protocols which function at the network layer of the OSI Reference Model. Thus, the primary mechanism used for filtering is based upon the use of the destination and source address fields within Token-Ring and Ethernet/IEEE 802.3 frames. For example, consider the IEEE Token-Ring functional addresses listed in Table 2.4 in Chapter 2. Assume that you wanted to preclude the transmission of Token-Ring functional address frames from being forwarded onto the Ethernet network illustrated in Figure 10.1 because those frames normally are irrelevant to stations on the Ethernet network. To do so you would set your bridge to filter all frames with destination addresses equivalent to the block of destination addresses assigned by the IEEE to the Token-Ring functional addresses listed in Table 2.4.

To illustrate the effect of functional address filtering, consider the active monitor address listed in Table 2.4. The active monitor on a Token-Ring network transmits an active monitor frame every seven seconds, or 12 343 times each day. This frame is used to notify the standby monitors that the active monitor is operational and the frame is irrelevant to an Ethernet network. Thus, the filtering of just this one frame reduces the flow of data from a Token-Ring network onto an Ethernet network by approximately 13 000 frames per day. Even when two Token-Ring networks are interconnected active monitor frames should be filtered, as each network has its own active monitor. Thus, this filtering example is applicable to both Token-Ring to Ethernet as well as Token-Ring to Token-Ring bridging.

Service access point filtering

Filtering based upon destination and source address fields is supported by essentially all bridges. A more sophisticated level of filtering supported by some bridges is based upon the DSAP and SSAP addresses carried within the information field of Token-Ring and Ethernet/IEEE 802.3 frames.

Figure 10.2 illustrates the general format of the conversion of a Token-Ring frame into an Ethernet frame. The DSAP and SSAP can be considered as post office boxes which identify locations where information is left and received to and from higher level layers of the OSI Reference Model. For example, the transportation of an electronic mail message used by a higher network process would have a defined DSAP. Thus, a bridge which includes the capability to perform filtering based upon DSAP and SSAP addresses would provide you with the ability to perform filtering at the application level, as well as to add a degree of security to your internet if you wish to restrict the movement of frames carrying certain types of information between networks.

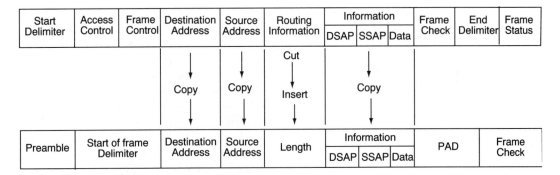

Figure 10.2 Token-Ring to IEEE 802.3 frame conversion. The conversion of a Token-Ring frame to an IEEE 802.3 frame results in the copying of the contents of the destination and source address fields as well as the subfields within the information field

10.2 PRECEDENCE AND EXPRESS QUEUING

In Chapter 4 we examined the use of waiting line analysis or queuing to determine an optimum line operating rate to link remote bridges and routers, the effect of single- and dual-port equipment upon internet performance, and buffer memory requirements of network devices. In doing so we assumed that the servicing of queues was based upon a first-in, first-out basis. That is, the arrival of frame n followed by frame $n + 1$ into a queue would result in a remote bridge or router transmitting frame n prior to transmitting frame $n + 1$. Although most remote bridges and routers operate on a first-in, first-out service basis, other devices may support precedence and/or express queuing. In doing so they provide a level of performance which may considerably exceed the performance of other devices that do not support such queuing options during periods of peak network activity. To illustrate the advantages of precedence and express queuing, let us first focus our attention upon the operation of first-in, first-out queuing and some of the problems associated with this queuing method.

10.2.1 First-in, first-out queuing

When first-in, first-out queuing is used messages are queued in the order in which they are received. This is the simplest method of queuing, as a single physical and logical buffer area is used to store data and all messages are assumed to have the same priority of service. The software used by the bridge or router

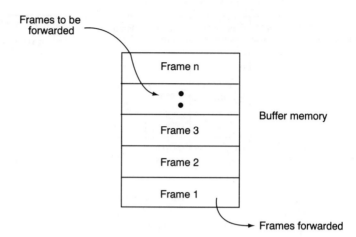

Figure 10.3 First-in, first-out queuing, in which frames are forwarded in their order of arrival into buffer memory

simply extracts each frame based upon its position in the queue. Figure 10.3 illustrates first-in, first-out queuing.

Queuing problems

The major problems associated with first-in, first-out queuing involve the effect of this queuing method upon a mixture of interactive and batch internet transmission during peak network utilization periods. To illustrate the problems associated with first-in, first-out queuing, consider the internet illustrated in Figure 8.4 in which a Token-Ring network is connected to an Ethernet network through the use of a pair of remote bridges.

Mixing file transfer and interactive sessions

Let us assume that station E on the Ethernet initiates a file transfer to station C on the Token-Ring. Let us also assume that the Ethernet network is a 10BASE-T network operating at 10 Mbps and the wide area network transmission facility operates at 56 kbps.

If the stations on the Ethernet are IBM PC or compatible computers with industry standard architecture (ISA) Ethernet adapter boards, the maximum transfer rate is normally less than 300 000 bytes per second. Using that figure and assuming that station E transmitted for one second in which each frame was the maximum length of 1500 information field bytes, not including

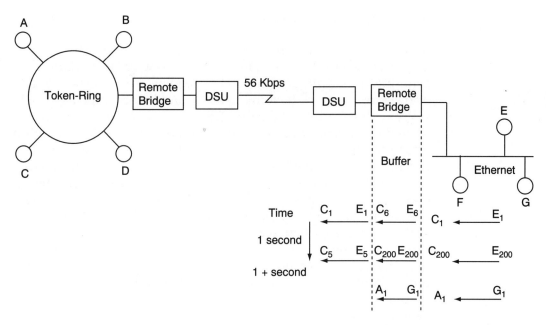

Figure 10.4 First-in, first-out queuing delays. First-in, first-out queuing can seriously degrade transmission when an interactive query occurs after the initiation of a long file transfer operation

frame overhead, a total of 300 000 bytes/1500 bytes per frame, or 200 frames, would be presented to the remote bridge. At 56 kbps the bridge would forward 56 000/(8 × 1500), or approximately five frames, not considering the WAN protocol and frame overhead. Thus, at the end of one second there could be 195 frames in the bridge's buffer, as illustrated in the lower right portion of Figure 10.4.

Now let us assume that slightly after this one second has passed, station G on the Ethernet transmits a query to an application operating on station A on the Token-Ring. The 195 frames in the buffer of the remote bridge would require approximately 40 seconds (195 frames × 1500 bytes/frame × 8 bits/byte ÷ 56 000 bps) to be emptied from the buffer and placed onto the line prior to the frame from station G being placed onto the line. Thus, first-in, first-out queuing can seriously degrade transmission from an Ethernet to another Ethernet or to a Token-Ring network when file transfer and interactive transmission occurs between networks. The reverse situation in which transmission is from a Token-Ring to an Ethernet or between two Token-Ring networks does not result in such significant problems, since a priority mechanism is built into the Token-Ring frame, which results in a more equitably shared use of the network bandwidth than is achievable on an Ethernet network.

Workstation retransmissions

In the preceding example we noted the potential for the delay of 40 seconds until data from station G were transmitted. In actuality this will almost never happen, since most remote bridges and routers have installation guidelines which typically suggest that you configure buffer memory to store only a few seconds' worth of data. However, doing so results in a workstation attempting to transfer a file retransmitting frames that were not accepted by the bridge or router, adding to network traffic as well as the level of network utilization. This will have a detrimental effect upon a series of stations attempting concurrent file transfer operations as well as stations performing interactive client–server activities when file transfer operations are in effect. In certain situations buffer queuing delays added to frame retransmission time can result in file transfer timeouts, which result in the termination of the file transfer session. In other situations, random delays in interactive sessions will frustrate network users. Due to such problems, some remote bridge and router manufacturers have incorporated precedence queuing and express queuing into their products.

10.2.2 Precedence queuing

Precedence queuing was probably the first method used by remote bridge and router manufacturers to enhance the transmission of internet traffic through device buffer memory. Under precedence queuing data entering a communications device, such as a remote bridge or router, are sorted by priority into separate queues, as illustrated in Figure 10.5. Because a bridge operates at the MAC sublayer of the OSI Reference Model's data link layer, a logical question concerns the method by which a bridge can recognize different frame priorities.

Methods used

In actuality, a remote bridge performing precedence queuing does not look for a priority byte, as there is none to look for. Instead, the bridge can use one of two methods: examining the DSAP address in a frame or the frame length. The examination of DSAP addresses permits the bridge to recognize certain predefined applications and prioritize the routing of frames onto the wide area network transmission facility based upon those priorities.

The second method, which is based upon the frame length, presumes that interactive traffic is carried by shorter length frames than file transfer and program load traffic.

Operation

Figure 10.5 illustrates the operation of precedence queuing based upon frame length within the buffer area of a remote bridge. In this example the physical buffer area is subdivided into logical partitions, with each partition used to queue frames whose length falls within a predefined range of values.

Frames from the attached local area network are placed into logical partitions based upon the length of the frame. For an Ethernet network this could entail subdivision of the maximum length of 1500 bytes of the information field of that frame. Once logical queues have formed the servicing of the queues can occur on a round-robin or a priority basis. The lower portion of Figure 10.5 illustrates a priority extraction process in which for every

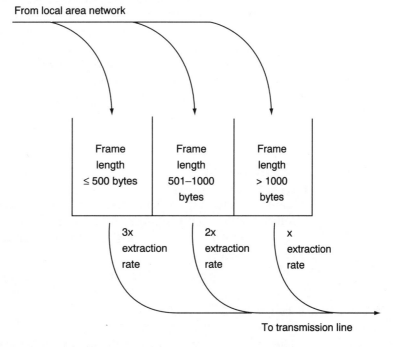

Figure 10.5 Precedence queuing based upon frame length. Frames are placed into logical queues based upon their length. In this example, the Ethernet information field length was used as the queue placement variable. Service of the queues can be on a round-robin or a priority basis, with the latter shown in this example

frame whose length exceeds 1000 bytes which is serviced and placed on the transmission line, two frames with a length of 501 to 1000 bytes and three frames whose length is less than or equal to 500 bytes are serviced from their queues and placed on the transmission line.

10.2.3 Express queuing

Express queuing is a term used by one bridge and router manufacturer to represent the allocation of transmission bandwidth based upon the destination address of frames in the queue, as well as the number of frames with the same destination address in the queue. That is, under express queuing transmission bandwidth is allocated so that in any given interval of time each destination address will be assigned to either a fixed portion of the WAN bandwidth or a smaller portion if there are fewer frames queued with that destination address. This technique recognizes the fact that interactive transmission is represented by a low rate of frame flow. Therefore, this type of transmission only requires a portion of the total transmission bandwidth to obtain an acceptable flow over the wide area transmission facility. The actual method by which bandwidth is allocated is based upon an algorithm designed not only to provide interactive transmission priority service but also to ensure that multiple concurrent file transfers share the majority of the remaining bandwidth in an equitable manner which prevents timeouts from occurring.

10.3 DATA COMPRESSION

Unless data are purely random they contain a degree of redundancy. Data compression can be considered a process which uses one or more algorithms to reduce or eliminate data redundancies.

10.3.1 Compression ratio

The efficiency of compression is referred to as the compression ratio, which represents the ratio of the number of original bytes in a frame to the number of compressed bytes. A high compression ratio represents either efficient compression, data with a high level of redundancy, or both.

Since data carried by information frames vary over time with respect to their content and the amount of data redundancy, the compression ratio will also vary over time. Normally you can expect a compression-performing remote bridge or router to have an average compression ratio between 2.0 and 2.5. Allowing for the fact that the wide area network transmission protocol has a 10–20% overhead, the effect of compression typically results in the doubling of the information-carrying capacity of a circuit. That is, as a general rule you can expect a 56 kbps digital circuit to transfer an average of 112 kbps of LAN frame data when compression-performing remote bridges or routers are used.

10.3.2 Compression methods

There are three main categories into which compression methods fall: byte-oriented, statistical, and table lookup or dictionary-based.

Byte-oriented

Byte-oriented compression techniques examine the bit composition of each byte, comparing the composition of the current byte with one or more succeeding bytes. If redundancies are noted, the algorithm replaces a series of bytes with a new sequence which eliminates those redundancies. Some of the more popular byte-oriented compression techniques include run length encoding, half-byte encoding, and null suppression.

Null suppression simply results in the substitution of a compression-indicating character and null count character for a sequence of nulls. In comparison, run length encoding permits any character sequence to be reduced by the use of a three-character sequence to replace a repeated run of any character. The three-character sequence includes a compression-indicating character, the character in the run, and a count character.

Half-byte encoding is a compression technique which results in the replacement of a sequence of characters that has the same half-byte bit composition, such as a string of numerics, by encoding two numerics into a byte. Then the reduced byte sequence is prefixed by a compression-indicating character and a count byte. Readers are referred to the author's book *Data and Image Compression (fourth edition)*, published by John Wiley & Sons, for detailed information concerning the operation of byte-oriented, statistical, and dictionary-based compression algorithms as well as for examples of program code used to implement different compression techniques.

Statistical

Statistical compression algorithms replace frequently occurring bytes by short codes and less frequently occurring bytes by longer codes. The net result of this replacement process is to reduce the average number of bits required to represent a character from eight to a lesser number, typically between four and five, resulting in a compression ratio of 2:1 or less. In replacing each fixed length byte of eight bits, the replacement process results in the use of a variable length code. This variable length code is constructed based upon a statistical compression algorithm, the Huffman coding technique being the most popular method employed. This technique results in the encoded compressed data bits having a prefix property which makes it instantaneously decodable. Thus, decompression performed according to the Huffman algorithm minimizes delays in comparison to the use of other compression methods. Although this was an important consideration during the era of Intel 8088 microprocessors, the widespread availability of Intel 80486 and other modern high-performance microprocessors has reduced the decompression times associated with other compression techniques to the point where they do not adversely affect the throughput of data. Readers are again referred to the author's book *Data and Image Compression (fourth edition)*, published by John Wiley & Sons, for information concerning Huffman coding of data and the instantaneous decoding of such data.

Dictionary-based

Since the replacement of frequently occurring bytes by short codes and less frequently occurring bytes by longer codes results in a reduction in the average number of bits required to represent a character, it is logical to assume greater efficiencies can be obtained by substituting codes for strings of characters. This logic resulted in the development of dictionary-based compression algorithms in which transmitted data are placed into a dictionary and the location of characters and strings of characters (pointers) is transmitted instead of the actual data.

The most popular dictionary-based compression algorithm originates from the work of Jacob Ziv and Abraham Lempel at Haifa University during the late 1970s. More modern versions of their algorithm are referred to as Lempel–Ziv or LZ-based and they differ in the method used to flush the dictionary, the number of pointers and size of the dictionary, and how pointers are coded in the compressed output.

One popular version of LZ coding is more commonly known as Lempel–Ziv–Welsh and is the method used in the CCITT V.42bis modem compression standard.

10.3.3 Performance considerations

Although compression is standardized for use in modems, the same is not true for its use in remote bridges and routers. This means not only that vendor compression performing equipment will more likely than not fail to interoperate but, in addition, you may have to rely upon vendor performance data. Unfortunately, some vendors have a tendency to place their equipment performance in the best possible light by transmitting files with a considerable degree of data redundancy and then claiming a high compression ratio, such as 4:1 or 5:1. If compression is an important equipment acquisition consideration, the author suggests that you create a set of files that are representative of your internet traffic and have each vendor under consideration transfer those files and provide you with either their transmission time at a fixed WAN rate or their compression ratio.

10.4 ETHERNET FRAME TRUNCATION

As noted in Chapter 2, Ethernet frames require a minimum length of 64 bytes even when the frame carries just one information character. Thus, a query/response client–server communications session in which a workstation user on an Ethernet initiates queries by entering a few search characters results in the transmission of a frame with a large number of pad characters to ensure the minimum packet size of 64 bytes is reached.

10.4.1 Overhead

Although the overhead associated with the use of pad characters is relatively insignificant on a 10 Mbps 10BASE-T network, those pad characters become more significant when frames are directed across a wide area transmission facility operating at a fraction of the local area network operating rate. Recognizing the effect of padded Ethernet frames upon communications over WAN facilities, Advanced Computer Communications was among the first vendors to offer Ethernet frame truncation in their remote bridge and router products.

The use of frame truncation results in Ethernet padded frames having their pad characters removed prior to transmission over a WAN. This results in the transmission of reduced length frames which require less time to transmit. This technique also permits the remote bridge or router to strip pad characters from minimum length Ethernet frames as they are placed in memory, permitting more frames to be stored in memory, as well as the faster servicing of frames when they are packeted and placed on the transmission line.

10.4.2 Utilization example

As an example of the potential benefit obtained from the use of Ethernet frame truncation, consider a situation in which 20 stations on a 10 Mbps Ethernet have users interactively working with a program located on a remote Token-Ring network through remote bridges communicating at 19 200 bps. Let us assume a worst-case scenario in which each user simultaneously enters a query using a five-digit invoice number. Then, instead of five characters in the information field, each frame must contain 46 characters including pad characters to comply with the Ethernet minimum packet length standard. Without considering the overhead of the protocol used for transmitting frames from the Ethernet to the Token-Ring network, this worst-case situation results in 20×46, or 920 bytes, being presented to the remote bridge or router when only 20×5, or 100 bytes, actually require transmission. Then the interactive traffic would use $920 \times 8/19\,200$, or approximately 38%, of the WAN bandwidth without Ethernet frame truncation. With Ethernet frame truncation, transmission would be reduced to 100 bytes which would use $100 \times 8/19\,200$, or approximately 4%, of the WAN bandwidth.

10.5 SWITCHED NETWORK USE FOR OVERCOMING CONGESTION

One problem frequently encountered by network designers, managers, and analysts is in determining the operating rate of a wide area network transmission facility. Almost all WAN transmission facilities are either leased analog or digital lines whose monthly cost is proportional to the data transmission rate they provide. Most organizations typically attempt to determine their busy hour traffic and obtain a wide area network transmission facility which provides an acceptable level of performance during the busy hour. Although this is a valid network design technique, it does not consider the use of a new class of equipment known as bandwidth-on-demand inverse multiplexers (BODM), nor the fact that in many organizations busy hour transmission may considerably exceed normal transmission.

10.5.1 Using bandwidth-on-demand inverse multiplexers

To illustrate the use of bandwidth-on-demand inverse multiplexers, as well as a feature known as dial-on congestion incorporated into some remote bridges and routers, let us assume that our network analysts have determined that a fractional T1 line operating at 128 kbps was required to interconnect two remote bridges at a cost of $4500 per month. Let us also assume that the cost of switched 56 kbps transmission is $30 per hour and that during an eight-hour day the WAN facility requires only 128 kbps of bandwidth for 90 minutes, and for the remainder of the workday a bandwidth of 64 kbps or less provides an acceptable level of performance.

Figure 10.6 illustrates the use of bandwidth-on-demand inverse multiplexers which examine the flow of packets between remote bridges. As the flow of packets increases to the point where there is essentially no available bandwidth on the leased line for a predefined period of time, the multiplexer initiates a switched

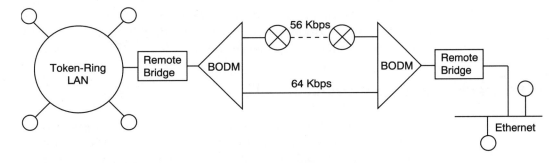

Figure 10.6 Using bandwidth-on-demand inverse multiplexers. A bandwidth-on-demand inverse multiplexer can be configured to support a leased line and initiate one or more switched 56 kbps calls when the activity on the leased line exceeds a predefined threshold for a defined period of time

56 kbps call to the distant multiplexer. Based upon our assumed cost of $30 per hour, switched 56 kbps transmission for 90 minutes per day would result in a daily cost of $45, or $990 if there are 22 working days in the month. If a 64 kbps fractional T1 line costs $2800 per month, the total cost of using a 64 kbps leased line and supplementing its capacity via the use of switched 56 kbps service would be $3790, not including the cost of the bandwidth-on-demand inverse multiplexers. Thus, in this example the use of BODM equipment would result in a monthly line cost reduction of $710.

10.5.2 Dial-on congestion

To alleviate the cost of separate bandwidth-on-demand inverse multiplexers, several vendors manufacturing remote bridges and routers have incorporated a dial-on-congestion capability into their products. This feature results in the use of a second port on a remote bridge or router for switched dial use during peak periods of activity. Users are referred to the author's book *Data Communications Networking Devices (third edition)*, published by John Wiley & Sons, for additional information concerning the use of inverse multiplexers.

10.6 NETWORK INTERFACE CARD

The network interface card is a circuit board designed for insertion into the expansion slot of a specific type of computer, such as an IBM PC or compatible computer, a Micro Channel IBM PS/2 computer, or an Apple Macintosh. This card contains a series of chips or an integrated chip set which implements the network access protocol, as well as RAM memory, and other chips designed to perform specific functions which can have a considerable bearing upon the ability of the adapter card to transfer data onto and receive data from the network.

10.6.1 Performance considerations

The key to the ability of a network interface card to transfer data onto and from a network is the method by which data transfer occurs between the adapter card and the computer in which it is inserted. Data transfer between the adapter card and the computer can be implemented in several ways, including direct memory access (DMA), I/O mapped and shared memory.

DMA interface

A direct memory access (DMA) interface is a data transfer technique in which the transfer of data between the adapter card and the computer's memory can occur simultaneously with other operations. To accomplish this the DMA transfer is initiated by a board processor storing a starting and ending address and then initiating a DMA transfer operation, after which the processor can perform other operations during which data is transferred from the adapter card's memory to the workstation's memory. If the adapter card does not include an onboard processor, circuitry can be used to implement a DMA transfer. To accomplish this, an on-board buffer area on the adapter card receives data from the network. As the buffer fills, circuitry on the adapter recognizes this condition as a signal to generate a DMA transfer.

Although a DMA transfer permits the simultaneous transfer of data from the NIC to the computer's memory to occur with other operations, it is generally slow in comparison to other methods of data transfer. The reason for this is due to the time required to set up and initiate a DMA transfer. A second factor which limits the capability of a DMA transfer is the fact that it requires contiguous memory in the host computer for its transfer operations. Since frames are often assembled from several different areas in memory, each DMA transfer may be limited to the amount of data that can be transferred.

I/O mapping

I/O mapping is a data transfer mechanism based upon the shared use of an I/O port between the adapter card and the host computer. This method of data transfer is faster than the use of a DMA transfer as it occurs at the I/O channel speed and eliminates the DMA transfer setup time.

Shared memory

In a shared memory method of data transfer, a portion of the computer's memory is set up so that it can be used by both the adapter card and the computer. This results in a frame avoiding an actual transfer between the adapter and the computer, enhancing the data transfer between the computer and the network.

Most modern high-performance network adapter cards use some type of shared memory scheme to expedite the transfer of data from the computer to the network and vice versa.

Typically, shared memory can be set up in increments of 16 kbytes, from 16 to 64 kbytes. Since the use of a LAN program and an application program will typically use a majority of conventional memory, many computers are limited to a setup in which only 16 kbytes are used as shared memory. Although this amount of memory will not adversely affect the operation of NICs connected to a 4 Mbps Token-Ring or a 10 Mbps Ethernet network, the opposite can occur if you are connected to a 16 Mbps Token-Ring network. This is because the 16 Mbps Token-Ring network can have an information frame whose length can exceed 16 kbytes.

In comparing the method used by the NIC for transferring data, performance can significantly differ depending upon the technique used. Although you may be tempted to simply select a vendor's adapter card based upon their stated data transfer rate, there is one additional item that you should consider prior to doing so. That additional item is the transfer rate of the hard disk of the computer in which you intend to install the network interface card.

The transfer rate of the hard disk will vary with the type of disk and disk controller used as well as with the bus interface of your computer. For example, older PC XT computers have a disk I/O transfer capability under 1 Mbps. Thus, installing a shared memory network interface card with a 2 Mbps transfer capability would probably be extravagant, because any sustained transfer of data to or from the computer's hard disk would be limited to 1 Mbps regardless of the type of NIC used. Thus, you should select a network interface card in conjunction with the performance characteristics of the computer in which it is to be installed.

10.7 CHANGE NETWORK ROUTING AND ADVERTISING PROTOCOLS

The development of local area networks can be traced to the 1970s, a period when internetworking for many organizations consisted of linking two networks in the same building together. Protocols developed during that time period fall primarily into a category of protocols referred to as distance vector algorithms and have certain inefficiencies associated with their use that can adversely effect the level of performance when used with large networks. In this concluding section we will examine how changing your routing and advertising protocol can enhance the efficiency of your network. However, prior to doing so let us discuss the difference between routing and advertising protocols so we have an understanding of why they consume bandwidth, and under certain network topologies can adversely effect communications between interconnected networks.

10.7.1 Routing protocol

A routing protocol transfers information between network devices which provides them with the information necessary to route frames through a network. In a NetWare environment the Routing Information Protocol (RIP) is an example of a routing protocol which facilitates the exchange of IPX packets.

RIP can be classified as a distance vector algorithm, in that it exchanges routing table information through periodic broadcasts to make network routers and servers aware of the current topology of the network. Distance vector algorithms use information stored and retrieved based upon the distance in terms of the number of hops between networks, with each router considered to represent one hop.

The RIP used by Novell was based on the distance vector algorithm developed by Xerox and was originally designed for connecting small LANs together. Novell modified RIP to include a cost metric based upon the original IBM PCs timer tick of about $\frac{1}{18}$th of a second. When a RIP request is transmitted the round trip acknowledgement time is counted in terms of timer ticks as a decision criteria when two or more routes have the same hop count.

10.7.2 Advertising protocol

In comparison to a routing protocol which seeks to find an optimum path through a network, an advertising protocol makes other devices aware of the presence of the device using the advertising protocol. One common example of an advertising protocol is NetWare's Service Advertisement Protocol (SAP).

In a NetWare environment different types of server advertise their presence by broadcasting a SAP every 60 seconds. Although the bytes contained in a SAP packet have a minimal effect on network bandwidth, even when a network has 10, 20 or more servers, when two networks are interconnected by a wide area network the effect of transmitting SAP packets becomes more pronounced and can considerably effect internetwork communications.

To illustrate how SAP packets can adversely effect inter-LAN communications that occur via wide area network transmission facilities consider Figure 10.7 which shows four LANs interconnected via three WAN circuits. In Figure 10.7 the arrows indicate the flow of SAP packets between networks, and squares with the letter S and a subscript number are used to identify a specific server. The table in the lower portion of Figure 10.7 indicates the SAP flow by circuit. As indicated, the six server internetwork will result in 12 SAP packets being transmitted every minute, or a total of 720 per hour, every hour.

Although the effect of a SAP upon network users is negligible when transmission occurs on the LAN at an operating rate expressed in Mbps, when forwarding occurs across WAN circuits the effect becomes more pronounced. For example, a 64 kbps WAN represents approximately one 156th of the bandwidth of a 10 Mbps Ethernet LAN. Since NetWare's Service Advertisement Protocol is implemented as a distance vector algorithm, each server maintains a table of servers it knows and the routes to those servers. Thus, as an internetwork increases the tables maintained by each server that increase, resulting in longer data exchanges every 60 seconds or whenever there is a change in network topology.

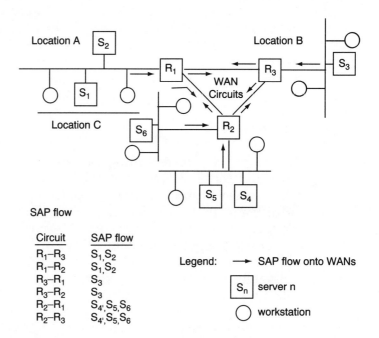

SAP flow

Circuit	SAP flow
R_1-R_3	S_1,S_2
R_1-R_2	S_1,S_2
R_3-R_1	S_3
R_3-R_2	S_3
R_2-R_1	$S_{4'},S_5,S_6$
R_2-R_3	$S_{4'},S_5,S_6$

Legend: → SAP flow onto WANs
S_n server n
○ workstation

Figure 10.7 Examining the effect of Service Advertising Protocol broadcasts on WAN circuits

10.7.3 NLSP

Recognizing the problems associated with distance vector protocols, several internetwork protocols were developed that result in the exchange of information by lengthening the interval between routing updates. In a NetWare environment Novell developed a routing protocol called NetWare Link Services Protocol (NLSP) which significantly reduces bandwidth during router and server exchanges. To accomplish this NLSP employs three databases: adjacency, link state and forwarding.

The adjacency database keeps track of a router's immediate neighbors, including servers and routers on the same LAN segment and the operational status of directly connected circuits. When a circuit becomes operational the router periodically transmits 'Hello' packets and listens for messages from its directly attached neighbors, with responses recorded in its adjacency databases.

Once neighbors have been noted for each LAN segment, NLSP selects a designated router. Here the designated router represents all routers that provide traffic to a common circuit. Thus, a designated router can reduce traffic caused when two or more routers provide traffic onto a common circuit. In addition, the designated router maintains a link state database which includes portions of adjacency databases. Thus, the link state database can include information about other routers, which reduces the number of tables that have to be exchanged. In addition, a link state database is only exchanged when changes to the database occur, further reducing overhead traffic.

The third database, the forwarding database, contains circuit costs based on an algorithm which identifies the shortest path between network nodes. Thus, this database which is created from information in the link state database governs how frames are forwarded.

In addition to significantly reducing the overhead required to perform routing on relatively low capacity WAN circuits, NLSP has several additional advantages. Those advantages include the use of IPX header compression which further reduces overhead as well as reduced router processing. The latter results from a decrease in routing table updates which provides more CPU time for frame processing.

Because NLSP eliminates both SAP and RIP traffic, it can provide additional bandwidth for low-speed WAN links that might otherwise require a costly upgrade. Owing to its relative efficiency in comparison to RIP and SAP, people operating NetWare should consider the use of this relatively new protocol.

APPENDIX A

P(N) AND P(N > K) VALUES FOR SINGLE-CHANNEL, SINGLE-SERVER SYSTEM

The program SSERVER.BAS whose statements are listed in Figure A.1 was developed to provide a listing of the probability of N units and the probability of K or more units in a single-channel, single-server system based upon different server utilization levels. The results obtained from the execution of SSERVER.BAS are contained in the remaining portion of this appendix and can be used by readers to determine the buffer storage requirements of remote bridges and routers. Readers are referred to Chapter 4 for specific information concerning the use of the tables of $P(N)$ and $P(N > K)$ presented in this appendix.

```
REM PROGRAM SSERVER.BAS
CLS
PRINT "SINGLE CHANNEL SINGLE SERVER QUEUING COMPUTATION PROGRAM"
INPUT "Enter number of transactions             : ", T
INPUT "Enter time period of transactions in hours: ", H
INPUT "Enter operating rate of server in bps     : ", BPS
INPUT "Enter average frame size in bytes         : ", BYTES
ARRIVAL = T / (H * 60 * 60)
MST = BYTES * 8 / BPS
SERVICERATE = 1 / MST
UTILIZATION = ARRIVAL / SERVICERATE
PO = 1 - UTILIZATION
L = ARRIVAL / (SERVICERATE - ARRIVAL)
LQ = UTILIZATION ^ 2 / (1 - UTILIZATION)
W = 1 / (SERVICERATE - ARRIVAL)
WQ = ARRIVAL / (SERVICERATE * (SERVICERATE - ARRIVAL))
PRINT
PRINT USING "ARRIVAL RATE = ###.#### FRAMES PER SEC "; ARRIVAL
PRINT USING "SERVICE RATE = ###.#### FRAMES PER SEC "; SERVICERATE
PRINT USING "UTILIZATION  = ###.#### PERCENT"; UTILIZATION * 100
PRINT
PRINT USING "MEAN NUMBER OF FRAMES IN SYSTEM = ###.#### "; L
PRINT USING "MEAN NUMBER OF FRAMES IN QUEUE  = ###.#### "; LQ
PRINT
PRINT USING "MEAN TIME IN THE SYSTEM IN SEC =  ###.#### "; W
PRINT USING "MEAN TIME IN THE QUEUE IN SEC  =  ###.#### "; WQ
PRINT
END
```

Figure A.1

Probability of *N* units and *K* or more units in system based upon server utilization level ranging from 10 to 95%

For a utilization level of 10%

Probability of *N* units		Probability of *K* or more units	
N	*P(N)*	*K*	*P(N > K)*
0	0.89999998	0	1.00000000
1	0.09000000	1	0.10000000
2	0.00900000	2	0.01000000
3	0.00090000	3	0.00100000
4	0.00009000	4	0.00010000
5	0.00000900	5	0.00001000
6	0.00000090	6	0.00000100
7	0.00000009	7	0.00000010
8	0.00000001	8	0.00000001
9	0.00000000	9	0.00000000
10	0.00000000	10	0.00000000
11	0.00000000	11	0.00000000
12	0.00000000	12	0.00000000
13	0.00000000	13	0.00000000
14	0.00000000	14	0.00000000
15	0.00000000	15	0.00000000
16	0.00000000	16	0.00000000
17	0.00000000	17	0.00000000
18	0.00000000	18	0.00000000
19	0.00000000	19	0.00000000
20	0.00000000	20	0.00000000
21	0.00000000	21	0.00000000
22	0.00000000	22	0.00000000
23	0.00000000	23	0.00000000
24	0.00000000	24	0.00000000
25	0.00000000	25	0.00000000

For a utilization level of 15%

Probability of *N* units		Probability of *K* or more units	
N	*P(N)*	*K*	*P(N > K)*
0	0.85000002	0	1.00000000
1	0.12750000	1	0.15000001
2	0.01912500	2	0.02250000
3	0.00286875	3	0.00337500
4	0.00043031	4	0.00050625
5	0.00006455	5	0.00007594
6	0.00000968	6	0.00001139
7	0.00000145	7	0.00000171
8	0.00000022	8	0.00000026
9	0.00000003	9	0.00000004
10	0.00000000	10	0.00000001
11	0.00000000	11	0.00000000
12	0.00000000	12	0.00000000
13	0.00000000	13	0.00000000
14	0.00000000	14	0.00000000
15	0.00000000	15	0.00000000
16	0.00000000	16	0.00000000
17	0.00000000	17	0.00000000
18	0.00000000	18	0.00000000
19	0.00000000	19	0.00000000
20	0.00000000	20	0.00000000
21	0.00000000	21	0.00000000
22	0.00000000	22	0.00000000
23	0.00000000	23	0.00000000
24	0.00000000	24	0.00000000
25	0.00000000	25	0.00000000

For a utilization level of 20%

Probability of N units		Probability of K or more units	
N	P(N)	K	P(N > K)
0	0.80000001	0	1.00000000
1	0.16000000	1	0.20000000
2	0.03200000	2	0.04000000
3	0.00640000	3	0.00800000
4	0.00128000	4	0.00160000
5	0.00025600	5	0.00032000
6	0.00005120	6	0.00006400
7	0.00001024	7	0.00001280
8	0.00000205	8	0.00000256
9	0.00000041	9	0.00000051
10	0.00000008	10	0.00000010
11	0.00000002	11	0.00000002
12	0.00000000	12	0.00000000
13	0.00000000	13	0.00000000
14	0.00000000	14	0.00000000
15	0.00000000	15	0.00000000
16	0.00000000	16	0.00000000
17	0.00000000	17	0.00000000
18	0.00000000	18	0.00000000
19	0.00000000	19	0.00000000
20	0.00000000	20	0.00000000
21	0.00000000	21	0.00000000
22	0.00000000	22	0.00000000
23	0.00000000	23	0.00000000
24	0.00000000	24	0.00000000
25	0.00000000	25	0.00000000

For a utilization level of 25%

Probability of N units		Probability of K or more units	
N	P(N)	K	P(N > K)
0	0.75000000	0	1.00000000
1	0.18750000	1	0.25000000
2	0.04687500	2	0.06250000
3	0.01171875	3	0.01562500
4	0.00292969	4	0.00390625
5	0.00073242	5	0.00097656
6	0.00018311	6	0.00024414
7	0.00004578	7	0.00006104
8	0.00001144	8	0.00001526
9	0.00000286	9	0.00000381
10	0.00000072	10	0.00000095
11	0.00000018	11	0.00000024
12	0.00000004	12	0.00000006
13	0.00000001	13	0.00000001
14	0.00000000	14	0.00000000
15	0.00000000	15	0.00000000
16	0.00000000	16	0.00000000
17	0.00000000	17	0.00000000
18	0.00000000	18	0.00000000
19	0.00000000	19	0.00000000
20	0.00000000	20	0.00000000
21	0.00000000	21	0.00000000
22	0.00000000	22	0.00000000
23	0.00000000	23	0.00000000
24	0.00000000	24	0.00000000
25	0.00000000	25	0.00000000

For a utilization level of 30%

Probability of N units		Probability of K or more units	
N	$P(N)$	K	$P(N > K)$
0	0.69999999	0	1.00000000
1	0.21000001	1	0.30000001
2	0.06300000	2	0.90000000
3	0.01890000	3	0.02700000
4	0.00567000	4	0.00810000
5	0.00170100	5	0.00243000
6	0.00051030	6	0.00072900
7	0.00015309	7	0.00021870
8	0.00004593	8	0.00006561
9	0.00001378	9	0.00001968
10	0.00000413	10	0.00000590
11	0.00000124	11	0.00000177
12	0.00000037	12	0.00000053
13	0.00000011	13	0.00000016
14	0.00000003	14	0.00000005
15	0.00000001	15	0.00000001
16	0.00000000	16	0.00000000
17	0.00000000	17	0.00000000
18	0.00000000	18	0.00000000
19	0.00000000	19	0.00000000
20	0.00000000	20	0.00000000
21	0.00000000	21	0.00000000
22	0.00000000	22	0.00000000
23	0.00000000	23	0.00000000
24	0.00000000	24	0.00000000
25	0.00000000	25	0.00000000

For a utilization level of 35%

Probability of N units		Probability of K or more units	
N	$P(N)$	K	$P(N > K)$
0	0.64999998	0	1.00000000
1	0.22750001	1	0.35000002
2	0.07962501	2	0.12250002
3	0.02786876	3	0.04287501
4	0.00975406	4	0.01500625
5	0.00341392	5	0.00525219
6	0.00119487	6	0.00183827
7	0.00041821	7	0.00064339
8	0.00014637	8	0.00022519
9	0.00005123	9	0.00007882
10	0.00001793	10	0.00002759
11	0.00000628	11	0.00000965
12	0.00000220	12	0.00000338
13	0.00000077	13	0.00000118
14	0.00000027	14	0.00000041
15	0.00000009	15	0.00000014
16	0.00000003	16	0.00000005
17	0.00000001	17	0.00000002
18	0.00000000	18	0.00000001
19	0.00000000	19	0.00000000
20	0.00000000	20	0.00000000
21	0.00000000	21	0.00000000
22	0.00000000	22	0.00000000
23	0.00000000	23	0.00000000
24	0.00000000	24	0.00000000
25	0.00000000	25	0.00000000

For a utilization level of 40%

Probability of N units			Probability of K or more units	
N	$P(N)$		K	$P(N > K)$
0	0.59999996		0	1.00000000
1	0.24000001		1	0.40000004
2	0.09600001		2	0.16000003
3	0.03840001		3	0.06400002
4	0.01536000		4	0.02560001
5	0.00614400		5	0.01024000
6	0.00245760		6	0.00409600
7	0.00098304		7	0.00163840
8	0.00039322		8	0.00065536
9	0.00015729		9	0.00026214
10	0.00006291		10	0.00010486
11	0.00002517		11	0.00004194
12	0.00001007		12	0.00001678
13	0.00000403		13	0.00000671
14	0.00000161		14	0.00000268
15	0.00000064		15	0.00000107
16	0.00000026		16	0.00000043
17	0.00000010		17	0.00000017
18	0.00000004		18	0.00000007
19	0.00000002		19	0.00000003
20	0.00000001		20	0.00000001
21	0.00000000		21	0.00000000
22	0.00000000		22	0.00000000
23	0.00000000		23	0.00000000
24	0.00000000		24	0.00000000
25	0.00000000		25	0.00000000

For a utilization level of 45%

Probability of N units			Probability of K or more units	
N	$P(N)$		K	$P(N > K)$
0	0.54999995		0	0.00000000
1	0.24750000		1	0.45000005
2	0.11137501		2	0.20250005
3	0.05011876		3	0.09112503
4	0.02255345		4	0.04100627
5	0.01014905		5	0.01845282
6	0.00456707		6	0.00830377
7	0.00205518		7	0.00373670
8	0.00092483		8	0.00168151
9	0.00041617		9	0.00075668
10	0.00018728		10	0.00034051
11	0.00008428		11	0.00015323
12	0.00003792		12	0.00006895
13	0.00001707		13	0.00003103
14	0.00000768		14	0.00001396
15	0.00000346		15	0.00000628
16	0.00000156		16	0.00000283
17	0.00000070		17	0.00000127
18	0.00000031		18	0.00000057
19	0.00000014		19	0.00000026
20	0.00000006		20	0.00000012
21	0.00000003		21	0.00000005
22	0.00000001		22	0.00000002
23	0.00000001		23	0.00000001
24	0.00000000		24	0.00000000
25	0.00000000		25	0.00000000

For a utilization level of 50%

Probability of N units		Probability of K or more units	
N	$P(N)$	K	$P(N > K)$
0	0.49999994	0	1.00000000
1	0.25000000	1	0.50000006
2	0.12500001	2	0.25000006
3	0.06250001	3	0.12500004
4	0.03125001	4	0.06250003
5	0.01562501	5	0.03125002
6	0.00781250	6	0.01562501
7	0.00390625	7	0.00781251
8	0.00195313	8	0.00390625
9	0.00097656	9	0.00195313
10	0.00048828	10	0.00097656
11	0.00024414	11	0.00048828
12	0.00012207	12	0.00024414
13	0.00006104	13	0.00012207
14	0.00003052	14	0.00006104
15	0.00001526	15	0.00003052
16	0.00000763	16	0.00001526
17	0.00000381	17	0.00000763
18	0.00000191	18	0.00000381
19	0.00000095	19	0.00000191
20	0.00000048	20	0.00000095
21	0.00000024	21	0.00000048
22	0.00000012	22	0.00000024
23	0.00000006	23	0.00000012
24	0.00000003	24	0.00000006
25	0.00000001	25	0.00000003

For a utilization level of 55%

Probability of N units		Probability of K or more units	
N	$P(N)$	K	$P(N > K)$
0	0.44999993	0	1.00000000
1	0.24749999	1	0.55000007
2	0.13612501	2	0.30250007
3	0.07486877	3	0.16637507
4	0.04117783	4	0.09150629
5	0.02264781	5	0.05032847
6	0.01245630	6	0.02768066
7	0.00685096	7	0.01522437
8	0.00376803	8	0.00837340
9	0.00207242	9	0.00460537
10	0.00113983	10	0.00253296
11	0.00062691	11	0.00139313
12	0.00034480	12	0.00076622
13	0.00018964	13	0.00042142
14	0.00010430	14	0.00023178
15	0.00005737	15	0.00012748
16	0.00003155	16	0.00007011
17	0.00001735	17	0.00003856
18	0.00000954	18	0.00002121
19	0.00000525	19	0.00001167
20	0.00000289	20	0.00000642
21	0.00000159	21	0.00000353
22	0.00000087	22	0.00000194
23	0.00000048	23	0.00000107
24	0.00000026	24	0.00000059
25	0.00000015	25	0.00000032

For a utilization level of 60%

Probability of N units		Probability of K or more units	
N	P(N)	K	P(N > K)
0	0.39999992	0	1.00000000
1	0.23999998	1	0.60000008
2	0.14400001	2	0.36000010
3	0.08640002	3	0.21600010
4	0.05184002	4	0.12960008
5	0.03110402	5	0.07776006
6	0.01866241	6	0.04665604
7	0.01119745	7	0.02799363
8	0.00671847	8	0.01679618
9	0.00403108	9	0.01007771
10	0.00241865	10	0.00604663
11	0.00145119	11	0.00362798
12	0.00087071	12	0.00217679
13	0.00052243	13	0.00130607
14	0.00031346	14	0.00078364
15	0.00018807	15	0.00047019
16	0.00011284	16	0.00028211
17	0.00006771	17	0.00016971
18	0.00004062	18	0.00010156
19	0.00002437	19	0.00006094
20	0.00001462	20	0.00003656
21	0.00000877	21	0.00002194
22	0.00000526	22	0.00001316
23	0.00000316	23	0.00000790
24	0.00000190	24	0.00000474
25	0.00000114	25	0.00000284

For a utilization level of 65%

Probability of N units		Probability of K or more units	
N	P(N)	K	P(N > K)
0	0.34999990	0	1.00000000
1	0.22749998	1	0.65000010
2	0.14787500	2	0.42250013
3	0.09611876	3	0.27462512
4	0.06247721	4	0.17850636
5	0.04061019	5	0.11602915
6	0.02639663	6	0.07541896
7	0.01715781	7	0.04902233
8	0.01115258	8	0.03186452
9	0.00724918	9	0.02071194
10	0.00471197	10	0.01346276
11	0.00306278	11	0.00875080
12	0.00199081	12	0.00568802
13	0.00129402	13	0.00369721
14	0.00084112	14	0.00240319
15	0.00054673	15	0.00156207
16	0.00035537	16	0.00101535
17	0.00023099	17	0.00065998
18	0.00015014	18	0.00042898
19	0.00009759	19	0.00027884
20	0.00006344	20	0.00018125
21	0.00004123	21	0.00011781
22	0.00002680	22	0.00007658
23	0.00001742	23	0.00004977
24	0.00001132	24	0.00003235
25	0.00000736	25	0.00002103

For a utilization level of 70%

Probability of N units		Probability of K or more units	
N	P(N)	K	P(N > K)
0	0.29999989	0	1.00000000
1	0.20999996	1	0.70000011
2	0.14700000	2	0.49000016
3	0.10290001	3	0.34300014
4	0.07203002	4	0.24010015
5	0.05042102	5	0.16807012
6	0.03529472	6	0.11764911
7	0.02470631	7	0.08235439
8	0.01729442	8	0.05764808
9	0.01210609	9	0.04035366
10	0.00847427	10	0.02824757
11	0.00593199	11	0.01977330
12	0.00415239	12	0.01384131
13	0.00290667	13	0.00968892
14	0.00203467	14	0.00678225
15	0.00142427	15	0.00474757
16	0.00099699	16	0.00332330
17	0.00069789	17	0.00232631
18	0.00048853	18	0.00162842
19	0.00034197	19	0.00113989
20	0.00023938	20	0.00079793
21	0.00016756	21	0.00055855
22	0.00011729	22	0.00039098
23	0.00008211	23	0.00027369
24	0.00005747	24	0.00019158
25	0.00004023	25	0.00013411

For a utilization level of 75%

Probability of N units		Probability of K or more units	
N	P(N)	K	P(N > K)
0	0.24999988	0	1.00000000
1	0.18749994	1	0.75000012
2	0.14062497	2	0.56250018
3	0.10546875	3	0.42187521
4	0.07910158	4	0.31640646
5	0.05932619	5	0.23730488
6	0.04449465	6	0.17797868
7	0.03337099	7	0.13348404
8	0.02502825	8	0.10011304
9	0.01877119	9	0.07508479
10	0.01407839	10	0.05631360
11	0.01055880	11	0.04223521
12	0.00791910	12	0.03167641
13	0.00593933	13	0.02375731
14	0.00445449	14	0.01781799
15	0.00334087	15	0.01336349
16	0.00250565	16	0.01002262
17	0.00187924	17	0.00751697
18	0.00140943	18	0.00563773
19	0.00105707	19	0.00422830
20	0.00079281	20	0.00317122
21	0.00059460	21	0.00237842
22	0.00044595	22	0.00178381
23	0.00033446	23	0.00133786
24	0.00025085	24	0.00100340
25	0.00018814	25	0.00075255

For a utilization level of 80%

Probability of N units		Probability of K or more units	
N	P(N)	K	P(N > K)
0	0.19999987	0	1.00000000
1	0.15999992	1	0.80000013
2	0.12799996	2	0.64000022
3	0.10239998	3	0.51200026
4	0.08192000	4	0.40960026
5	0.06553601	5	0.32768026
6	0.05242882	6	0.26214427
7	0.04194306	7	0.20971544
8	0.03355445	8	0.16777238
9	0.02684357	9	0.13421793
10	0.02147486	10	0.10737436
11	0.01717989	11	0.08589950
12	0.01374391	12	0.06871961
13	0.01099513	13	0.05497570
14	0.00879611	14	0.04398056
15	0.00703689	15	0.03518446
16	0.00562951	16	0.02814757
17	0.00450361	17	0.02251806
18	0.00360289	18	0.01801445
19	0.00288231	19	0.01441156
20	0.00230585	20	0.01152925
21	0.00184468	21	0.00922340
22	0.00147574	22	0.00737872
23	0.00118060	23	0.00590298
24	0.00094448	24	0.00472239
25	0.00075558	25	0.00377791

For a utilization level of 85%

Probability of N units		Probability of K or more units	
N	P(N)	K	P(N > K)
0	0.14999986	0	1.00000000
1	0.12749989	1	0.85000014
2	0.10837493	2	0.72250026
3	0.09211871	3	0.61412531
4	0.07830092	4	0.52200663
5	0.06655579	5	0.44370568
6	0.05657243	6	0.37714991
7	0.04808657	7	0.32057747
8	0.04087359	8	0.27249089
9	0.03474256	9	0.23161730
10	0.02953118	10	0.19687474
11	0.02510151	11	0.16734356
12	0.02133629	12	0.14224204
13	0.01813585	13	0.12090576
14	0.01541547	14	0.10276991
15	0.01310315	15	0.08735444
16	0.01113768	16	0.07425129
17	0.00946703	17	0.06311361
18	0.00804698	18	0.05364657
19	0.00683993	19	0.04559959
20	0.00581394	20	0.03875966
21	0.00494185	21	0.03294572
22	0.00420058	22	0.02800386
23	0.00357049	23	0.02380329
24	0.00303492	24	0.02023280
25	0.00257969	25	0.01719788

For a utilization level of 90%

Probability of N units		Probability of K or more units	
N	P(N)	K	P(N > K)
0	0.09999985	0	1.00000000
1	0.08999988	1	0.90000015
2	0.08099990	2	0.81000030
3	0.07289992	3	0.72900039
4	0.06560995	4	0.65610045
5	0.05904896	5	0.59049052
6	0.05314407	6	0.53144157
7	0.04782967	7	0.47829747
8	0.04304671	8	0.43046781
9	0.03874205	9	0.38742110
10	0.03486785	10	0.34867904
11	0.03138107	11	0.31381118
12	0.02824297	12	0.28243011
13	0.02541868	13	0.25418717
14	0.02287681	14	0.22876848
15	0.02058913	15	0.20589167
16	0.01853022	16	0.18530253
17	0.01667720	17	0.16677231
18	0.01500949	18	0.15009511
19	0.01350854	19	0.13508561
20	0.01215769	20	0.12157708
21	0.01094192	21	0.10941938
22	0.00984773	22	0.09847746
23	0.00886296	23	0.08862973
24	0.00797667	24	0.07976677
25	0.00717900	25	0.07179011

For a utilization level of 95%

Probability of N units		Probability of K or more units	
N	P(N)	K	P(N > K)
0	0.04999983	0	1.00000000
1	0.04749985	1	0.95000017
2	0.04512487	2	0.90250033
3	0.04286863	3	0.85737544
4	0.04072521	4	0.81450683
5	0.03868895	5	0.77378160
6	0.03675451	6	0.73509264
7	0.03491679	7	0.69833815
8	0.03317096	8	0.66342139
9	0.03151242	9	0.63025039
10	0.02993680	10	0.59873801
11	0.02843997	11	0.56880116
12	0.02701797	12	0.54036123
13	0.02566708	13	0.51334327
14	0.02438373	14	0.48767617
15	0.02316455	15	0.46329245
16	0.02200632	16	0.44012791
17	0.02090601	17	0.41812158
18	0.01986071	18	0.39721557
19	0.01886768	19	0.37735486
20	0.01792430	20	0.35848719
21	0.01702809	21	0.34056288
22	0.01617669	22	0.32353479
23	0.01536785	23	0.30735812
24	0.01459946	24	0.29199025
25	0.01386949	25	0.27739078

APPENDIX B

4 AND 16 MBPS TOKEN-RING NETWORK PERFORMANCE BASED UPON THE NETWORK OPERATING RATE, NUMBER OF NETWORK STATIONS, FRAME LENGTH AND TOTAL CABLE LENGTH

Frame rate of 4 Mbps Token-Ring network based upon the network operating rate, number of stations, frame length and total cable length

Number of stations	Avg frame length	Cable length ×000 feet	Frame rate in fps	Number of stations	Avg frame length	Cable length ×000 feet	Frame rate in fps
20	512	2	914	10	64	2	5301
20	512	4	911	10	64	4	5210
20	512	6	909	10	64	6	5123
20	512	8	906	10	64	8	5038
20	512	10	903	10	64	10	4956
20	1024	2	472	10	128	2	3158
20	1024	4	471	10	128	4	3126
20	1024	6	471	10	128	6	3094
20	1024	8	470	10	128	8	3063
20	1024	10	469	10	128	10	3032
20	2048	2	240	10	256	2	1746
20	2048	4	240	10	256	4	1736
20	204B	6	240	10	256	6	1726
20	2048	8	239	10	256	8	1717
20	2048	10	239	10	256	10	1707
20	4096	2	121	10	512	2	922
20	4096	4	121	10	512	4	919
20	4096	6	121	10	5l2	6	916
20	4096	8	121	10	512	8	914
20	4096	10	121	10	512	10	911
30	64	2	4821	10	1024	2	474
30	64	4	4746	10	1024	4	473
30	64	6	4674	10	1024	6	473
30	64	8	4603	10	1024	8	472
30	64	10	4535	10	1024	10	471
30	128	2	2981	10	2048	2	241
30	128	4	2953	10	2048	4	240
30	128	6	2924	10	2048	6	240
30	128	8	2896	10	2048	8	240
30	128	10	2869	10	2048	10	240
30	256	2	1691	10	4096	2	121
30	256	4	1682	10	4096	4	121
30	256	6	1672	10	4096	6	121
30	256	8	1663	10	4096	8	121
30	256	10	1654	10	4096	10	121
30	512	2	906	20	64	2	5050
30	512	4	904	20	64	4	4967
30	512	6	901	20	64	6	4888
30	512	8	898	20	64	8	4811
30	512	10	896	20	64	10	4736
30	1024	2	470	20	128	2	3067
30	1024	4	469	20	128	4	3037
30	1024	6	469	20	128	6	3007
30	1024	8	468	20	128	8	2977
30	1024	10	467	20	128	10	2949
30	2048	2	239	20	256	2	1718
30	2048	4	239	20	256	4	1708
30	2048	6	239	20	256	6	1699
30	2048	8	239	20	256	8	1690
30	2048	10	239	20	256	10	1680

Number of stations	Avg frame length	Cable length ×000 feet	Frame rate in fps	Number of stations	Avg frame length	Cable length ×000 feet	Frame rate in fps
30	4096	2	121	50	256	2	1639
30	4096	4	121	50	256	4	1630
30	4096	6	121	50	256	6	1621
30	4096	8	121	50	256	8	1613
30	4096	10	121	50	256	10	1604
40	64	2	4613	50	512	2	891
40	64	4	4544	50	512	4	889
40	64	6	4477	50	512	6	886
40	64	8	4413	50	512	8	883
40	64	10	4350	50	512	10	881
40	128	2	2900	50	1024	2	466
40	128	4	2873	50	1024	4	465
40	128	6	2846	50	1024	6	465
40	128	8	2820	50	1024	8	464
40	128	10	2794	50	1024	10	463
40	256	2	1665	50	2048	2	238
40	256	4	1655	50	2048	4	238
40	256	6	1647	50	2048	6	238
40	256	8	1638	50	2048	8	238
40	256	10	1629	50	2048	10	238
40	512	2	899	50	4096	2	121
40	512	4	896	50	4096	4	121
40	512	6	893	50	4096	6	121
40	512	8	891	50	4096	8	120
40	512	10	888	50	4096	10	120
40	1024	2	468	60	64	2	4246
40	1024	4	467	60	64	4	4187
40	1024	6	467	60	64	6	4131
40	1024	8	466	60	64	8	4075
40	1024	10	465	60	64	10	4022
40	2048	2	239	60	128	2	2751
40	2048	4	239	60	128	4	2726
40	2048	6	239	60	128	6	2702
40	2048	8	238	60	128	8	2678
40	2048	10	238	60	128	10	2655
40	4096	2	121	60	256	2	1614
40	4096	4	121	60	256	4	1606
40	4096	6	121	60	256	6	1597
40	4096	8	121	60	256	8	1589
40	4096	10	121	60	256	10	1581
50	64	2	4422	60	512	2	884
50	64	4	4359	60	512	4	881
50	64	6	4297	60	512	6	879
50	64	8	4237	60	512	8	876
50	64	10	4179	60	512	10	874
50	128	2	2824	60	1024	2	464
50	128	4	2798	60	1024	4	463
50	128	6	2772	60	1024	6	463
50	128	8	2747	60	1024	8	462
50	128	10	2723	60	1024	10	461

Number of stations	Avg frame length	Cable length ×000 feet	Frame rate in fps	Number of stations	Avg frame length	Cable length ×000 feet	Frame rate in fps
60	2048	2	238	80	128	2	2616
60	2048	4	238	80	128	4	2594
60	2048	6	238	80	128	6	2572
60	2048	8	237	80	128	8	2550
60	2048	10	237	80	128	10	2529
60	4096	2	120	80	256	2	1567
60	4096	4	120	80	256	4	1559
60	4096	6	120	80	256	6	1551
60	4096	8	120	80	256	8	1543
60	4096	10	120	80	256	10	1535
70	64	2	4083	80	512	2	869
70	64	4	4029	80	512	4	867
70	64	6	3977	80	512	6	864
70	64	8	3925	80	512	8	862
70	64	10	3876	80	512	10	860
70	128	2	2682	80	1024	2	460
70	128	4	2658	80	1024	4	459
70	128	6	2635	80	1024	6	459
70	128	8	2613	80	1024	8	458
70	128	10	2591	80	1024	10	457
70	256	2	1590	80	2048	2	237
70	256	4	1582	80	2048	4	237
70	256	6	1574	80	2048	6	236
70	256	8	1566	80	2048	8	236
70	256	10	1558	80	2048	10	Z36
70	512	2	876	80	4096	2	120
70	512	4	874	80	4096	4	120
70	512	6	871	80	4096	6	120
70	512	8	869	80	4096	8	120
70	512	10	867	80	4096	10	120
70	1024	2	462	90	64	2	3793
70	1024	4	461	90	64	4	3746
70	1024	6	461	90	64	6	3701
70	1024	8	460	90	64	8	3656
70	1024	10	459	90	64	10	3613
70	2048	2	237	90	128	2	2553
70	2048	4	237	90	128	4	2532
70	2048	6	237	90	128	6	2511
70	2048	8	237	90	128	8	2491
70	2048	10	237	90	128	10	2471
70	4096	2	120	90	256	2	1544
70	4096	4	120	90	256	4	1536
70	4096	6	120	90	256	6	1529
70	4096	8	120	90	256	8	1521
70	4096	10	120	90	256	10	1513
80	64	2	3933	90	512	2	862
80	64	4	3883	90	512	4	860
80	64	6	3834	90	512	6	857
80	64	8	3786	90	512	8	855
80	64	10	3740	90	512	10	853

Number of stations	Avg frame length	Cable length ×000 feet	Frame rate in fps	Number of stations	Avg frame length	Cable length ×000 feet	Frame rate in fps
90	1024	2	458	110	64	2	3541
90	1024	4	457	110	64	4	3500
90	1024	6	457	110	64	6	3461
90	1024	8	456	110	64	8	3422
90	1024	10	455	110	64	10	3384
90	2048	2	236	110	128	2	2437
90	2048	4	236	110	128	4	2417
90	2048	6	236	110	128	6	2398
90	2048	8	236	110	128	8	2380
90	2048	10	236	110	128	10	2361
90	4096	2	120	110	256	2	1501
90	4096	4	120	110	256	4	1493
90	4096	6	120	110	256	6	1486
90	4096	8	120	110	256	8	1479
90	4096	10	120	110	256	10	1472
100	64	2	3663	110	512	2	849
100	64	4	3619	110	512	4	846
100	64	6	3577	110	512	6	844
100	64	8	3535	110	512	8	842
100	64	10	3495	110	512	10	839
100	128	2	2494	110	1024	2	454
100	128	4	2473	110	1024	4	453
100	128	6	2453	110	1024	6	453
100	128	8	2434	110	1024	8	452
100	128	10	2415	110	1024	10	451
100	256	2	1522	110	2048	2	235
100	256	4	1514	110	2048	4	235
100	256	6	1507	110	2048	6	235
100	256	8	1500	110	2048	8	235
100	256	10	1492	110	2048	10	235
100	512	2	855	110	4096	2	120
100	512	4	853	110	4096	4	120
100	512	6	851	110	4096	6	120
100	512	8	848	110	4096	8	120
100	512	10	846	110	4096	10	120
100	1024	2	456	120	64	2	3427
100	1024	4	455	120	64	4	3389
100	1024	6	455	120	64	6	3352
100	1024	8	454	120	64	8	3315
100	1024	10	453	120	64	10	3280
100	2048	2	236	120	128	2	2382
100	2048	4	236	120	128	4	2364
100	2048	6	235	120	128	6	2346
100	2048	8	235	120	128	8	2328
100	2048	10	235	120	128	10	2310
100	4096	2	120	120	256	2	1480
100	4096	4	120	120	256	4	1473
100	4096	6	120	120	256	6	1466
100	4096	8	120	120	256	8	1459
100	4096	10	120	120	256	10	1452

Number of stations	Avg frame length	Cable length ×000 feet	Frame rate in fps	Number of stations	Avg frame length	Cable length ×000 feet	Frame rate in fps
120	512	2	842	130	4096	2	120
120	512	4	840	130	4096	4	119
120	512	6	837	130	4096	6	119
120	512	8	835	130	4096	8	119
120	512	10	833	130	4096	10	119
120	1024	2	452	140	64	2	3220
120	1024	4	451	140	64	4	3187
120	1024	6	451	140	64	6	3154
120	1024	8	450	140	64	8	3121
120	1024	10	449	140	64	10	3090
120	2048	2	235	140	128	2	2280
120	2048	4	235	140	128	4	2263
120	2048	6	234	140	128	6	2247
120	2048	8	234	140	128	9	2230
120	2048	10	234	140	128	10	2214
120	4096	2	120	140	256	2	1440
120	4096	4	120	140	256	4	1433
120	4096	6	120	140	256	6	1426
120	4096	8	120	140	256	8	1420
120	4096	10	119	140	256	10	1413
130	64	2	3321	140	512	2	829
130	64	4	3285	140	512	4	827
130	64	6	3250	140	512	6	824
130	64	8	3215	140	512	8	822
130	64	10	3182	140	512	10	820
130	128	2	2330	140	1024	2	448
130	128	4	2312	140	1024	4	448
130	128	6	2295	140	1024	6	447
130	128	8	2278	140	1024	8	446
130	128	10	2261	140	1024	10	446
130	256	2	1460	140	2048	2	234
130	256	4	1453	140	2048	4	234
130	256	6	1446	140	2048	6	233
130	256	8	1439	140	2048	8	233
130	256	10	1432	140	2048	10	233
130	512	2	835	140	4096	2	119
130	512	4	833	140	4096	4	119
130	512	6	831	140	4096	6	119
130	512	8	829	140	4096	8	119
130	512	10	826	140	4096	10	119
130	1024	2	450	150	64	2	3126
130	1024	4	450	150	64	4	3094
130	1024	6	449	150	64	6	3063
130	1024	8	448	150	64	8	3033
130	1024	10	448	150	64	10	3003
130	2048	2	234	150	128	2	2233
130	204S	4	234	150	128	4	2216
130	2048	6	234	150	128	6	2200
130	2048	8	234	150	128	8	2185
130	2048	10	234	150	128	10	2169

Number of stations	Avg frame length	Cable length ×000 feet	Frame rate in fps	Number of stations	Avg frame length	Cable length ×000 feet	Frame rate in fps
150	256	2	1421	160	2048	2	233
150	256	4	1414	160	2048	4	233
150	256	6	1408	160	2048	6	232
150	256	8	1401	160	2048	8	232
150	256	10	1395	160	2048	10	232
150	512	2	822	160	4096	2	119
150	512	4	820	160	4096	4	119
150	512	6	818	160	4096	6	119
150	512	8	816	160	4096	8	119
150	512	10	814	160	4096	10	119
150	1024	2	446	170	64	2	2953
150	1024	4	446	170	64	4	2925
150	1024	6	445	170	64	6	2897
150	1024	8	444	170	64	8	2869
150	1024	10	444	170	64	10	2843
150	2048	2	233	170	128	2	2143
150	2048	4	233	170	128	4	2128
150	2048	6	233	170	128	6	2113
150	2048	8	233	170	128	8	2099
150	2048	10	233	170	128	10	2084
150	4096	2	119	170	256	2	1384
150	4096	4	119	170	256	4	1378
150	4096	6	119	170	256	6	1371
150	4096	8	119	170	256	8	1365
150	4096	10	119	170	256	10	1359
160	64	2	3037	170	512	2	810
160	64	4	3007	170	512	4	808
160	64	6	2978	170	512	6	806
160	64	8	2949	170	512	8	804
160	64	10	2921	170	512	10	801
160	128	2	2187	170	1024	2	443
160	128	4	2171	170	1024	4	442
160	128	6	2156	170	1024	6	441
160	128	8	2141	170	1024	8	441
160	128	10	2126	170	1024	10	440
160	256	2	1402	170	2048	2	232
160	256	4	1396	170	2048	4	232
160	256	6	1389	170	2048	6	232
160	256	8	1383	170	2048	8	232
160	256	10	1377	170	2048	10	231
160	512	2	816	170	4096	2	119
160	512	4	814	170	4096	4	119
160	512	6	812	170	4096	6	119
160	512	8	810	170	4096	8	119
160	512	10	807	170	4096	10	119
160	1024	2	445	180	64	2	2873
160	1024	4	444	180	64	4	2846
160	1024	6	443	180	64	6	2820
160	1024	8	443	180	64	8	2794
160	1024	10	442	180	64	10	2769

Number of stations	Avg frame length	Cable length ×000 feet	Frame rate in fps	Number of stations	Avg frame length	Cable length ×000 feet	Frame rate in fps
180	128	2	2101	190	1024	2	439
180	128	4	2086	190	1024	4	438
180	128	6	2072	190	1024	6	438
180	128	8	2058	190	1024	8	437
180	128	10	2044	190	1024	10	437
180	256	2	1366	190	2048	2	231
180	256	4	1360	190	2048	4	231
180	256	6	1354	190	2048	6	231
180	256	8	1348	190	2048	8	231
180	256	10	1342	190	2048	10	230
180	512	2	804	190	4096	2	119
180	512	4	802	190	4096	4	119
180	512	6	800	190	4096	6	119
180	512	8	798	190	4096	8	119
180	512	10	795	190	4096	10	119
180	1024	2	441	200	64	2	2726
180	1024	4	440	200	64	4	2702
180	1024	6	440	200	64	6	2679
180	1024	8	439	200	64	8	2655
180	1024	10	438	200	64	10	2632
180	2048	2	232	200	128	2	2021
180	2048	4	232	200	128	4	2008
180	2048	6	231	200	128	6	1995
180	2048	8	231	200	128	8	1982
180	2048	10	231	200	128	10	1969
180	4096	2	119	200	256	2	1332
180	4096	4	119	200	256	4	1326
180	4096	6	119	200	256	6	1320
180	4096	8	119	200	256	8	1315
180	4096	10	119	200	256	10	1309
190	64	2	2798	200	512	2	792
190	64	4	2773	200	512	4	790
190	64	6	2748	200	512	6	788
190	64	8	2723	200	512	8	786
190	64	10	2699	200	512	10	784
190	128	2	2060	200	1024	2	437
190	128	4	2046	200	1024	4	437
190	128	6	2033	200	1024	6	436
190	128	8	2019	200	1024	8	435
190	128	10	2006	200	1024	10	435
190	256	2	1349	200	2048	2	231
190	256	4	1343	200	2048	4	231
190	256	6	1337	200	2048	6	230
190	256	8	1331	200	2048	8	230
190	256	10	1325	200	2048	10	230
190	512	2	798	200	4096	2	119
190	512	4	796	200	4096	4	119
190	512	6	794	200	4096	6	119
190	512	8	792	200	4096	8	118
190	512	10	790	200	4096	10	118

Number of stations	Avg frame length	Cable length ×000 feet	Frame rate in fps	Number of stations	Avg frame length	Cable length ×000 feet	Frame rate in fps
210	64	2	2658	220	512	2	780
210	64	4	2635	220	512	4	778
210	64	6	2613	220	512	6	776
210	64	8	2591	220	512	8	774
210	64	10	2569	220	512	10	772
210	128	2	1984	220	1024	2	434
210	128	4	1971	220	1024	4	433
210	128	6	1958	220	1024	6	433
210	128	8	1946	220	1024	8	432
210	128	10	1933	220	1024	10	431
210	256	2	1316	220	2048	2	230
210	256	4	1310	220	2048	4	230
210	256	6	1304	220	2048	6	229
210	256	8	1299	220	2048	8	229
210	256	10	1293	220	2048	10	229
210	512	2	786	220	4096	2	118
210	512	4	784	220	4096	4	118
210	512	6	782	220	4096	6	118
210	512	8	780	220	4096	8	118
210	512	10	778	220	4096	10	118
210	1024	2	436	230	64	2	2532
210	1024	4	435	230	64	4	2511
210	1024	6	434	230	64	6	2491
210	1024	8	434	230	64	8	2471
210	1024	10	433	230	64	10	2451
210	2048	2	230	230	128	2	1912
210	2048	4	230	230	128	4	1900
210	2048	6	230	230	128	6	1889
210	2048	8	230	230	128	8	1877
210	2048	10	230	230	128	10	1866
210	4096	2	118	230	256	2	1284
210	4096	4	118	230	256	4	1278
210	4096	6	118	230	256	6	1273
210	4096	8	118	230	256	8	1268
210	4096	10	118	230	256	10	1263
220	64	2	2594	230	512	2	775
220	64	4	2572	230	512	4	773
220	64	6	2550	230	512	6	771
220	64	8	2529	230	512	8	769
220	64	10	2508	230	512	10	767
220	128	2	1947	230	1024	2	432
220	128	4	1935	230	1024	4	431
220	128	6	1923	230	1024	6	431
220	128	8	1911	230	1024	8	430
220	128	10	1899	230	1024	10	430
220	256	2	1299	230	2048	2	229
220	256	4	1294	230	2048	4	229
220	256	6	1289	230	2048	6	229
220	256	8	1283	230	2048	8	229
220	256	10	1278	230	2048	10	229

Number of stations	Avg frame length	Cable length ×000 feet	Frame rate in fps	Number of stations	Avg frame length	Cable length ×000 feet	Frame rate in fps
230	4096	2	118	250	512	2	764
230	4096	4	118	250	512	4	762
230	4096	6	118	250	512	6	760
230	4096	8	118	250	512	8	758
230	4096	10	118	250	512	10	756
240	64	2	2474	250	1024	2	429
240	64	4	2454	250	1024	4	428
240	64	6	2434	250	1024	6	427
240	64	8	2415	250	1024	8	427
240	64	10	2396	250	1024	10	426
240	128	2	1879	250	2048	2	228
240	128	4	1867	250	2048	4	228
240	128	6	1856	250	2048	6	228
240	128	8	1845	250	2048	8	228
240	128	10	1834	250	2048	10	228
240	256	2	1269	250	4096	2	118
240	256	4	1263	250	4096	4	118
240	256	6	1258	250	4096	6	118
240	256	8	1253	250	4096	8	118
240	256	10	1248	250	4096	10	118
240	512	2	769	260	64	2	2364
240	512	4	767	260	64	4	2346
240	512	6	765	260	64	6	2328
240	512	8	763	260	64	8	2310
240	512	10	761	260	64	10	2293
240	1024	2	430	260	128	2	1815
240	1024	4	430	260	128	4	1804
240	1024	6	429	260	128	6	1793
240	1024	8	428	260	128	8	1783
240	1024	10	428	260	128	10	1773
240	2048	2	229	260	256	2	1239
240	2048	4	229	260	256	4	1234
240	2048	6	228	260	256	6	1229
240	2048	8	228	260	256	8	1224
240	2048	10	228	260	256	10	1219
240	4096	2	118	260	512	2	758
240	4096	4	118	260	512	4	756
240	4096	6	118	260	512	6	754
240	4096	8	118	260	512	8	753
240	4096	10	118	260	512	10	751
250	64	2	2417	260	1024	2	427
250	64	4	2398	260	1024	4	426
250	64	6	2380	260	1024	6	426
250	64	8	2361	260	1024	8	425
250	64	10	2343	260	1024	10	424
250	128	2	1846	260	2048	2	228
250	128	4	1835	260	2048	4	228
250	128	6	1824	260	2048	6	227
250	128	8	1813	260	2048	8	227
250	128	10	1803	260	2048	10	227
250	256	2	1254	260	4096	2	118
250	256	4	1249	260	4096	4	118
250	256	6	1243	260	4096	6	118
250	256	8	1238	260	4096	8	118
250	256	10	1233	260	4096	10	118

Frame rate of 16 Mbps Token-Ring network based upon the network operating rate, number of stations, frame length and total cable length

Number of stations	Avg frame length	Cable length ×000 feet	Frame rate in fps	Number of stations	Avg frame length	Cable length ×000 feet	Frame rate in fps
10	64	2	20152	20	512	2	3624
10	64	4	18902	20	512	4	3581
10	64	6	17799	20	512	6	3539
10	64	8	16817	20	512	8	3499
10	64	10	15938	20	512	10	3459
10	128	2	12251	20	1024	2	1880
10	128	4	11778	20	1024	4	1868
10	128	6	11340	20	1024	6	1857
10	128	8	10933	20	1024	8	1846
10	128	10	10555	20	1024	10	1835
10	256	2	6867	20	2048	2	958
10	256	4	6716	20	2048	4	955
10	256	6	6571	20	2048	6	952
10	256	8	6432	20	2048	8	949
10	256	10	6299	20	2048	10	946
10	512	2	3655	20	4096	2	484
10	512	4	3611	20	4096	4	483
10	512	6	3569	20	4096	6	482
10	512	8	3528	20	4096	8	481
10	512	10	3487	20	4096	10	481
10	1024	2	1888	30	64	2	18412
10	1024	4	1877	30	64	4	17364
10	1024	6	1865	30	64	6	16428
10	1024	8	1854	30	64	8	15588
10	1024	10	1842	30	64	10	14830
10	2048	2	960	30	128	2	11586
10	2048	4	957	30	128	4	11162
10	2048	6	954	30	128	6	10768
10	2048	8	951	30	128	8	10400
10	2048	10	948	30	128	10	10057
10	4096	2	484	30	256	2	6653
10	4096	4	483	30	256	4	6511
10	4096	6	483	30	256	6	6375
10	4096	8	482	30	256	8	6244
10	4096	10	481	30	256	10	6119
20	64	2	19243	30	512	2	3593
20	64	4	18100	30	512	4	3551
20	64	6	17086	30	512	6	3510
20	64	8	16179	30	512	8	3470
20	64	10	15364	30	512	10	3431
20	128	2	11909	30	1024	2	1872
20	128	4	11462	30	1024	4	1860
20	128	6	11046	30	1024	6	1849
20	128	8	10660	30	1024	8	1838
20	128	10	10300	30	1024	10	1827
20	256	2	6758	30	2048	2	956
20	256	4	6612	30	2048	4	953
20	256	6	6471	30	2048	6	950
20	256	8	6337	30	2048	8	947
20	256	10	6208	30	2048	10	944

Number of stations	Avg frame length	Cable length ×000 feet	Frame rate in fps	Number of stations	Avg frame length	Cable length ×000 feet	Frame rate in fps
30	4096	2	483	50	256	2	6452
30	4096	4	482	50	256	4	6318
30	4096	6	481	50	256	6	6190
30	4096	8	481	50	256	8	6067
30	4096	10	480	50	256	10	5948
40	64	2	17651	50	512	2	3534
40	64	4	16685	50	512	4	3493
40	64	6	15819	50	512	6	3454
40	64	8	15039	50	512	8	3415
40	64	10	14332	50	512	10	3377
40	128	2	11280	50	1024	2	1855
40	128	4	10877	50	1024	4	1844
40	128	6	10503	50	1024	6	1833
40	128	8	10153	50	1024	8	1822
40	128	10	9826	50	1024	10	1811
40	256	2	6551	50	2048	2	951
40	256	4	6413	50	2048	4	949
40	256	6	6281	50	2048	6	946
40	256	8	6154	50	2048	8	943
40	256	10	6032	50	2048	10	940
40	512	2	3563	50	4096	2	482
40	512	4	3522	50	4096	4	481
40	512	6	3482	50	4096	6	480
40	512	8	3442	50	4096	8	480
40	512	10	3404	50	4096	10	479
40	1024	2	1863	60	64	2	16302
40	1024	4	1852	60	64	4	15474
40	1024	6	1841	60	64	6	14727
40	1024	8	1830	60	64	8	14048
40	1024	10	1819	60	64	10	13430
40	2048	2	954	60	128	2	10713
40	2048	4	951	60	128	4	10350
40	2048	6	948	60	128	6	10010
40	2048	8	945	60	128	8	9692
40	2048	10	942	60	128	10	9393
40	4096	2	482	60	256	2	6356
40	4096	4	482	60	256	4	6226
40	4096	6	481	60	256	6	6101
40	4096	8	480	60	256	8	5981
40	4096	10	479	60	256	10	5866
50	64	2	16950	60	512	2	3505
50	64	4	16057	60	512	4	3465
50	64	6	15253	60	512	6	3426
50	64	8	14527	60	512	8	3388
50	64	10	13866	60	512	10	3351
50	128	2	10989	60	1024	2	1847
50	128	4	10607	60	1024	4	1836
50	128	6	10250	60	1024	6	1825
50	128	8	9917	60	1024	8	1814
50	128	10	9604	60	1024	10	1804

Number of stations	Avg frame length	Cable length ×000 feet	Frame rate in fps	Number of stations	Avg frame length	Cable length ×000 feet	Frame rate in fps
60	2048	2	949	80	128	2	10201
60	2048	4	946	80	128	4	9871
60	2048	6	943	80	128	6	9561
60	2048	8	941	80	128	8	9270
60	2048	10	938	80	128	10	8997
60	4096	2	481	80	256	2	6172
60	4096	4	481	80	256	4	6049
60	4096	6	480	80	256	6	5932
60	4096	8	479	80	256	8	5818
60	4096	10	478	80	256	10	5709
70	64	2	15702	80	512	2	3448
70	64	4	14933	80	512	4	3409
70	64	6	14236	80	512	6	3372
70	64	8	13601	80	512	8	3335
70	64	10	13020	80	512	10	3299
70	128	2	10451	80	1024	2	1831
70	128	4	10104	80	1024	4	1820
70	128	6	9780	80	1024	6	1810
70	128	8	9476	80	1024	8	1799
70	128	10	9191	80	1024	10	1788
70	256	2	6262	80	2048	2	945
70	256	4	6136	80	2048	4	942
70	256	6	6015	80	2048	6	939
70	256	8	5899	80	2048	8	936
70	256	10	5787	80	2048	10	934
70	512	2	3476	80	4096	2	480
70	512	4	3437	80	4096	4	480
70	512	6	3399	80	4096	6	479
70	512	8	3361	80	4096	8	478
70	512	10	3324	80	4096	10	477
70	1024	2	1839	90	64	2	14625
70	1024	4	1828	90	64	4	13956
70	1024	6	1817	90	64	6	13345
70	1024	8	1807	90	64	8	12785
70	1024	10	1796	90	64	10	12271
70	2048	2	947	90	128	2	9963
70	2048	4	944	90	128	4	9648
70	2048	6	941	90	128	6	9352
70	2048	8	939	90	128	8	9073
70	2048	10	936	90	128	10	8811
70	4096	2	481	90	256	2	6084
70	4096	4	480	90	256	4	5965
70	4096	6	479	90	256	6	5850
70	4096	8	479	90	256	8	5740
70	4096	10	478	90	256	10	5634
80	64	2	15145	90	512	2	3420
80	64	4	14428	90	512	4	3382
80	64	6	13776	90	512	6	3345
80	64	8	13180	90	512	8	3309
80	64	10	12634	90	512	10	3273

Number of stations	Avg frame length	Cable length ×000 feet	Frame rate in fps	Number of stations	Avg frame length	Cable length ×000 feet	Frame rate in fps
90	1024	2	1824	110	64	2	13687
90	1024	4	1813	110	64	4	13099
90	1024	6	1802	110	64	6	12559
90	1024	8	1791	110	64	8	12063
90	1024	10	1781	110	64	10	11603
90	2048	2	943	110	128	2	9518
90	2048	4	940	110	128	4	9230
90	2048	6	937	110	128	6	8959
90	2048	8	934	110	128	8	8703
90	2048	10	932	110	128	10	8462
90	4096	2	480	110	256	2	5915
90	4096	4	479	110	256	4	5802
90	4096	6	478	110	256	6	5694
90	4096	8	478	110	256	8	5590
90	4096	10	477	110	256	10	5489
100	64	2	14141	110	512	2	3366
100	64	4	13514	110	512	4	3330
100	64	6	12940	110	512	6	3294
100	64	8	12413	110	512	8	3258
100	64	10	11928	110	512	10	3224
100	128	2	9735	110	1024	2	1808
100	128	4	9434	110	1024	4	1797
100	128	6	9151	110	1024	6	1787
100	128	8	8884	110	1024	8	1777
100	128	10	8633	110	1024	10	1766
100	256	2	5998	110	2048	2	939
100	256	4	5882	110	2048	4	936
100	256	6	5771	110	2048	6	933
100	256	8	5664	110	2048	8	930
100	256	10	5561	110	2048	10	927
100	512	2	3393	110	4096	2	479
100	512	4	3356	110	4096	4	478
100	512	6	3319	110	4096	6	477
100	512	8	3283	110	4096	8	476
100	512	10	3248	110	4096	10	476
100	1024	2	1816	120	64	2	13262
100	1024	4	1805	120	64	4	12709
100	1024	6	1794	120	64	6	12200
100	1024	8	1784	120	64	8	11731
100	1024	10	1774	120	64	10	11296
100	2048	2	941	120	128	2	9311
100	2048	4	938	120	128	4	9035
100	2048	6	935	120	128	6	8775
100	2048	8	932	120	128	8	8529
100	2048	10	930	120	128	10	8297
100	4096	2	479	120	256	2	5834
100	4096	4	478	120	256	4	5725
100	4096	6	478	120	256	6	5619
100	4096	8	477	120	256	8	5517
100	4096	10	476	120	256	10	5419

Number of stations	Avg frame length	Cable length ×000 feet	Frame rate in fps	Number of stations	Avg frame length	Cable length ×000 feet	Frame rate in fps
130	4096	2	478	120	512	2	3340
130	4096	4	477	120	512	4	3304
130	4096	6	476	120	512	6	3268
130	4096	8	475	120	512	8	3234
130	4096	10	475	120	512	10	3200
140	64	2	12486	120	1024	2	1800
140	64	4	11994	120	1024	4	1790
140	64	6	11540	120	1024	6	1779
140	64	8	11119	120	1024	8	1769
140	64	10	10728	120	1024	10	1759
140	128	2	8921	120	2048	2	937
140	128	4	8668	120	2048	4	934
140	128	6	8428	120	2048	6	931
140	128	8	8201	120	2048	8	928
140	128	10	7986	120	2048	10	925
140	256	2	5679	120	4096	2	478
140	256	4	5575	120	4096	4	477
140	256	6	5475	120	4096	6	477
140	256	8	5378	120	4096	8	476
140	256	10	5285	120	4096	10	475
140	512	2	3288	130	64	2	12862
140	512	4	3253	130	64	4	12341
140	512	6	3219	130	64	6	11861
140	512	8	3185	130	64	8	11417
140	512	10	3152	130	64	10	11005
140	1024	2	1785	130	128	2	9112
140	1024	4	1775	130	128	4	8847
140	1024	6	1765	130	128	6	8598
140	1024	8	1755	130	128	8	8362
140	1024	10	1745	130	128	10	8139
140	2048	2	933	130	256	2	5755
140	2048	4	930	130	256	4	5649
140	2048	6	927	130	256	6	5546
140	2048	8	924	130	256	8	5447
140	2048	10	921	130	256	10	5351
140	4096	2	477	130	512	2	3314
140	4096	4	476	130	512	4	3278
140	4096	6	476	130	512	6	3244
140	4096	8	475	130	512	8	3209
140	4096	10	474	130	512	10	3176
150	64	2	12131	130	1024	2	1793
150	64	4	11666	130	1024	4	1782
150	64	6	11236	130	1024	6	1772
150	64	8	10837	130	1024	8	1762
150	64	10	10465	130	1024	10	1752
150	128	2	8738	130	2048	2	935
150	128	4	8495	130	2048	4	932
150	128	6	8265	130	2048	6	929
150	128	8	8047	130	2048	8	926
150	128	10	7840	130	2048	10	923

Number of stations	Avg frame length	Cable length ×000 feet	Frame rate in fps	Number of stations	Avg frame length	Cable length ×000 feet	Frame rate in fps
150	256	2	5604	160	2048	2	929
150	256	4	5503	160	2048	4	926
150	256	6	5406	160	2048	6	923
150	256	8	5311	160	2048	8	920
150	256	10	5220	160	2048	10	918
150	512	2	3263	160	4096	2	476
150	512	4	3229	160	4096	4	475
150	512	6	3195	160	4096	6	475
150	512	8	3162	160	4096	8	474
150	512	10	3129	160	4096	10	473
150	1024	2	1778	170	64	2	11478
150	1024	4	1768	170	64	4	11061
150	1024	6	1757	170	64	6	10674
150	1024	8	1747	170	64	8	10313
150	1024	10	1737	170	64	10	9976
150	2048	2	931	170	128	2	8395
150	2048	4	928	170	128	4	8170
150	2048	6	925	170	128	6	7956
150	2048	8	922	170	128	8	7754
150	2048	10	919	170	128	10	7562
150	4096	2	477	170	256	2	5461
150	4096	4	476	170	256	4	5365
150	4096	6	475	170	256	6	5272
150	4096	8	474	170	256	8	5182
150	4096	10	474	170	256	10	5096
160	64	2	11795	170	512	2	3214
160	64	4	11356	170	512	4	3181
160	64	6	10948	170	512	6	3148
160	64	8	10569	170	512	8	3116
160	64	10	10215	170	512	10	3084
160	128	2	8563	170	1024	2	1763
160	128	4	8329	170	1024	4	1753
160	128	6	8108	170	1024	6	1743
160	128	8	7898	170	1024	8	1733
160	128	10	7698	170	1024	10	1723
160	256	2	5532	170	2048	2	927
160	256	4	5433	170	2048	4	924
160	256	6	5338	170	2048	6	921
160	256	8	5246	170	2048	8	918
160	256	10	5157	170	2048	10	916
160	512	2	3239	170	4096	2	475
160	512	4	3205	170	4096	4	475
160	512	6	3171	170	4096	6	474
160	512	8	3139	170	4096	8	473
160	512	10	3107	170	4096	10	473
160	1024	2	1771	180	64	2	11177
160	1024	4	1760	180	64	4	10782
160	1024	6	1750	180	64	6	10414
160	1024	8	1740	180	64	8	10070
160	1024	10	1730	180	64	10	9748

Number of stations	Avg frame length	Cable length ×000 feet	Frame rate in fps	Number of stations	Avg frame length	Cable length ×000 feet	Frame rate in fps
180	128	2	8233	190	1024	2	1749
180	128	4	8016	190	1024	4	1739
180	128	6	7811	190	1024	6	1729
180	128	8	7616	190	1024	8	1719
180	128	10	7430	190	1024	10	1710
180	256	2	5392	190	2048	2	923
180	256	4	5298	190	2048	4	920
180	256	6	5208	190	2048	6	917
180	256	8	5120	190	2048	8	914
180	256	10	5036	190	2048	10	912
180	512	2	3190	190	4096	2	474
180	512	4	3157	190	4096	4	474
180	512	6	3125	190	4096	6	473
180	512	8	3093	190	4096	8	472
180	512	10	3062	190	4096	10	471
180	1024	2	1756	200	64	2	10621
180	1024	4	1746	200	64	4	10263
180	1024	6	1736	200	64	6	9929
180	1024	8	1726	200	64	8	9616
180	1024	10	1716	200	64	10	9322
180	2048	2	925	200	128	2	7927
180	2048	4	922	200	128	4	7726
180	2048	6	919	200	128	6	7535
180	2048	8	916	200	128	8	7353
180	2048	10	914	200	128	10	7180
180	4096	2	475	200	256	2	5259
180	4096	4	474	200	256	4	5170
180	4096	6	473	200	256	6	5083
180	4096	8	473	200	256	8	5000
180	4096	10	472	200	256	10	4919
190	64	2	10892	200	512	2	3143
190	64	4	10516	200	512	4	3111
190	64	6	10166	200	512	6	3080
190	64	8	9838	200	512	8	3049
190	64	10	9530	200	512	10	3019
190	128	2	8077	200	1024	2	1742
190	128	4	7868	200	1024	4	1732
190	128	6	7670	200	1024	6	1722
190	128	8	7482	200	1024	8	1712
190	128	10	7303	200	1024	10	1703
190	256	2	5324	200	2048	2	921
190	256	4	5233	200	2048	4	918
190	256	6	5145	200	2048	6	915
190	256	8	5059	200	2048	8	912
190	256	10	4977	200	2048	10	910
190	512	2	3166	200	4096	2	474
190	512	4	3134	200	4096	4	473
190	512	6	3102	200	4096	6	472
190	512	8	3071	200	4096	8	472
190	512	10	3040	200	4096	10	471

Number of stations	Avg frame length	Cable length ×000 feet	Frame rate in fps	Number of stations	Avg frame length	Cable length ×000 feet	Frame rate in fps
210	64	2	10363	220	512	2	3097
210	64	4	10022	220	512	4	3066
210	64	6	9703	220	512	6	3036
210	64	8	9404	220	512	8	3006
210	64	10	9123	220	512	10	2977
210	128	2	7782	220	1024	2	1728
210	128	4	7588	220	1024	4	1718
210	128	6	7404	220	1024	6	1708
210	128	8	7229	220	1024	8	1699
210	128	10	7061	220	1024	10	1689
210	256	2	5195	220	2048	2	917
210	256	4	5108	220	2048	4	914
210	256	6	5024	220	2048	6	911
210	256	8	4942	220	2048	8	909
210	256	10	4863	220	2048	10	906
210	512	2	3120	220	4096	2	473
210	512	4	3089	220	4096	4	472
210	512	6	3058	220	4096	6	471
210	512	8	3027	220	4096	8	471
210	512	10	2997	220	4096	10	470
210	1024	2	1735	230	64	2	9883
210	1024	4	1725	230	64	4	9572
210	1024	6	1715	230	64	6	9281
210	1024	8	1705	230	64	8	9007
210	1024	10	1696	230	64	10	8748
210	2048	2	919	230	128	2	7508
210	2048	4	916	230	128	4	7328
210	2048	6	913	230	128	6	7156
210	2048	8	910	230	128	8	6992
210	2048	10	908	230	128	10	6835
210	4096	2	473	230	256	2	5071
210	4096	4	473	230	256	4	4988
210	4096	6	472	230	256	6	4908
210	4096	8	471	230	256	8	4830
210	4096	10	470	230	256	10	4755
220	64	2	10117	230	512	2	3075
220	64	4	9792	230	512	4	3044
220	64	6	9487	230	512	6	3014
220	64	8	9201	230	512	8	2985
220	64	10	8932	230	512	10	2956
220	128	2	7643	230	1024	2	1721
220	128	4	7456	230	1024	4	1711
220	128	6	7278	230	1024	6	1701
220	128	8	7108	230	1024	8	1692
220	128	10	6946	230	1024	10	1683
220	256	2	5132	230	2048	2	915
220	256	4	5047	230	2048	4	912
220	256	6	4965	230	2048	6	909
220	256	8	4886	230	2048	8	907
220	256	10	4809	230	2048	10	904

Number of stations	Avg frame length	Cable length ×000 feet	Frame rate in fps	Number of stations	Avg frame length	Cable length ×000 feet	Frame rate in fps
230	4096	2	472	250	512	2	3031
230	4096	4	472	250	512	4	3002
230	4096	6	471	250	512	6	2972
230	4096	8	470	250	512	8	2944
230	4096	10	469	250	512	10	2916
240	64	2	9659	250	1024	2	1707
240	64	4	9362	250	1024	4	1697
240	64	6	9083	250	1024	6	1688
240	64	8	8821	250	1024	8	1679
240	64	10	8573	250	1024	10	1669
240	128	2	7378	250	2048	2	911
240	128	4	7204	250	2048	4	908
240	128	6	7038	250	2048	6	905
240	128	8	6879	250	2048	8	903
240	128	10	6727	250	2048	10	900
240	256	2	5012	250	4096	2	471
240	256	4	4931	250	4096	4	471
240	256	6	4852	250	4096	6	470
240	256	8	4776	250	4096	8	469
240	256	10	4703	250	4096	10	468
240	512	2	3053	260	64	2	9241
240	512	4	3023	260	64	4	8969
240	512	6	2993	260	64	6	8713
240	512	8	2964	260	64	8	8470
240	512	10	2936	260	64	10	8241
240	1024	2	1714	260	128	2	7132
240	1024	4	1704	260	128	4	6969
240	1024	6	1695	260	128	6	6813
240	1024	8	1685	260	128	8	6664
240	1024	10	1676	260	128	10	6522
240	2048	2	913	260	256	2	4897
240	2048	4	910	260	256	4	4819
240	2048	6	907	260	256	6	4744
240	2048	8	905	260	256	8	4672
240	2048	10	902	260	256	10	4601
240	4096	2	472	260	512	2	3010
240	4096	4	471	260	512	4	2981
240	4096	6	470	260	512	6	2952
240	4096	8	470	260	512	8	2923
240	4096	10	469	260	512	10	2896
250	64	2	9445	260	1024	2	1700
250	64	4	9161	260	1024	4	1691
250	64	6	8894	260	1024	6	1681
250	64	8	8642	260	1024	8	1672
250	64	10	8404	260	1024	10	1663
250	128	2	7253	260	2048	2	909
250	128	4	7084	260	2048	4	906
250	128	6	6924	260	2048	6	904
250	128	8	6770	260	2048	8	901
250	128	10	6623	260	2048	10	898
250	256	2	4954	260	4096	2	471
250	256	4	4874	260	4096	4	470
250	256	6	4798	260	4096	6	469
250	256	8	4723	260	4096	8	469
250	256	10	4651	260	4096	10	468

INDEX

A/B/C notation 72–3
access control field 26–9
active monitor 29
adapter cards 136, 177–8
address values 32
advertising protocol 231–2
AR/MSR 64
arrival rate 73–4
ATM port 203–5
  availability
  computation 91
  computation automation 103–7
  definition 90
  levels 4–5, 89–107
AVAIL.BAS program 103–7
AVAIL.BAS program execution 105–7
AVAIL.BAS program listing 104

bandwidth-on-demand inverse
  multiplexers (BODM) 227–8
BASIC 7
BASICA 4
bit rate (bps) 42, 47
BMP 160
bridges 6, 121–8
  local 144–6
  remote 3–4, 55–88, 146–53
    connections 125–8
    network applications 59–67
  switching operation 184–5
buffer memory 55, 80–8
  average memory 81
  using probability 81–2

collision detection network access
  protocol 5

color reduction 174–5
column entries 41–3
component availability 90–2
compression ratio 222–3
conventional hub bottlenecks 180–3
conventional hub dataflow 181
CSMA/CD network 123, 129
  access protocol 5, 109
  frame format 12
  frame rate 110–16
  performance 110–21
cyclic redundancy check (CRC) 18,
  190–1

data compression 148–50, 222–5
  byte-oriented techniques 223
  dictionary-based 224–5
  performance considerations 225
  statistical compression algorithms
    224
data field 17
data service units (DSUs) 71
data transfer time estimation 124–5
destination address field 14, 30–3
dial-on congestion 228
dictionary-based data compression
  224–5
Differential Manchester encoding 23–4
direct memory access (DMA) interface
  229
disk mirroring 100–3
distance vector algorithms 230–1
dual circuits 75–6
dual hardware versus dual transmission
  facilities 98–100
dual-port equipment 71–80

EITR.BAS program execution 120
EITR.BAS program listing 119
End of Stream Delimiter (ESD) 19, 20
EPERFORM.BAS program 113–16
EPERFORM.BAS program execution
   115
EPERFORM.BAS program listing 113
Ethernet 1–2
  frame composition 12–19
  frame operations 2–3, 11–21
  frame overhead 19–21
  frame processing capability 112
  frame truncation 225–6
  hub operation 180–2
  information transfer rate 118–21
  network performance 5–6
  network performance estimation
    109–28
  network utilization 117–18
  operating rate 116–21
express queuing 222

Fast Ethernet 100BASE-TX network
   110, 114
  frame format 12, 18–19
  frame processing requirement 114
  frame rate 110
fat pipe 202–3
FDDI port 203–5
file formats, image formats 160
filtering 214–16
  address field 215–16
  local versus remote 214
  methods 215–16
  service access point 216
first-in, first-out queuing 217–20
Frame Check Sequence (FCS) 18, 25,
   191
frame determination 64–5
frame length versus information
   transfer rate 121
functional address indicator (FAI) 31–2
functional addresses 32–3

GIF (Graphical Interchange Format)
   162
graphic versus text transfer 47–8
GW-BASIC 4

half-byte encoding 223
HDLC 24

IEEE 802.3 12–19, 18, 84, 110
IEEE 802.5 24, 29, 30
I/G subfield 14–15
image-based applications 7, 155–78
  basics 156
  data storage problem 158
  examining visual image differences
    170–1
  hardware considerations 176–8
  transmission delays 159–60
  vector images 157
  see also raster images
image cropping 173–4
image formats 160–73
  common storage and viewing
    methods 160
  file formats 160
    comparisons 168–70
  storage requirements 166–73
image management operations 173–5
Image Manager 166–73
information field 34
information transfer rate versus frame
   length 121
intelligent switches 8, 179–212
  100BASE-T port support 203
  ATM port 203–5
  backplane throughput 199
  backpressure 205–6
  basic components 185–6
  cross-point switching 188–90
  delay times 186–7
  fat pipe 202–3
  FDDI port 203–5
  flow control support 205–6
  high-speed port operation 200–5
  hub development 183–4
  hub features 197–208
  hub hierarchy 204
  hubs 185–8
  hybrid 193
  key advantages of use 187–8
  networking techniques 208–12
  port-based switching 194–5
  port support 200
  segment-based switching 195–6
  server software module 206
  statistics 206
  store-and-forward 190–3
  switching method 197–9
  switching operations 183–96

intelligent switches (*continued*)
  switching techniques 188–97
  virtual LAN 206–8
Internet traffic flow 150–3
inter-network versus intra-network
    communications 52–3
I/O mapping 229

Joint Picture Experts Group (JPEG)
    163
JPG 163–4, 171–3

LANs
  infrastructure upgrading 178
  linked 123–4
  performance issues 1–9
  segmentation 176–7
  virtual LAN creation support 206–8
Lempel-Ziv based dictionary-based
    compression algorithm 224–5
Lempel-Ziv-Welsh technique 162–3
Lempel-Ziv-Welsh coding 225
length field 17
line speed versus utilization level 68–9
locally administered address 15–16, 31
logical link control (LLC) 29, 34

Manchester encoding 23–4
maximum frame size 84
mean time before failure (MTBF) 1–1, 5,
    90–2, 93, 103, 105
mean time to repair (MTTR) 5, 90–2,
    93, 102, 103, 105, 106
media access control (MAC) 29, 34
mirrored disk system 102
mixed serial/parallel connection 96–8
M/M/1 notation 72–3
M/M/2 queuing system 75
monitor bit 27–9
MTBR 106
multiple-channel, single-phase system
    75
multiple-channel waiting line system
    57
multiple-phase service facility 57
Multistation Access Unit (MAU) 180

NetWare Link Services Protocol (NLSP)
    233
network basics 1–2
network bottlenecks 183
network growth planning 49

network interface card (NIC) 15–16,
    228–30
network linking 230
network modification 49–53
network performance issues 1–9
network printing 45–6
network redistribution 208–9
network segmentation 211–12
network subdivision 50–2
network traffic estimation 3, 39–53
  worksheet 40–3, 43–8
network utilization 48–9
non-data symbols 24–6
non-return to zero (NRZ) 23
null suppression 223
number of stations 40

operating rate selection 69–70

parallel connection 94–6
PCX 164
performance issues 1–9
preamble field 13
precedence queuing 220–1
priority bit field 27
priority bit settings 26
Priority-Hold state 27
probability density function (pdf) 72
propagation delay 131
protocol overhead 148

QUEUE.BAS program 67
QUEUE.BAS program execution 69
QUEUE.BAS program listing 68
QUEUE2.BAS program execution 80
QUEUE2.BAS program listing 79
queue length 64
  versus server utilization 87
queuing
  express 222
  first-in, first-out 217–20
  precedence 220–1
queuing model 60–1
queuing storage requirements 83–4
queuing theory 56, 58–64
  application 61–3
  designators 63–4
QuickBASIC 4
QVU.BAS program 84
QVU.BAS program execution 85
QVU.BAS program listing 85

raster images 156–7
  color depth 156
  data storage problem 158
reference physical link functions 29
remote bridges 3–4, 55–88, 146–53
  connections 125–8
  network applications 59–67
reservation bit field 27
routers 3–4, 6, 55
  network applications 59–67
  remote 146–53
routing information field (RIF) 34
Routing Information Protocol (RIP) 231
routing protocol 231
Run Length Encoding (RLE) 160–2

series connection 92–4
server segmentation 209–10
Service Advertisement Protocol (SAP)
  231–2
service rate 74
shared memory 229–30
single disk system 102
single-channel, single-phase system 87
single-channel, single-phase waiting
  line system 57
single-channel, single-server system 81
single circuit communications link
  72–5
single-port equipment 71–80
source address field 16, 33–4
start of frame delimiter field 13–14
Start of Stream Delimiter (SSD) 19, 20
starting/ending delimiters 23
statistical compression algorithms 224
statistics, intelligent switches 206
switched networks 226–8
system availability 92–8
  comparison 98

Tag Image File Format (TIFF) 164–5
throughput prediction 123–8
TIF 164–6
time computations 65–7
Token-Ring networks 1–2
  4 Mbps 131–3, 135, 140
  16 Mbps 131, 141
  frame check sequence field 35–6
  frame composition 22–36

frame control field 29–30
frame formats 21–37
frame operations 2–3
frame overhead 36–7
frame size variation 134–6
frame status field 36
hub operation 182–3
model development 130–3
network modification 134
network performance 6–7
network performance estimation
  129–53
station effect upon network
  performance 142–3
traffic modeling 130–43
TPERFORM.BAS program 139
TPERFORM.BAS program listing 138
transmission gaps 77
transmission optimization 8–9
  techniques 213–33
TRWAN.BAS program 147–50
TRWAN.BAS program execution 148
TRWAN.BAS program listing 147
two-byte length field 17
two-byte type field 17
type field 17

U/L subfield 15
UNITS.BAS program 81
UNITS.BAS program execution 83
UNITS.BAS program listing 82
universally administered address
  15–16, 30–1
utilization level versus line speed
  68–9
utilization of service facility (p) 63–4,
  74, 75

vector images 157

waiting line analysis 56–67
waiting line system, basic components
  56–8
waiting time relationships 67
waiting times 78
wide area networks (WANs), operating
  rate 146–53
workstation class 40

Index compiled by Geoffrey C. Jones

LOCAL AREA NETWORKING

PROTECTING LAN RESOURCES
A Comprehensive Guide to Securing, Protecting and Rebuilding a Network

With the evolution of distributed computing, security is now a key issue for network users. This comprehensive guide will provide network managers and users with a detailed knowledge of the techniques and tools they can use to secure their data against unauthorised users. Gil Held also provides guidance on how to prevent disasters such as self-corruption of data and computer viruses.

1995   0 471 95407 1

TOKEN- RING NETWORKS
Characteristics, Operation, Construction and Management

This timely book provides the reader with a comprehensive understanding of how Token-Ring networks operate, the constraints and performance issues that affect their implementation, and how their growth and use can be managed both locally and as part of an Enterprise network.

1993 0 471 94041 0

ETHERNET NETWORKS
Design, Implementation, Operation, and Management

1994 0 471 59717 1

REFERENCE

DICTIONARY OF COMMUNICATIONS TECHNOLOGY
Terms, Definitions and Abbreviations

1995 0 471 95126 9 (Paper)
**   0 471 95542 6 (Cloth)**

THE COMPLETE MODEM REFERENCE
2nd Edition

1994 0 471 00852 4

THE COMPLETE PC AT AND COMPATIBLES REFERENCE MANUAL

1991 0 471 53315 7